THE ENNEAGRAM JOUR

July 2012

Volume V
Number 1

Published by International Enneagram Association Publications

ISBN 978 – 0 – 9857861 – 1 – 3

www.internationalenneagram.org

TABLE OF CONTENTS

FROM THE EDITORS

Welcome to CJ Fitzsimons as the new co-editor-in-chief. The "in-chief" part means CJ gets to do the reading and the work while J.P. (Wagner) gets to do the reading. Thanks, CJ, for taking this on.

I'm writing this editorial to get some discussion going. We've always encouraged *Enneagram Journal* readers to send in their comments as a point-counterpoint dialogue. The topic is: How sacrosanct is the Enneagram figure?

Is it a universal diagram that ought not to be tampered with? Has its author(s) hit upon a map that accurately portrays the territory and so we should stay with its outline? Just how set in stone is this Rosetta?

Or is the Enneagram a "useful fiction" like any other theory and, in the words of Karl Popper the philosopher of science, its present status is "not yet disconfirmed." All theories are waiting to be replaced by better theories.

Do we need to honor the tradition and preserve the form as it is? Or can we be creative and rearrange the diagram since maybe its original designers didn't see all that there is to see and we now have a better -- or at least different -- perspective.

I have heard some Enneagram authors working within the system and I have noticed other authors rearranging the diagram.

Or is the Enneagram both/and? a *tertium quid* that fails to fit into a dichotomy? Is it a flexible figure that can accommodate new configurations as well as maintain its original shape? I haven't seen enough *Transformer* movies to know if this is what they do.

I'm ambivalent about this issue. While I lean towards preserving the Enneagram design, and here would prefer assimilation (interpreting new information with established schemas), I'm also open to updating maps and accommodating prior schemas to fit new data. Either way works for Piaget.

What think ye? Send your reflections to the editors at journal@internationalenneagram.org. We'll collect your comments and print them in the next *Enneagram Journal*.

Jerome P. Wagner
Co-Editor, Enneagram Journal

You're holding Volume 5 of the Enneagram Journal in your hands. Without Bea Chestnut's vision and drive there would be no Enneagram Journal in the first place. The last two editions of the Journal were carefully and diligently guided by Merrie Monks. They've left good footprints for me to follow and hard shoes to fill.

My special thanks to JP for being a pleasure to work with. He does a lot more to make the Enneagram Journal what it is than he lets on – or else I really need to thank his dear wife, Bernie.

My primary research background is in Mathematics – an area with a different standard of what counts as research and scholarship than all others. So I'd like to explain a little what criteria we've been applying when evaluating articles.

The basic criterion for an article in the Journal is that the authors can bring a convincing line of argument for their scholarship. If we whittled down the Enneagram to the tried and tested, we'd save a lot of trees and lose a lot of its richness. We would also be in danger of fixating on a dogma. I have a difficulty with the word dogma, with its normative and religious connotations. Even scientists can get tripped up by the word dogma. Crick and Watson formulated a Central Dogma about the primacy of DNA in the 1950s – this delayed the development of epi-genetics by a good thirty years. As the composer Gustav Mahler put it, "Tradition is tending the flame, it's not worshipping the ashes". New ideas need to link back to what reasonable people recognize as the accepted body of theory (if they can set their preferences and prejudices aside for a moment). Of course this can be experimented with!

This year's Journal offers a wide variety of solid scholarship from around the world, with contributions from the Brazil, Denmark, England, Germany, and the USA. They offer a spectrum of interesting ideas to trigger further thinking about the ongoing development of the Enneagram, its application and its combination with other models and systems.

As my good friend Roland Ottmann would say, I hope it offers you good brain food.

CJ Fitzsimons
Co-Editor, Enneagram Journal

PRESIDENT'S MESSAGE

You hold in your hands a shining example of the value of the IEA.

At the time of this writing, a search on the words "Enneagram books" returns 690 items on Amazon.com. A search on the word "Enneagram" produces "about 2,360,000" results on Google.com. Information on the Enneagram is everywhere; but you will be hard-pressed to find information of this caliber brought together in one place anywhere.

Journal editors CJ Fitzsimons, PhD, and Jerome Wagner, PhD, have done a stellar job of scouring the Enneagram community for articles that are challenging, thought-provoking, and informative. Ideas that might not have been seen by a broad audience are now on display for the whole Enneagram community to sample and digest.

This issue also represents the diversity of thought about and application of the Enneagram in this community. The 2012 Journal covers topics as diverse Thomas Merton; NLP, Spiral Dynamics, and the work of Ken Wilber; the work of Schulz von Thun; Millon's personality theories; and psychometric validation of assessments. The 2012 Journal contains something for everyone and is a significant contribution to the field of Enneagram studies.

Thanks are due to CJ and Jerry for their tireless efforts in bringing this edition of the Journal to fruition. IEA members should be proud to be part of an organization that produces such a product and helps to move us all closer to the IEA's vision of a world where the Enneagram is widely understood and constructively used.

Mario Sikora
President, IEA Board of Directors

"BUT IS IT *REAL*?"
A REVIEW OF RESEARCH ON THE ENNEAGRAM

Anna Sutton, Ph.D.

One of the most common questions I am asked when introducing people to the Enneagram goes something along the lines of: "Yes, but is it *real*? What scientific evidence is there?" It was exactly that question that prompted me to do my PhD research a few years ago. I could see the Enneagram worked for me but I wanted to know if it could stand up to rigorous psychological research. In this article, I have tried to summarise the published research on the Enneagram so that next time someone asks you that question you can answer confidently, "Yes, there is good evidence of its validity, let me tell you about it..."

Why do research on the Enneagram?

Much of our Enneagram knowledge has been built up through narrative and experience. The use of panel interviews, books with quotes and stories, videos, anything that uses examples from other people's experience to make the types come alive is the way most of us learn about the Enneagram. We have deep, rich understandings and descriptions of the nine types. So why do research?

I believe solid research is important for two reasons. First, it helps to justify our use of the Enneagram. There are unfortunately a lot of fads and fashions out there, particularly when it comes to understanding and developing ourselves: "personality tests" on the web that can tell you what kind of animal you are, books aimed at improving your life based on nothing more than anecdotes of what worked for one person. Anecdotes are all very well and good in piquing someone's interest but as professional Enneagram practitioners, part of our role is to demonstrate that the Enneagram is not just another fad, that the stories and experiences we use to flesh out the types are not just convenient but are real illustrations of the similarities and differences between people. It is only through well constructed and rigorous research that we can build up this evidence base and establish the Enneagram as a reliable and valid model of human personality and development.

The second reason it is essential that we have good research is to sound a note of caution that we do not lose the reality of the Enneagram in idiosyncratic interpretations or conjecture. One of the things we know from the Enneagram (and in fact from a lot of psychological research) is that we all view the world in a slightly different way and that we tend to make what we see "fit" with what we expect or want. This does not just stop happening when we are learning about or using the Enneagram. We may find a particular story about a type really strikes home for us but how do we know it is actually typical of that type and not just an individual quirk? Without good research to identify and define the types, we are open to making assumptions about types based in our own unique perceptions.

Research is a way to keep different practitioners centred around the basis of the Enneagram – building our understanding certainly, but building on the same foundation so that our knowledge can be shared rather than fragmented.

I believe that, at its root, research is simply common sense. Of course we would want to check that a particularly fascinating story was true for other people of that type before using it as an illustration. Of course we would want to make sure we were not misleading people about how to understand themselves and others. Valuing research is no different from valuing authenticity in our practice. It is a journey of discovery, finding out new things and checking the things we think we know.

What makes a "good" theory of personality?

So on this journey of discovery, what are we trying to find out? What kind of things do we need to investigate if we are to be able to demonstrate that the Enneagram is a "real" model of personality? In my own work (Sutton, 2007), I found that researchers and theorists in the field of personality psychology are seeking to address three major criteria when evaluating personality theories. The first is a need for personality theory to be scientifically rigorous. That means a theory that makes clear, testable predictions. It may seem strange to say that a theory needs to be able to be proved wrong in order to be "good". But if we have a theory that is so vague that anything we can imagine can fit into it, it is not actually of any use. A theory of gravity that said "sometimes things fall to earth and sometimes they don't" would not be testable: if we dropped a rock and it floated, it would not have disproved the theory. This can be quite a problem with personality theories because we are dealing with such complicated objects – people's minds – and it can be very tempting to say "sometimes we are like this and sometimes not" and leave it at that. A scientifically rigorous theory will not pretend that complicated things are simple, but it will make clear and testable predictions about those complicated things. An example of this in the Enneagram would be the way it describes each type clearly but also describes how each type changes in times of security or stress. If we say that Sevens are typically optimistic and cheerful but that under stress they will become more critical and pessimistic, that is a specific, testable prediction drawn from the theory.

The second criterion that is used for judging a personality theory is its usefulness. As Kurt Lewin, one of the earliest applied psychologists said, "There is nothing so practical as a good theory." Particularly in my own field of work psychology, there is a desire for a theory that will be useful rather than an abstract description which cannot be applied to improve people's everyday lives. We only have to look at the proliferation of books and courses based on the Enneagram to see the many different ways it is being applied. Research to prove the utility of a theory needs to check these claims. Instead of simply claiming, for example, that learning about the Enneagram can help teams to work together better, we need to demonstrate that it does and be able to specify exactly how it does so. *How* do people work together better? *What* has improved for them since they learnt about the Enneagram?

And finally, there is the search for a comprehensive theory, one which can encompass all that researchers have discovered so far within the field. This is personality psychology's wish for a "Theory of Everything" and it has a lot of ground to cover because it needs to able to describe how each of us is similar to and different from every other person on the planet, how we got that way and what we might be like in the future. Here we run into a problem. Investigation of the differences between people necessitates a "broad" approach, looking at averages across lots of people so we can tell how they are more or less different from everyone else, and losing sight of the individual. On the other hand, trying to understand individuals in detail, their personal histories and development, requires a "deep" approach, a detailed analysis of individual case studies that loses generalisability. I believe the Enneagram can provide a way of integrating the two. The Enneagram typology describes both how people of the same type share an internal structuring of personality as well as how they are different from others. Research can help to show that the Enneagram works for everyone but also that it tells us detailed things about individuals.

So a "good" personality theory is one that is scientifically testable, useful and comprehensive. The reason I was excited by the Enneagram when I first came across it, and still am now, is that I believe it meets those criteria as well as, if not better than, any other model of personality I have come across. That belief, however, and theoretical explanations of how good the Enneagram *might* be, is not enough. We need research to back it up.

What have we learnt so far?

Most Enneagram authors have tended to concentrate on how the Enneagram can help us to develop rather than conducting research to test the model itself, and while there has been some interest in publishing theoretical papers about the Enneagram, there has been less interest in conducting scientifically rigorous testing of the model. Combined with this is the unfortunate fact that there is still a disappointing level of prejudice against the Enneagram from many psychologists, which may well be limiting the publication of good research. This means that there is a relatively small pool of research dissertations and peer-reviewed papers to review. However, what we have so far makes for an interesting and convincing beginning to the research base for the Enneagram.

Theoretical publications

Several theoretical papers have attempted to develop the possible applications of the Enneagram. In the business field, for example, the Enneagram was incorporated into a dense theoretical paper presenting a new framework for knowledge acquisition and sense-making by Cutting and Kouzmin (2004), proposing that the Enneagram be used as part of an overall model to develop and integrate knowledge in the social sciences. A paper on market segmentation suggested using the Enneagram typology (Kamineni, 2005) to create different marketing strategies for each of the types as consumers. Suggestions on improving workplace spirituality (Kale and Shrivastava, 2003) recommended introducing the Enneagram to organisations as a way for companies to create a more harmonious and profitable company. And Brugha (1998) included the Enneagram in a proposal for a system for analysing development decision making in management. All of these papers, however, focused on theoretical developments or applications and while they indicated interesting areas for future work, did not conduct research to test these suggestions.

Similarly, in the counselling literature, Wyman (1998) presented a psychotherapy model aimed at the counselling practitioner which combined the MBTI and the Enneagram, suggesting that the former captured the "core self" and the latter described a person's typical defence system. Given that Enneagram Types are already described in terms of a "core self", it is hard to justify ignoring these descriptions in favour of the Myers-Briggs types without supporting evidence, which this paper unfortunately did not provide. The theoretical associations between the Enneagram and other psychological models was also discussed by Naranjo (1994) who drew parallels with models such as the interpersonal circumplex and the DSM-IV categories of mental illness. Again, although his theorising is detailed and seems theoretically sound, it also has not yet been tested.

We now turn to consider the practical research on the Enneagram that has been carried out over the past few decades. While my focus here is on the Enneagram in psychology, broadly defined, it is worth acknowledging that published research covers a range of areas, from Religious Philosophy to Education.

Enneagram Questionnaire studies

In line with much personality research, several studies have focused on constructing a reliable questionnaire to identify the 9 personality types. Several of these questionnaire studies have also had as their goal a demonstration of the reliability or validity of the Enneagram theory itself, rather than just the particular questionnaire under investigation. It is of course difficult to separate tests of the theory from tests of the instruments but this is a problem common to personality research, where the measure of a concept can become a proxy for the concept itself.

When we are constructing a psychological measure, we have two main concerns. The first is that the measure must be reliable. Just like if we were to measure how tall someone was on two different occasions, we would expect to get the same height, if someone completes the questionnaire on two different occasions, we would expect to get the same results. The second concern is that the questionnaire should be valid: it should actually measure what we say it measures. To continue the example of height, a valid measurement would be centimetres but not kilograms. It is more difficult to demonstrate validity for psychological concepts than physical ones, but one of the ways we can do it is by demonstrating that the Enneagram types are different from each other in theoretically expected ways on other, already established, personality measures. In our example of height, this would be like saying that we expect that someone who is short in centimetres would also be short when measured in inches.

These theoretically expected and type-distinctive personality profiles have, in fact, been demonstrated for the Enneagram types on several established measures of personality.

First steps in validating the Riso-Hudson Enneagram Type Indicator (RHETI) were made by Warling (1995) when she collected data from 153 students who completed the RHETI and an already established questionnaire, Cattell's 16PF, which measures 16 different personality traits. She found significant correlations between the scales on the RHETI and comparable traits on the 16PF, as well as support for the distinctions between the Enneagram types. Dameyer (2001) undertook further research on the RHETI and demonstrated that test-retest reliability was high: 82% of her 135 respondents were identified as the same type the second time they completed the questionnaire. However, there was only weak agreement (42%) between a person's type as identified by the RHETI and the Wagner Enneagram Personality Styles Scale (WEPSS). In addition, relationships between the RHETI and the Adjective Checklist, which asks respondents to choose adjectives to describe themselves, were also not strong. This indicates that the two Enneagram questionnaires are not describing the types consistently, either with each other or in a way that can be captured clearly by an outside measure.

In recent years, the Big Five personality traits (Extraversion, Agreeableness, Conscientiousness, Emotional Stability and Openness to Experience) have become the standard way of capturing the broad differences between people in the personality research literature. Further work on the RHETI, with a sample of 287 participants who completed the RHETI and a measure of the Big Five, showed that the nine type scales generally had theoretically predicted relationships with the Big Five (Newgent et al., 2004). Although there is still room for improvement in the RHETI, as some of the scales are less reliable than others, this provides some evidence that the differences between the Enneagram personality types can be demonstrated on the "industry standard" measure of personality traits.

Sharp (1994) conducted a study to test three other Enneagram questionnaires (the Wagner Inventory, the Cohen-Palmer Inventory and the Zinkle Inventory) and compare them with the Holland Vocational Preference Inventory, on the basis that personality type would have an influence on the kind of career environments people prefer. He asked 340 people to complete all four questionnaires and his analyses provided evidence that the Enneagram questionnaires had a valid structure. However, the results showed that there was only a weak relationship between Enneagram type, as measured by these questionnaires, and vocational preference.

In summary, while several Enneagram questionnaires have been developed and can show reasonable levels of reliability, demonstrating validity is more difficult. Using a personality questionnaire as a measure of someone's real Enneagram type is, of course, fraught with difficulty. Part of what makes the Enneagram so useful in application is the fact that it describes often-unconscious processes and motivations that we may initially not have easy access to. Asking people to complete a self-report questionnaire will of necessity miss out on this deeper understanding. Self-report questionnaires are only able to tap a respondent's conscious self-concept; those who have not yet recognised their subconscious processes or default ways of operating will simply not be able to report accurately on them. It is therefore to be expected that Enneagram questionnaires may show lower reliabilities than questionnaires which measure explicit personality. While we can still use questionnaires as perhaps a first indication or a basis for guidance in discovering one's type, I would suggest that using self-report questionnaires on people who have never come across the Enneagram before is unlikely to provide convincing evidence for the model as a whole.

A reliable "criterion measure"

This brings us on to a constantly recurring problem facing Enneagram researchers: the lack of a standard (criterion measure) against which to assess the effectiveness of questionnaires or other approaches to determining type. Gamard (1986) focused his doctoral research on this problem by evaluating the level of agreement among "expert judges" who watched videoed interviews and were asked to type the interviewee. However, Gamard's research compared the expert judges' type decisions to a criterion rating based on a joint decision between himself and another Enneagram practitioner. So although the judges showed highly significant agreement among themselves, their agreement with the criterion rating was not high enough to reach significance. It seems strange that the author then interpreted this as not providing evidence for the reliability of expert judgements. A more reasonable interpretation would seem to be that there was consensus among the judges on the types that differed from the researchers' joint judgements. Additionally, the inter-rater agreement for the Enneagram was comparable to that found in research for inter-rater reliability in DSM-IV categories (which are used to classify mental illnesses) (Skodol et al., 2005), indicating that expert judges are able to make clinically valid judgements. However, Gamard's results also indicated that the judges were more confident of their intuitive rating of participants than was really warranted, and this sounds a note of caution when evaluating future research.

As Thrasher (1994) pointed out, Gamard's research used expert judges who, although very familiar with the Enneagram, were completely unacquainted with the participants. She suggested that people who were familiar with the participants ("significant others") might make better judges of type and asked her participants to nominate a significant other, who was then given a description of the nine types and asked to type their corresponding partner. Perhaps not surprisingly, results indicated that in this group of 118 pairs, significant others were only good judges of type if they were already very familiar with the Enneagram system.

Taking Gamard's and Thrasher's results together seems to indicate that maximising the accuracy of judgements by others can be done by increasing a judge's familiarity with both the person and the system. This is, of course, what the longer-term Enneagram workshops already do. A further complication for the self-report questionnaire approach is that there is some indication that our Enneagram type might have an influence on how we report our personality on other instruments, like the MBTI (Wyman and Magidson, 2008). This research showed that there was a significant relationship between Enneagram type and "misreporting" of a preference on the MBTI. This opens up an interesting area for further research in how our different conceptions of personality may interact.

Questionnaires tested against self-identified type

Having identified some of the difficulties we face in identifying an accurate criterion measure, it is worth mentioning a couple that have used either self- or other-identified type as a standard against which to assess their accuracy. The Essential Enneagram test, developed by Daniels and Price (2000) is interesting in that it uses a more narrative-based approach than the traditional questionnaire style adopted by others. Instead of answering a series of questions that are then scored to give a likely Enneagram type, in this test the respondent chooses between paragraph-length descriptions of each type. The descriptions include essential information about the type (including worldview and attentional style) and were reviewed by representatives of each type to ensure their accuracy. Subsequently, a large sample of 970 people who did not yet know their type completed the test. Each person's initial paragraph choice was compared to their type as determined by either a typing interview or their own re-evaluation after a 10 week Enneagram course to determine how well the paragraphs identified a person's type. They found a statistically significant degree of agreement between respondents' original paragraph choice and their final type decision, with accuracy ranging from 37% for the Type 8 paragraph to 68% for Type 9. Although this is well above chance (we would only expect to be able to get classification right 1 in 9 times or 11% if it was pure chance), it is certainly not perfect and the test is presented more as a first step in self-discovery than a definitive means of identifying type. In line with this, the authors analysed how likely it was that a person who chose one paragraph was ultimately identified as each of the other eight types. This is developed in their book as a way of helping respondents to more correctly identify their type by describing the similarities and differences between these connected or look-a-like types.

Similarly, the Wagner Enneagram Personality Style Scales (WEPPS) has been developed over many years as an attempt to help people find their type using a self-report inventory. The WEPPS consists of items measuring both the "resourceful" (positive or adaptive) and "non-resourceful" (negative or non-adaptive) aspects of each of the 9 types (Wagner, 1999). On completion, a respondent has a score for how like them each type is (with the highest referred to as the *core style*), as well as a measure of how much they identify with both the resourceful and non-resourceful aspects of the type. The psychometric properties of the test were assessed on a large sample of 1,429 people and found a good level of reliability, comparable to that of other personality questionnaires. Validity was demonstrated by showing theoretically expected relationships between the WEPPS and other measures, such as conflict-handling modes, and also by finding a high level of agreement between scores on the WEPPS and self-determined type. Assuming that respondents' core style is an accurate representation of their Enneagram type, which these results indicate is a reasonable assumption, we can draw some interesting observations from this large sample. First, there were approximately 5% more type 9s than other types. Second, there were sex differences on some of the types: women were more likely than men to be type 2, 4 or 7 while the reverse was true for types 3, 5 and 8.

Although primarily aimed at developing reliable and valid questionnaires, these studies show us how using a good criterion measure can develop our understanding and application of the Enneagram. We can start to identify typical confusions between types and thereby be more equipped to help clients or students when first introducing the model. And we can also start to understand what some of the group differences might be – a first step in finding out why those differences exist and whether they have any practical implications.

Studies using self-identified Enneagram Type

Research based around Enneagram questionnaires makes up the majority of the work so far in the field. However, there are a few other studies that use a reliable criterion measure involving more complex or detailed methods of identifying type that provide us with some solid findings.

Wagner's (1981) doctoral dissertation and subsequent publication (1983) is a good example of this and was one of the first studies concerned with establishing the reliability and validity of the Enneagram as a typology of personality. In this, 390 participants established their Enneagram type on a workshop and then completed the Millon Illinois Self-Report Inventory scales and the Myers-Briggs Type Indicator. The workshop involved detailed oral explanations and descriptions of the types, written type descriptions, listening to people of each type sharing their experiences, discussion with others of the same type as the participant and discussions with the workshop leader. In summary, decisions about type were based on a combination of self, peer and expert judgements. All of this was designed to ensure the typing process was as accurate as possible.

Wagner was able to demonstrate two important things. The first was that there were statistically significant differences between the types on the scales from these different personality questionnaires, indicating that the Enneagram captured distinct personality types. The second important finding was an indication that people's Enneagram type remained stable over time. The percentage of people whose initial type judgement remained the same ranged from 79% to 100%, depending on type, with an average stability of 85%. Interestingly, over half of those who did change their judgements settled on a type that was a neighbour of the original type, providing some initial support for the concept of the "wings".

Research by Brown and Bartram (2005) used a similar robust typing strategy to Wagner, establishing type for the people in their sample through courses and interviews. Their 241 respondents completed the OPQ (Occupational Personality Questionnaire) and found very encouraging results. Firstly, there were significant differences between the nine types on the Big Five traits that were in line with theoretically expected results and secondly, analysis could classify people into the correct type 75% of the time.

My own research was along a similar line but I tried to capture more than just personality traits in testing the descriptions of the types (Sutton et al., 2009). I asked over 400 people who knew their Enneagram type – established through a minimum of a week-long course – to complete 3 different personality questionnaires. These were: the Big Five, personal values (things people report as important in guiding their lives, such as security or self-direction) and a measure of implicit (that is, unconscious) motives. The latter is obviously difficult to measure but one approach is to use projective tests, where the respondent explains what they think is happening in an ambiguous picture. As the picture itself is ambiguous, the respondent has to project meaning onto it from within themselves and analysis of their responses can tell us something about their implicit motives.

I developed hypotheses of how each type would be expected to score on each trait, value or motive from reading the descriptions in published books and collating expectations from qualified Enneagram teachers and then tested these hypotheses with the results from my respondents. (e.g. Type 2 will score higher than others on Extraversion). Out of a total of 62 individual hypotheses, 53 were confirmed and only one showed the opposite result to that expected. Going back to our discussion earlier about what makes a "good" personality theory, this and the studies above provide excellent support for the Enneagram in terms of its ability to make testable predictions.

Stress and security points

Besides the descriptions of the personality types themselves, one of the other testable predictions the Enneagram makes is the idea that we change in type-related ways when we are under stress or in times of security and that these changes are represented on the Enneagram diagram by the arrows. Although they may be referred to by different names, such as integration / disintegration (Riso and Hudson, 1999), these changes are a central part of Enneagram theory and there have been a couple of studies that have tried to investigate them further.

Thrasher (1994) addressed this issue in her doctoral thesis by asking nearly 120 participants who knew their Enneagram type to complete an anxiety measure to assess the degree to which they were feeling stressed or secure. She also asked participants' "significant others" to type the participants as they were "usually, under stress and when doing well". Unfortunately, she did not find any support for the concept of movement between types, either from the individuals themselves or from their significant others, though the results might be confounded by the fact, noted earlier, that significant others were found only to be reliable at choosing type when they were already familiar with the Enneagram. At around the same time, Twomey (1995) also made an attempt to address this issue. She asked 185 participants to complete a measure of ego strength to represent how "secure" the individuals felt and a measure of anxiety for how "stressed" they were, and then compared scores on these measures with their scores on the resourceful and non-resourceful scales of the WEPSS. Unfortunately she also did not find support for the idea that movement along the arrows in the Enneagram is a good representation for how we change in stress or security.

While these initial results are cause for caution in our understanding of stress and security changes, they should not be taken as definitive evidence that these changes do not happen. It is likely that the lack of support in these two studies could be simply down to methodological issues. As Thrasher (1994) suggests, future research in this area should use longitudinal studies and more sophisticated measures of stress or self-actualisation.

Applications

An essential part of the Enneagram teaching is its emphasis on self-actualisation, growth towards fulfilling one's potential. The Enneagram is a great tool to help people develop their self-awareness, giving us insight into our own and others' behaviour and motivations, easing personal and work relationships. It allows us to respond to the other person's intention rather than misinterpret their behaviour, and so lends itself to team-building and relationship development. Integral to the Enneagram is the guidance it provides in overcoming one's personality bias, loosening the limitations of personality. Despite this remarkable array of potential applications, there is very little research testing whether these promises can be fulfilled.

The use of the Enneagram in developing professional practice has been addressed in a couple of papers. Luckcock (2007) for example, recommends a combination of appreciative inquiry and the Enneagram in developing practitioner research and learning for education professionals. He demonstrates how this combination can provide a way to explore the subjective aspects of one's own experience and engage with others in collaborative dialogue. In addition, Ball (2009) promotes the use of the Enneagram in developing problem-solving approaches in nursing, particularly when dealing with inter-professional issues.

Using a case study approach, Ormond (2007) looked at whether Enneagram training could improve team effectiveness and outcomes such as emotional intelligence and interpersonal skills for a small team of eight people. While team effectiveness was improved, there was no measurable effect on the other outcomes, though this is likely to be due to the small sample size. Participants did comment on improved self-awareness and personal growth in interviews however, so it may be a larger sample will be able to capture these changes in the future.

Another aspect of my own research was addressing the utility of the Enneagram for various work applications. I found clear and theoretically-justified relationships between the Enneagram types and work attitudes and outcomes, like job satisfaction, enthusiasm and even type of occupation (Sutton et al., 2007). In addition, I tested the effects of a 4 hour introductory Enneagram workshop on work attitudes and personal development by asking over 80 participants to complete questionnaires before and after the workshops. Similarly to Ormond's work, the measures I used did not demonstrate a significant difference in self-awareness but participants did report a variety of positive outcomes, including improved understanding of themselves, a greater appreciation of diversity, improved communication with colleagues and increased confidence (Sutton et al., 2011).

Although we are making our first steps towards demonstrating the utility of the Enneagram in applied situations, there is still great scope for further work.

The Enneagram as a theory of personality

In summary, the research we have so far gives us a good indication that the Enneagram could fulfil the three criteria personality psychologists are looking for: we can make clear, testable hypotheses from it, it is practically useful and it is comprehensive. In practical terms, this is what we have learnt from the research:

The personality types described by the Enneagram can be clearly differentiated from each other using other established personality measures. (For an example, see the table which summarises findings on the Big Five.)

Enneagram personality questionnaires like the RHETI and WEPSS are reasonably reliable but we should still be cautious about their validity. That means, we're likely to get the same results on different occasions but there's no guarantee that's really our type.

The types are reasonably equally distributed in the population, though there are some small differences.

Trained practitioners are pretty good at typing people in interview, but not as good as they think they are!

It may seem obvious, but the best way to make an accurate decision on a person's type is by a combination of good knowledge of the person and good knowledge of the Enneagram. Just one or the other won't do.
Once people identify their type, it seems to be very stable.
There is good evidence that learning about the Enneagram has a positive impact on self-acceptance, self-development and understanding of others.

The evidence so far is certainly promising, but by no means definitive. There is much that remains unanswered – or perhaps unasked? We do not yet have clear research on the centres, wings or subtypes, or evidence around personality development. We also still need further research to test the stress and security changes that the Enneagram proposes. We have good descriptions of the typical traits of each type, but it would be interesting to know what it's like for people who identify as that type and don't match the "average" trait profile. And clear evidence of the applications of the Enneagram is still in its infancy.

Personal conviction is a good starting point but it needs to be tempered with an understanding of what we have and haven't got evidence for. We have reason to be cautious in our claims for the Enneagram, but I also believe we are on to something good and have a solid basis for confidence in using the Enneagram in our own lives and introducing it to others.

Summary of the Enneagram Type scores on the Big Five

Three studies used the Big Five (Sutton, 2007, Newgent et al., 2004, Brown and Bartram, 2005) to investigate the Enneagram types, which means that we can start to see what trait profile is typical for each of the nine types. The following are brief definitions of the traits. It should be remembered that just like no Enneagram type is "better" or "worse" than any of the others, neither are different scores on these traits.

Extraversion: people scoring at the higher end tend to be outgoing, sociable and confident, while those at the lower end are more reserved, independent and private.

Agreeableness: higher scores indicate that people are trusting, altruistic and will tend to go along with those around them, while lower scores indicate that people are more sceptical, self-focused and tough-minded.

Conscientiousness: those at the higher end are more dutiful, organised and disciplined, while those at the lower end are likely to be more disorganised and spontaneous.

Emotional Stability: high scores indicate people are secure, calm and unflappable while lower scores indicate people are excitable, emotionally reactive and alert.

Openness to Experience: people scoring high on this trait tend to be curious, liberal and novelty-seeking, while those at the lower end are more practical and conservative.

The table below shows the average score for each type on each trait.

	Extraversion	Agreeableness	Conscientious	Emotional Stability	Openness to Experience
Type 1			**HIGH**	high	low
Type 2	**HIGH**	high			low
Type 3	**HIGH**	low	**HIGH**		?
Type 4	low	?	low	**LOW**	high
Type 5	**LOW**	**LOW**			
Type 6	**LOW**	high		**LOW**	low
Type 7	**HIGH**		**LOW**	high	**HIGH**
Type 8	**HIGH**	**LOW**	high	?	high
Type 9	low	**HIGH**	low	**HIGH**	**LOW**

CAPS = found in more than one study
Lower case = found in one study and not found in others
? = contradictory evidence in different studies: high in some, low in others

References

Ball, E. (2009) Do professions have distinct or singular personalities? Using the enneagram to support and facilitate inter-professional nursing. *Nurse Education Today,* 29, 365-366.

Brown, A. & Bartram, D. (2005) Relationships between OPQ and Enneagram Types. London: SHL Group plc.

Brugha, C. M. (1998) The structure of development decision-making. *European Journal of Operational Research,* 104, 77-92.

Cutting, B. & Kouzmin, A. (2004) A synthesis of knowing and governance: making sense of organizational and governance polemics. *Corporate Governance,* 4, 76-114.

Dameyer, J. J. (2001) *Psychometric evaluation of the Riso-Hudson Enneagram Type Indicator.* PhD, California Institute of Integral Studies.

Daniels, D. N. & Price, V. A. (2000) *The Essential Enneagram,* San Francisco, HarperCollins.

Gamard, W. S. (1986) Interrater reliability and validity of judgments of enneagram personality types. PhD, California Institute of Integral Studies.

Kale, S. H. & Shrivastava, S. (2003) The enneagram system for enhancing workplace spirituality. The Journal of Management Development, 22, 308-328.

Kamineni, R. (2005) The Next Stage of Psychographic Segmentation: Usage of the Enneagram. *Journal of American Academy of Business, Cambridge,* 6, 315-320.

Luckcock, T. (2007) The soul of teaching and professional learning: An appreciative inquiry into the Enneagram of reflective practice. *Educational Action Research,* 15, 127-145.

Naranjo, C. (1994) *Character and Neurosis: an integrative view,* Nevada City, Gateways / IDHHB, Inc.

Newgent, R. A., Parr, P. E., Newman, I. & Higgins, K. K. (2004) The Riso-Hudson Enneagram Type Indicator: Estimates of Reliability and Validity. *Measurement and Evaluation in Counseling and Development,* 36, 226-237.

Ormond, C. H. (2007) The effects of emotional intelligence and team effectiveness of a newly formed corporate team learning the Enneagram. *Dissertation Abstracts International: Section B: The Sciences and Engineering,* 68, 2699.

Riso, D. R. & Hudson, R. (1999) *The Wisdom of the Enneagram,* New York, Bantam Books.

Sharp, P. M. (1994) A factor analytic study of three Enneagram personality inventories and the Vocational Preference Inventory. EdD, Texas Tech University.

Skodol, A. E., Oldham, J. M., Bender, D. S., Dyck, I. R., Stout, R. L., Morey, L. C., Shea, M. T., Zanarini, M. C., Sanilsow, C. A., Grilo, C. M., Mcglashan, T. H. & Gunderson, J. G. (2005) Dimensional Representations of DSM-IV Personality Disorders: Relationships to Functional Impairment. *American Journal of Psychiatry,* 162, 1919-1925.

Sutton, A. (2007) Implicit and Explicit Personality in Work Settings: An Application of Enneagram Theory. PhD, University of Leeds.

Sutton, A., Williams, H. & Allinson, C. (2007) Hidden Personality at Work - Predicting occupational outcomes by combining knowledge of employees' implicit and explicit personality. *Division of Occupational Psychology.* Bristol: British Psychological Society.

Sutton, A., Williams, H. & Allinson, C. (2009) Capturing patterns of traits using a typology net. *British Psychological Society Division of Occupational Psychology Conference.*

Sutton, A., Williams, H. & Allinson, C. (2011) Is ignorance bliss? The relationship of self-awareness to job well-being and coping strategies at work. *Performance and Reward Conference.* Manchester.

Thrasher, P. (1994) The enneagram: Movement between types, an inventory, and a criterion measure. PhD, Loyola University of Chicago.

Twomey, J. A. (1995) *The Enneagram and Jungian archetypal images.* PsyD, Chicago School of Professional Psychology.

Wagner, J. (1981) A Descriptive, Reliability and Validity Study of the Enneagram Personality Typology. PhD, Loyola University of Chicago.

Wagner, J. (1983) Reliability and validity study of a Sufi personality typology: The Enneagram. *Journal of Clinical Psychology,* 39, 712-717.

Wagner, J. P. (1999) *Wagner Enneagram Personality Style Scales Manual,* Los Angeles, Western Psychological Services.

Warling, D. L. (1995) An examination fo the external validity of the Riso Hudson Enneagram Type Indicator. MSc, University of Guelph.

Wyman, P. (1998) Integrating the MBTI and the Enneagram in Psychotherapy: The Core Self and the Defense System. *Journal of Psychological Type,* 46, 28-40.

Wyman, P. & Magidson, J. (2008) The effect of the Enneagram on measurement of MBTIReg. extraversion-introversion dimension. *Journal of Psychological Type,* 68, 1-8.

A COMPARISON OF THE NINE ENNEAGRAM PERSONALITY STYLES AND THEODORE MILLONS' EIGHT PERSONALITY PATTERNS

Jerome Wagner, Ph.D.

There are several congenial correlations between the nine styles of the Enneagram and the eight personality patterns proposed by Theodore Millon, Ph.D. (1969) who is an influential personality theorist, personality and clinical test developer, and a member of the task force that formulated one of the earliest versions of the *Diagnostic and Statistical Manual of Mental Disorders* published by the American Psychiatric Association. Since the correlations are in the direction one would expect, given the dynamics of each typology, the results provide some concurrent validity for both systems.

Millon devised a typology which defines eight personality patterns. His formulation of the genesis of these personality patterns parallels in many ways the Enneagram conception of the development of ego-fixations, particularly along the lines of Claudio Naranjo's theorizing (1994). Millon suggests that personality patterns result from an interaction between our genetic dispositions and temperament and our social environment which reinforces, punishes, or ignores our behavioral experiments. Nature + nurture = personality.

In the first years of life, children engage in a wide variety of spontaneous behaviors. Although they display certain characteristics consonant with their innate or constitutional dispositions, their way of reacting to others and coping with their environment tends, at first, to be capricious and unpredictable; flexibility and changeability characterize their moods, attitudes, and behaviors. This seemingly random behavior serves an exploratory function; each child is 'trying out' and testing during this period alternative modes for coping with his environment. As time progresses, the child learns which techniques 'work,' that is, which of these varied behaviors enable him to achieve his desires and avoid discomforts. Endowed with a distinctive pattern of capacities, energies and temperaments, which serve as base, he learns specific preferences among activities and goals and, perhaps of greater importance, learns that certain types of behaviors and strategies are especially successful for him in obtaining these goals. In his interaction with parents, siblings, and peers, he learns to discriminate which goals are permissible, which are rewarded and which are not.

Throughout these years, then, a shaping process has taken place in which the range of initially diverse behaviors becomes narrowed, selective and, finally, crystallized into particular preferred modes of seeking and achieving. In time, these behaviors persist and become accentuated; not only are they highly resistant to extinction but they are reinforced by the restrictions and repetitions of a limited social environment, and are perpetuated and intensified by the child's own perceptions, needs, and actions. Thus, given a continuity in basic biological equipment, and a narrow band of experiences for learning behavioral alternatives, the child develops a distinctive pattern of characteristics that are deeply etched, cannot be eradicated easily and pervade every facet of his functioning. In short, these characteristics are the essence and sum of his personality, his automatic way of perceiving, feeling, thinking and behaving. (Millon, 1969, p. 221)

Millon describes a *personality pattern* as:

...those intrinsic and pervasive modes of functioning which emerge from the entire matrix of the individual's developmental history, and which now characterize his perceptions and ways of dealing with his environment. We have chosen the term pattern for two reasons: first, to focus on the fact that these behaviors and attitudes derive from the constant and pervasive interaction of both biological dispositions and learned experience; and second, to denote the fact that these personality characteristics are not just a potpourri of unrelated behavior tendencies, but a tightly knit organization of needs, attitudes and behaviors. People may start out in life with random and diverse reactions, but the repetitive sequence of reinforcing experiences to which they are exposed gradually narrows their repertoire to certain habitual strategies, perceptions and behavior which become prepotent, and come to characterize their distinctive and consistent way of relating to the world. (Millon, 1969, p. 221)

In Millon's theory the individual's personality pattern becomes the foundation for his or her capacity to function in a mentally healthy or unhealthy way:

When an individual displays an ability to cope with his environment in a flexible and adaptive manner and when his characteristic perceptions and behaviors foster increments in personal gratification, then he may be said to possess a normal and healthy personality pattern. Conversely, when average responsibilities and everyday relationships are responded to inflexibly or defectively, or when the individual's characteristic perceptions and behaviors foster increments in personal discomfort or curtail his opportunities to learn and grow, then a pathological personality pattern may be said to exist. (Millon, 1969, p. 222).

I think many Enneagram theorists would agree that health involves being flexible and adaptable enough to access the internal resources of all nine Enneagram styles to bring them to bear on whatever environmental exigencies are present. We have many tools in our toolkit, not just a hammer, to deal with our problems. Or to use another analogy, given the requirements of the situation, we have nine players on our inner team that we can bring into the game instead of just the two or three with whom we are most familiar and comfortable.

Sometimes we are required to be exact as when performing brain surgery; sometimes we need to be unfocused and brooding to allow a new solution to arise from our unconscious. There are times when we need to bring force to bear on a situation when justice requires an intervention; there are times when we need to go with the flow, allowing nature to take its course. Sometimes we need to keep the law to avoid intersection collisions; sometimes we need to break the law to overcome tyranny. Sometimes we need to use our head; and sometimes our heart. There is a time to be serious and a time to play; a time to weep and a time to rejoice.

The Study

Some time ago (Wagner, 1981) I conducted a research project comparing the nine Enneagram styles with Theodore Millon's (1969) eight personality types. While it's not easy squeezing nine into eight, I did find some significant correlations between the two systems with each Enneagram style showing a distinct profile of Millon's eight patterns. Among other things, the differences help tease out how Enneagram look-alikes are not-alike. And even though the study was done in the past, the comparisons should still hold up in the present.

The sample consisted of 390 subjects, combined from various groups. There were 311 women and 79 men, with ages ranging from 19-82. The age distribution of the sample followed a bell curve with most of the subjects in the 20-60 age range.

For this study I constructed a 135 item *Enneagram Personality Inventory*, (Wagner, 1981) to assess Enneagram styles and used the 150 item *Millon-Illinois Self-Report Inventory* (Millon, 1974) to determine Millon's types. The MISRI was designed for nonclinical normal adults. Millon went on to develop the *Millon Clinical Multiaxial Inventory* (MCMI) to measure a more pathological clinical population.

I eventually developed a questionnaire, the *Wagner Enneagram Personality Style Scales* (1999) with much more robust reliability and validity.

Even with the lower reliability and validity of these early instruments, all of the differences among the Enneagram types and Millon scales were significantly different beyond the .0001 level except on Millon's active-ambivalent scale 8 which at .05 was still statistically significant. Apparently a little ambivalence shows up even in testing.

I'll give a brief summary of Millon's theory of types along with his description of the eight patterns and then show how the Enneagram styles scored in his system.

Millon's Types

Millon describes eight personality patterns based on whether we *seek* comfort and satisfaction (positive reinforcement) or attempt to *avoid* emotional pain and distress (negative reinforcement); whether we seek satisfactions from *outside* or *within* ourselves; and whether we *actively* or *passively* go about maximizing rewards and minimizing pain. Individuals who seem aroused and attentive, arranging and manipulating life events to achieve gratification and avoid discomfort, display an *active* pattern; those who seem apathetic, restrained, yielding, resigned, or seemingly content to allow events to take their own course without personal regulation or control, possess a *passive* pattern.

Detached types are those persons who fail to seek positive reinforcements and who experience few rewards or satisfactions in life, be it from self or others.

1. Passive-detached/apathetic/asocial personalities seek neither to gain positive reinforcements nor to avoid negative reinforcements. Their self-image is *"I am complacent "*and their interpersonal attitude is *indifference*. They may come from an *impersonal* family background and their temperamental disposition is *phlegmatic* or anhedonic.

High scorers tend to keep to themselves, appearing rather quiet and unemotional. They are undemanding, even-handed, fair-minded and not easily excited. They tend not to get emotionally involved with others and do not often feel strongly about things. They do not avoid other people, but simply feel indifferent about having others around.

2. Active-detached/sensitive/avoidant personalities do not seek positive reinforcements from others or from themselves but do seek to avoid negative ones. Their self-image is *"I am alienated"* and their interpersonal attitude is *distrustful*. They may have experienced *parental rejection and deprecation* in their family background and their temperamental disposition is *threctic*, representing a fearfulness and vulnerability to threat, sensitivity to stimulation, and tenseness and hyperirritability.

High scorers tend to be quite shy or socially ill-at-ease with others. These persons would like to be close to people but have learned that it is better to maintain one's distance and not to trust the friendship of others. Although they often feel lonely, they avoid close interpersonal contact, often fearing rejection and tending to keep their sometimes very strong feelings to themselves. They may be tense and cranky and withdrawing and can provoke hostile and rejecting attitudes from others.

Dependent types are those individuals who experience reinforcements from sources other than themselves and who measure their satisfactions or discomforts by how others react to or feel about them.

3. Passive-dependent/cooperative/submissive personalities wait for others to provide reinforcements. Their self-image is *"I am inadequate"* and their interpersonal attitude is *compliance*. They may have had *over-protective parents* and their temperament is a combination of *melancholic* and *threctic*.

High scorers tend to be soft-hearted, sentimental and kindly in relationships with others. They are extremely reluctant to assert themselves, however, and avoid taking initiative or assuming a leadership role. They are inclined to be quite dependent on others, preferring to let them take the lead and give direction. It is typical of them to "play down" their own achievements and to underestimate their abilities. They present a gentle, sad, fearful visage and style that provokes warmth and over-protection from others.

4. Active-dependent/sociable/gregarious personalities manipulate and seduce others to provide reinforcements for them. Their self-image is *"I am sociable"* and their interpersonal attitude is *seductive*. In their families they experienced *irregular positive reinforcements* of good behaviors and *no negative reinforcement* for bad behavior. There was a variety of sources of gratification. Millon did not assign a temperamental label for this pattern – though sanguine might describe this approach.

High scorers are talkative, socially charming and frequently dramatic or emotionally expressive. They tend to have strong, but usually brief relationships with others. These persons always look for new excitements and interesting experiences. They often find themselves becoming bored with routine and longstanding relationships. They are active and responsive and provoke varied and stimulating reactions from others.

Independent types are persons who experience reinforcements primarily from themselves, whose gratification is gauged primarily in terms of their own values and desires with little reference to the concerns and wishes of others.

5. Passive-independent/self-assured/narcissistic personalities are self-satisfied and content to leave matters be. Their self image is *"I am admirable"* and their interpersonal attitude is *exploitive*. Pampered and indulged, they experienced *non-contingent positive reinforcement* in their families. Here, again, Millon assigns no temperamental disposition, though *sanguine* might fit.

High scorers tend to be quite confident in their abilities and are often seen by others as self-centered and egocentric. They rarely doubt their own self-worth and act in a self-assured manner. These persons tend to take others for granted and often do not share or concern themselves with the needs of those to whom they relate.

6. Active-independent/assertive/aggressive personalities seek to arrogate more power to themselves. Their self image is *"I am assertive"* and their interpersonal attitude is *vindictive*. They may have experienced *non-contingent punishment* in their families and their temperament is *choleric* and *parmic*, representing a fearless, aggressive, thick-skinned approach to life.

High scorers are strong-willed and tough minded, tending to lead and dominate others. They frequently question the abilities of others and prefer to take over responsibility and direction in most situations. They are often blunt and unkind, tending to be impatient with the problems of weaknesses of others. They are both suspicious of others and confident in their powers of self-sufficiency. Their acting out, aggressive, impulsive, intrusive, and incorrigible behavior provokes aggression from others.

Ambivalent types are those who have conflicting attitudes about dependence and independence, who experience considerable conflict over whether to be guided by what others say and wish or to follow their own opposing desires and needs.

7. Passive-ambivalent/disciplined/conforming personalities submerge their desire for independence and behave in an overly acquiescent manner. They are dependent on the outside and independent on the inside. Their self image is "*I am conscientious*" and their interpersonal attitude is *respectful*. They had *over-controlling parents* who scheduled them and experienced *regular contingent punishment*. Their temperament is a combination of *threctic-choleric-anhedonic.*

High scorers are very serious-minded, efficient, and rule-conscious persons who try to do the "right" and "proper" things. They tend to keep their emotions under check and dislike "showy" people. They prefer to live their lives in a very orderly and well-planned fashion, avoiding unpredictable and unexpected situations. They restrain their anger out of fear. They know what they should not do, but not what they can do.

8. Active-ambivalent/unpredictable/negativistic personalities vacillate erratic-ally from a position of dependence to a position of independence. Their self image is "*I am discontented*" and their interpersonal attitude is *vacillation*. They experienced *parental inconsistency* and so were unable to predict the consequences of their behavior. Their temperament is a combination of *threctic-melancholic-choleric*.

High scorers tend to be discontent and pessimistic. They often find themselves behaving unpredictably: sometimes being out-going and enthusiastic; then changing quickly to the opposite. They often feel guilt about their moodiness, apologize to the people involved, but soon are just as moody as ever. As children who were difficult to schedule, irritable, sullen, peevish, testy, fretful, and nervous, they provoked confusion and vacillation in their parents and now, as adults, in others.

Enneagram Types

Now let's take the Enneagram styles in turn and see how they correlated with Millon's types. Each Enneatype has a distinct configuration of Millon's patterns.

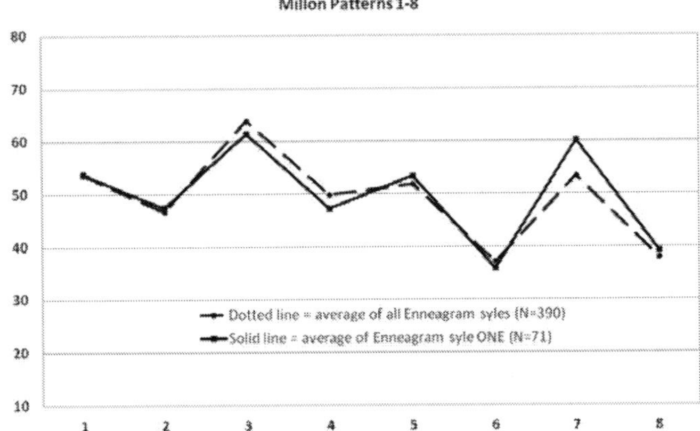

Enneagram Style One (N=71) practically paralleled the pattern of all the Enneagram types averaged together (N=390). In the graphs, the dotted line is the average of all the Enneatypes while the solid line is the average of each particular Enneagram type. Ones scored highest on Millon's passive-ambivalent scale (7), which is his disciplined or conforming pattern. These individuals are described by Millon as being serious-minded, efficient, and rule-conscious persons who try to do the "right" and "proper" things. They are perfectionistic, compulsive, legalistic, righteous, and moralistic. They adopt a "good boy," "good girl" image. In their childhood they were taught a deep sense of responsibility to others and a feeling of guilt when these responsibilities have not been met. As youngsters they were moralized to inhibit their natural inclinations toward frivolous play and impulse gratification. These are all remarkable One-like characterizations.

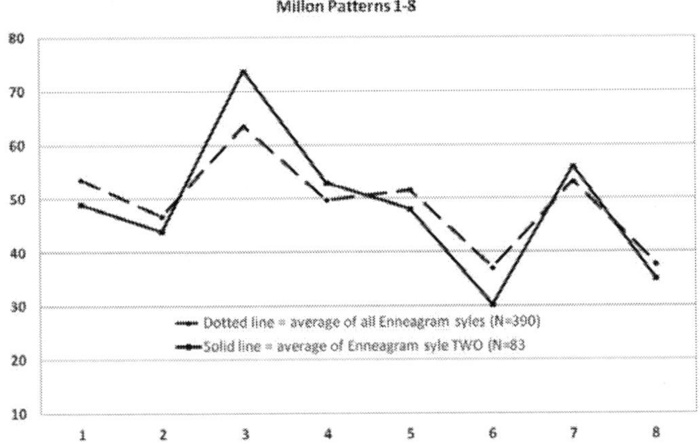

Enneagram Style Two (N=83) scored highest on Millon's passive-dependent personality scale (3). This is the cooperative or submissive type of person. High scorers tend to be soft-hearted, sentimental, and kindly in their relationships with others. They are inclined to be dependent on others for approval. Twos also scored higher on Millon's active-dependent scale (4). By their helping behavior, they are actively trying to solicit the approval of others. Twos scored lower on Millon's independent personality scales (Millon 5 and 6) and were also less detached (Millon scales 1 and 2) than the average Enneatype.

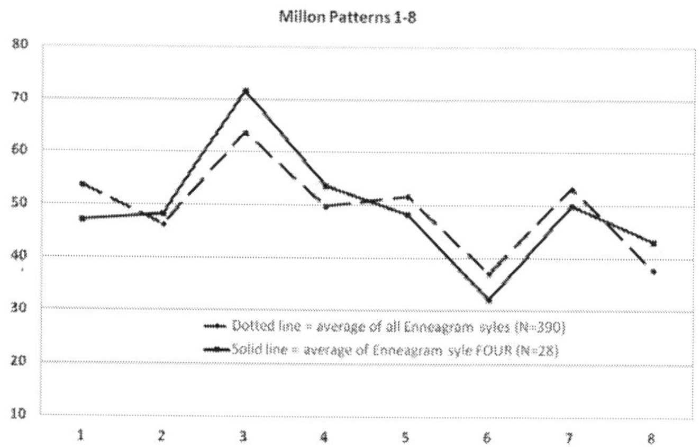

Enneagram Style Three (N=28) scored highest on Millon's passive-independent/self-assured/narcissistic personality pattern (5). High scorers here tend to be quite confident in their abilities and are often seen by others as self-centered and egocentric. They convey a calm, self-assured quality in their social behavior which is sometimes perceived by others as immodest, haughty, cocksure, and arrogant. They exaggerate their powers, transform failure into success, and inflate their self worth. Threes also scored high on Millon's active independent/gregarious/sociable scale (6). High scorers here are talkative, socially charming, and frequently dramatic or emotionally expressive. Not surprisingly, threes scored low on Millon's detached patterns (1 and 2) since they move towards and against, not away from people.

Enneagram Style Four (N=28) scored highest on the passive/dependent scale (3). They are dependent on others' approval and acceptance, but tend to stand off, waiting for others to notice them and invite them into the group. They are also high on the active/dependent scale (4). Through their suffering and specialness, they seek to draw others to them. Fours scored low on the independent scales (Millon 5 and 6). They were lower than the average on Millon's scale 7, the disciplined style. Fours want to be original, not conforming. Some of the Fours scored high on Millon's active-detached scale (2), the sensitive personality. These Fours (like Fives) actively avoid involvement to keep from being misunderstood and hurt.

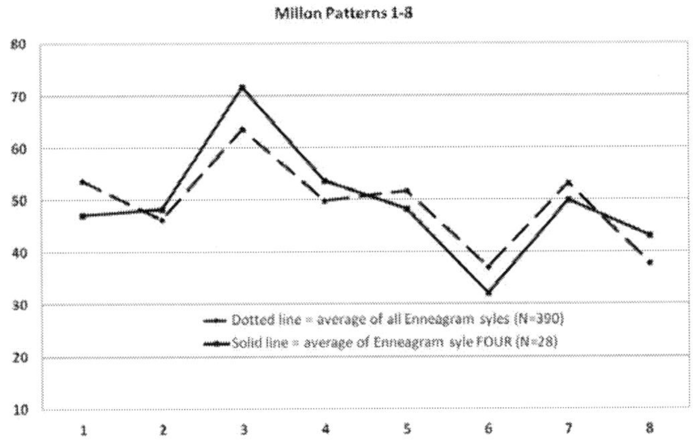

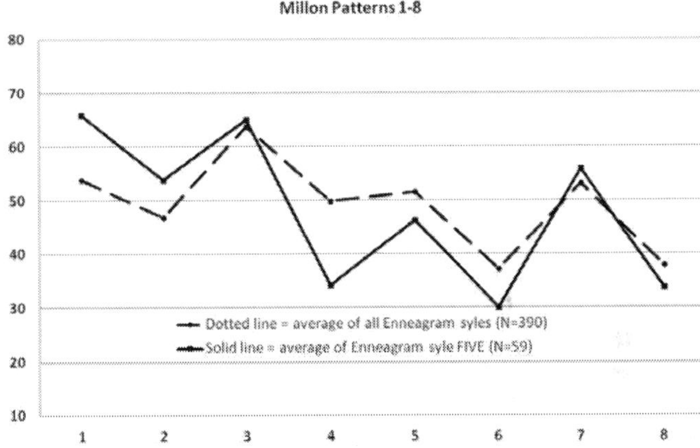

Enneagram Style Five (N=59) scored higher than the average Enneatypes on Millon's detached patterns (1 and 2) and lower on Millon's styles 4 (gregarious), 5 (self-assured) and 6 (assertive). High scorers on the passive-detached/apathetic pattern (Millon 1) tend to keep to themselves, appearing rather quiet and unemotional. They are even-handed, fair-minded, and not easily excited. They tend not to get emotionally involved with others and do not often feel strongly about things. As we shall see, Fives share some of this pattern with their look-alike Nines. Where they differ is their higher elevation on Millon's style 2 the active-detached/avoidant pattern. High scorers on this scale tend to be shy or socially ill-at-ease with others. These persons would like to be close to people but have learned that it is better to maintain one's distance and not to trust the friendship of others. This is in contrast to passive-detached asocial individuals (Millon scale 1) who do not avoid other people, but simply feel indifferent about having others around. Avoidant personalities (Millon scale 2) are highly alert to social stimuli and are oversensitive to the moods and feelings of others, especially those which portend rejection and humiliation. While passive-detached personalities (Nines) tend to drift to the shore, active-detached personalities (Fives) head for the hills.

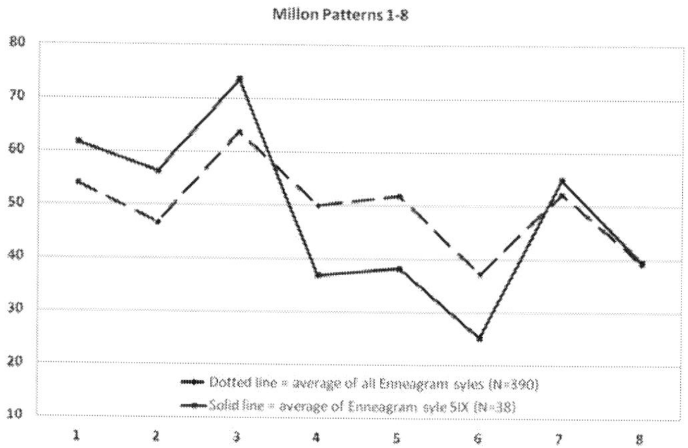

Enneagram Style Six (N=38) scored higher than the average on both the passive and active detached scales (1 and 2) and on the passive-dependent scale (Millon 3) where they competed with the Twos for the highest scores on this cooperative/submissive/compliant scale. Sixes (at least the fearful variety) want to belong in the group and want to be aligned with authority. Sixes were lower than average on the gregarious, self-assured, and assertive scales (Millon 4, 5, 6) and appeared the least aggressive of all the types. In contrast to their Five neighbors, Sixes were less passively-detached Millon scale 1), but more actively-detached (Millon scale 2). Perhaps their fear makes them even more wary and cautious than their hyper-alert neighbors. Sixes were more gregarious (Millon scale 4) but noticeably less self-assured (Millon scale 5) than Fives.

Enneagram Style Seven (N=19) came out less detached (Millon 1 and 2), dependent (Millon 3), and disciplined (Millon 7) than the other Enneagram styles and more gregarious, self-assured, and assertive (Millon 4, 5, 6). This appears to reflect the Sevens' self-image of "I am O.K.," their outgoing nature, their liking for parties and social events, and their tendency towards gluttony which would not lead them to a high disciplined score. Interestingly and fittingly the different groups that made up the Seven sample had the most variability amongst themselves of all the Enneagram types. This might have been due to the small sample size or this is what tracking a collection of butterflies looks like.

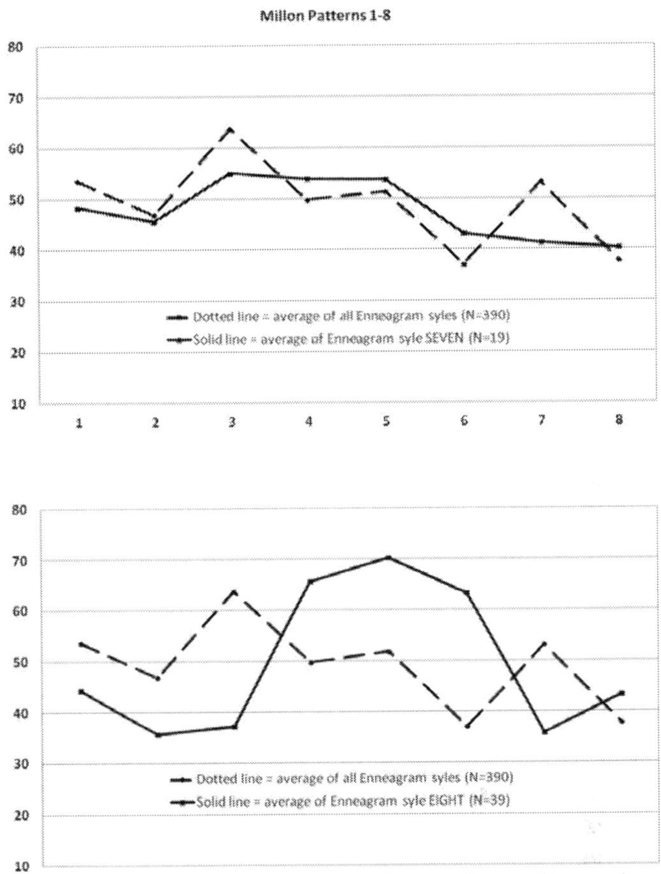

Enneagram Style Eight (N=39) profile came out almost the opposite of the other Enneagram types – giving new meaning to the term oppositional character. Eights were decidedly less detached (Millon scales 1 and 2), dependent (Millon scale 3), and conforming (Millon scale 7), while being more gregarious, self-assured, and assertive (Millon scales 4, 5, 6) than the average Enneatype. They displayed a 5 (passive independent), 4 (active dependent), 6 (active independent) pattern for their highest scales but were by far the highest scorers among the Enneagram types on the active independent assertive scale 6. Millon describes high scorers on this scale as strong-willed and tough-minded, tending to lead and dominate others. They frequently question the abilities of others and prefer to take over responsibility and direction in most situations. They are often blunt and unkind and are driven by a need to assert their own superiority. Independence for them stems not so much from a belief in self-worth, as from a fear and mistrust of others. They feel secure only when they are independent of those who may harm and humiliate them. These and further descriptions of the active-independent personality read like they are taken directly from the Eight's playbook.

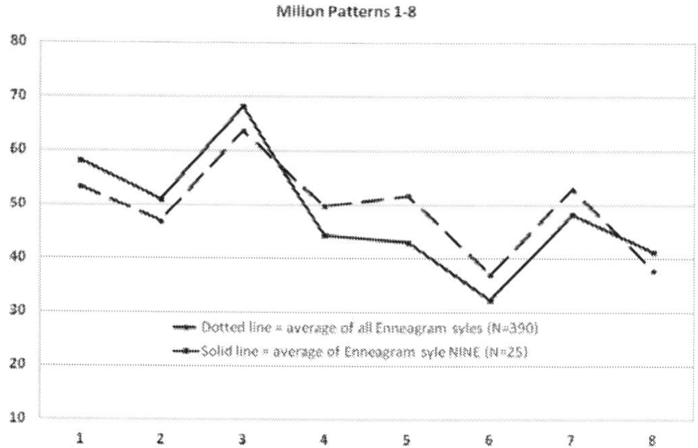

Enneagram Style Nine (N=25) profile, in contrast to the Eights but like the Ones, followed the general overall pattern of all the other styles. Apparently even on personality inventories, Nines do not like to differentiate themselves from others. The Nine profile has an affinity to the Enneagram type Five and Six configurations. Like the Fives and Sixes, Nines scored higher on the detached scales (Millon scales 1 and 2). They scored higher on the passive-dependent scale (Millon scale 3) than the average – more so than the Fives but less so than the Sixes. Nines scored lower than the average on the gregarious, self-assured, and assertive scales (Millon 4, 5, and 6). They were more gregarious and assertive than Enneatypes Five and Six and more self-assured than Sixes but less assured than Fives. Nines, Fives, and Sixes show different elevations in their scales which might help in differentiating them. Not surprisingly Nines scored lower than the average on the disciplined personality scale (Millon 7). Nines tend to be more "whatever", relaxed, and loose rather than rigid, uptight, and driven.

As can be seen in the accompanying figures, each Enneagram style has a profile distinct from all the other Enneatypes on Millon's typology, providing some confirmation that there might indeed be nine distinct Enneagram styles. Also the correlations among the Enneagram and Millon types are, for the most part, congenial by being in the direction one would expect. For example Ones are disciplined while Nines, not so much. This yields some concurrent validity to both systems. These varying profiles also point to some underlying dissimilarities among Enneatype look-alikes.

Enneagram Look-Alikes

Even a cursory knowledge of Millon's patterns might be useful in distinguishing between Enneagram look-alikes.

Ones and Sixes look alike in that both are conscientious, responsible, rule-abiding, accountable, etc.

But Sixes are more asocial and avoidant and more cooperative than Ones. And they are less sociable, self-assured, and assertive than Ones. Ones have an edge, however, on being disciplined.

Twos and Sevens look alike when Twos try to cheer you up if they can't help you and Sevens try to help you if they can't cheer you up.

Twos and Sevens are about the same when it comes to being asocial and avoidant. Both are below average. But Twos are much more cooperative and much less assertive than Sevens. And they are more disciplined.

Threes and Eights are both problem/solution/action oriented, assertive, energetic, etc.

Both are much less detached than the other Enneatypes. But Threes are more dependent and submissive than Eights; both are equally self-assured but Eights are more aggressive. Threes are considerably more disciplined and less unpredictable. So Eights would be more: "Let's step on it;" while Threes would be: "Let's calibrate it."

Fours and Sevens look alike when Fours are on the manic side of their mood swings though Sevens might decline the invitation to swing down to the melancholy side.

Fours tend to be a little more sensitive than Sevens but not as much as one might expect. Fours are more passive-dependent/cooperative than Sevens but just about as active-dependent/gregarious as Sevens. Fours are less assertive but more disciplined and unpredictable than Sevens.

Fives and Nines are alike in that both are on the sidelines. However Nines have drifted there, while Fives have headed there.

While both Fives and Nines are more detached than the other Enneagram styles, Fives are more asocial and a little more avoidant than Nines. Nines are more submissive than Fives and are more gregarious but a little less self-assured. Fives are more disciplined than Nines and not as unpredictable.

Readers are invited to explore these Enneagram-Millon profiles to see how Enneatypes differ in their underlying dynamics even though they may look alike on the surface.

Bibliography

Millon, T. (1969) *Modern psychopathology*. Philadelphia: W.B. Saunders Co.

Millon, T. (1974) *Millon-Illinois Self-Report Inventory (MISRI)*. Philadelphia: W.B. Saunders Co.

Naranjo, C. (1994) *Character and neurosis: An integrative view*. Nevada City, CA: Gateways/IDHHB.

Wagner, J. (1981) *A descriptive, reliability, and validity study of the Enneagram personality typology*. Ph.D., 1981, Loyola University, Chicago. 41/11A. GAX 81-09973.

Wagner, J. (1999) *Wagner Enneagram Personality Style Scales*: Los Angeles: Western Psychological Services. www.wepss.com

THOMAS MERTON
ANOTHER LOOK AT ENNEAGRAM TYPE

Virginia S. George

Abstract

Thomas Merton is a world-renowned writer and much beloved figure who has served as exemplar and guide to generations of American Catholics and to contemplatives of all faiths. In Enneagram circles, the conventional wisdom is that Merton is Type Four. Grounded in Don Richard Riso's and Russ Hudson's Insight Approach™ to the Enneagram of Personality, my master's thesis, Thomas Merton: Another Look at Enneagram Type, *is a case study that argues Merton is Type Seven. This article is based on my thesis.*

Thomas Merton is one of the great lights of the Twentieth Century. As a contemplative monk and prolific writer, he continues to be widely read and studied today. The conventional wisdom about Merton's Enneagram Type is that he is a Four (Zuercher, 1996; Russ Hudson, personal communication, April 2007; Rohr & Ebert, 2001).

To date, Enneagram Type has been discerned by a largely intuitive process, with the Type-*er* getting a sense of the individual to be typed based on his or her observation of the individual's style of being in the world. Since Merton is no longer with us—he died in 1968—observation of his style of being in the world appears to have been based on the style of the writing he published during his lifetime.

In my master's thesis, *Thomas Merton: Another Look at Enneagram Type*, it is my hypothesis that Merton is not a Four but a Seven. To prove my hypothesis, I relied not on my intuition but on evidence culled from thousands of pages written by and about Merton both before and after his death. In addition to Merton's posthumously published private journals and letters, I relied heavily on his official biography *The Seven Mountains of Thomas Merton* by Michael Mott (1984).

This article is based on my thesis. I present first a Factual Background or portrait of Thomas Merton, which summarizes my research, followed by my

Enneagram analysis, which is grounded in Don Richard Riso's and Russ Hudson's Insight Approach™ to the Enneagram of Personality.

Factual Background

Thomas Merton was born in 1915 in France to a New Zealander father and an American mother. He lost his mother at age 6 and his father at age 15. He was educated first in France, then in England. Before starting at Oxford University, he traveled on his own in Europe and fell in love with the churches in Rome. Oxford itself was a disaster for him. He spent his first year drinking and womanizing, barely passed his exams, and his scholarship was in jeopardy. He is said to have fathered a child out of wedlock, a shameful scandal in his day. (Mott, 1984)

His guardian recommended that he move to the United States, where his maternal grandparents lived, and where he resumed his education at Columbia University (Mott, 1984). He continued drinking and womanizing, but he was also a budding writer and Big Man on Campus, serving as editor of the yearbook and contributing to the literary and humor magazines (Mott, 1984). At the same time, Merton was doing a lot of spiritual reading, mostly in the Roman Catholic tradition, and also beginning to meditate (Mott, 1984). At age 23, he converted to Roman Catholicism, then, in 1941, at the age of 26, he entered Gethsemani, a monastery of the Cistercian Order of the Strict Observance (C.O.S.O), also known as the Trappists (Mott, 1984). "Some of Merton's friends wondered if he would remain in the monastery as long as a year. Merton liked people, he was gregarious, he liked women, he liked talk, lots of talk, argument, and laughter" (Mott, 1984, p. 202). But Merton took vows of poverty, chastity, obedience, and stability, the latter a vow to spend the rest of his life at Gethsemani (Merton, 1953).

In his early years at the monastery Merton was cloistered—confined to the monastery grounds. He was permitted to write for two hours a day and produced several books for his order as well as private journals. In 1946, he received permission to write *The Seven Storey Mountain* (SSM), his spiritual autobiography, which grew to 650 typed pages in less than a year—all in two hours a day (Mott, 1984, pp. 227-28). When published in 1948, SSM was a runaway hit, selling more than 600,000 copies in the year after its release. SSM made Merton famous and he began to receive fan mail.

The early years at Gethsemani were Merton's "Edenic period" (Mott, 1984, p. 208). Harford (2006) tells us that "Merton had been on a high for more than two years" after entering Gethsemani (p. 60). Beginning in 1949, however, Merton began to have crises of stability, in which he desired more privacy and greater solitude. He wrote to other orders and to other foundations of the Trappists looking for a place that he thought might bring him what he called perfect solitude. He began to dream of being a hermit and of having his own hermitage on land Gethsemani owned. He could have left Gethsemani at any time, but he had taken a vow of obedience and wanted whatever he did to be done with the permission of his order. (Mott, 1984)

Permission to leave Gethsemani was never granted, but Merton began to win accommodation to his desires for more privacy and solitude. He was named the Forester for Gethsemani, which gave him leave to roam the monastery woods alone. He was given an abandoned tool shed to use as a kind of day hermitage. At first, he feels he has arrived at the very place he has been longing for, only to experience crisis after crisis. Eventually he is given his own single room and again he believes he has found perfect solitude. But soon enough he is seeking permission to transfer, leave, or become a hermit on monastery grounds. At the end of 1960, Merton is allowed to become a part-time hermit in a small building on monastery grounds built for that purpose. Within months, however, he is again pressing for perfect solitude somewhere else. He writes to bishops seeking a hermitage in some remote part of their dioceses. He presses his Abbot for permission to transfer to monasteries in South America. In 1965, he is at last permitted to become a full-time hermit. Once again he feels that he has arrived at perfect solitude. Within two months, however, he is seeking transfer to South America. (Mott, 1984)

Merton continued to write throughout this period. By the time of his death at age 53 in 1968, he had written more than 36 books, including books of poetry, essays, and edited private journals, plus dozens of book reviews and magazine and journal articles, a play that was produced on TV, and the screenplay for a film (Mott, 1984). In addition, he continued with his private journals, most of which were not published until 25 years after his death, and wrote over ten thousand letters to more than two thousand correspondents around the world (Mott, 1984, p. 487; Shannon & Bochen, 2008, pp. vi-viii). He is said to have been an incredibly fast typist. One witness to Merton's typing said he would not have been surprised if the typewriter had burst into flames (Forest, 1984, pp. 54-55).

Merton was also highly advanced on the spiritual path. His *(New) Seeds of Contemplation* and *Thoughts in Solitude* are classics that bear witness to his mystical experience and understanding. He may even have attained nondual consciousness in the days before his death (Merton, 1973, pp. 233-36).

But what was Merton like? According to people who actually knew him, Merton was "a very different type than the image he projected in his writings" (Bamberger, 1983, p. 116). He was "both charming and interesting" (Mott, 1984, p. 96), "a very outgoing person with an obvious ease with relationships, very approachable, with a great sense of humor" (Bamberger, 1984, p. 116) and a "sharp and penetrating intellect" (Fox, 1983, p. 144). "His whole manner was open and...constantly enthusiastic" (Bamberger, 1983, p. 44). He had "tremendous energy and dynamism" (Bamberger, 1984, p. 116). There was "an air of dispatch in all he did" (Kelty, 1983, p. 22). He was "full of humor and jokes, and always buoyant" (Burns, 1984, p. 104), even "effervescent" (Kelty, 1983, p. 26), "bursting with fervor and enthusiasm" (Fox, 1983, p. 143). He was interested in everything, "a man churning with ideas" (Laughlin, 1984, p. 6). His friend Bob

Lax said Merton "walked with joy, bounced with joy" (Mott, 1984, p. 102). James Forest described Merton's laugh as "a monsoon of joy" (Mott, 1984, p. 381), and Merton's face as "unfettered in its expressiveness, the eyes bright and quick and sure, suggesting some strange balance between mischief and wisdom" (Mott, 1984, p. 386).

Typing Thomas Merton

Methodology

Exemplars of type are individuals from history, literature, or popular culture who are used to teach the characteristic energies of the Enneagram types. Exemplars have been typed to date by a largely intuitive process. Only rarely is evidence presented to justify an Enneagram diagnosis. Suzanne Zuercher (1996) is the only person I know of who has attempted an in-depth analysis of an exemplar. She chose Thomas Merton and concluded he was Type Four. Zuercher (1996) is an Enneagram teacher and author who states that her diagnosis of Merton has been based on her lifetime of reading Merton and the materials she had access to (pp. 8, 13). To a large extent, Zuercher and I had access to the same materials, except that the bulk of Merton's private journals, on which I heavily relied, were not published until after Zuercher had written her study.

In *Merton: An Enneagram Profile*, Zuercher (1996) says she focused on Merton's spiritual path, presumably as evidenced by his spiritual writings (p. 13). I adopted a case study approach and focused on Merton's behavior, as evidenced by his autobiography (SSM); his private journals; his letters; his official biography; and the witness of individuals who knew him. I then compared observed personality traits and behaviors to descriptions of type presented by Riso and Hudson (1996, 1999, 2000, 2003). Why not compare my observations to a variety of Enneagram authors? As Riso and Hudson (1999) tell us, there are, unfortunately, "inconsistencies and contradictions" among the various Enneagram authors (p. 389). This is because, as Riso and Hudson (1999) acknowledge, "For better or worse, there is no such thing as 'the Enneagram,'—only different interpretations of it by different authors" (p. 389). I decided to focus on Riso's and Hudson's interpretation, given their impressive body of work and long years in the Enneagram field. The works of two other leading Enneagram experts and teachers, Sandra Maitri (2000) and Helen Palmer (1988), were consulted on occasion both to confirm and augment the Riso and Hudson material.

The Difference Between Type Four and Type Seven

Generally speaking, Type Four is introverted and melancholic. Riso and Hudson (1999) describe the Four as the "Sensitive, Withdrawn Type: Expressive, Dramatic, Self-Absorbed, and Temperamental" (p. 180). They say that "Fours want to express themselves and their individuality, to create and surround themselves with beauty, to maintain certain moods and feelings, to withdraw to protect their vulnerabilities, to take care of emotional needs before attending to anything else, and to attract a 'rescuer' who will understand them" (Riso & Hudson, 2003, p. 118). Exemplars of the Four cited by Riso and Hudson (1999) include Sylvia Plath, Anne Rice, Bob Dylan, and Edgar Allen Poe.

Type Seven, on the other hand, tends to be ebullient, needing to constantly be on the go or engaged with stimulating mental activity. They fear being stuck without choices, without activities to keep their minds occupied. They are multi-talented generalists who enjoy learning about new things and easily pick up all kinds of skills (Riso & Hudson, 1996, pp. 269-270). They tend to be involved in a variety of projects at any one time (Riso & Hudson, 1999, p. 262), have a "wide-ranging curiosity" (Riso & Hudson, 1999, p. 263), and are "exhilarated by the rush of ideas" (Riso & Hudson, 1999, pp. 262-63). They are "exceptionally fast learners" (Riso & Hudson, 1999, p. 262), adept at languages (Riso & Hudson, 1996, p. 269), and tend to be dexterous in such manual skills as playing the piano and typing (Riso & Hudson, 1999, p. 262). Maitri (2000) describes Sevens as buoyant and curious, interested in everything, and youthful in spirit (p. 223). Exemplars of the Seven cited by Riso and Hudson (1999) include Jim Carrey, John F. Kennedy, and Steven Spielberg.

Although Type Four and Type Seven appear to be polar opposites, not easily mistaken, Riso and Hudson teach that Sevens who are depressed can present as (D. R. Riso, personal communication, April 2007) and may even mistake themselves for Fours (Riso & Hudson, 2000, p. 228). As considered elsewhere in this article, there is ample evidence that Merton suffered from depression throughout his life. I believe Merton may also have suffered from Bipolar Spectrum Disorder (BSD), also known as manic-depressive disorder. Those on the BSD spectrum can be psychologically normal most of the time and only occasionally suffer from depression, hypomania, or mania (Jamison, 1993). Riso and Hudson (1999) have indicated that Type Seven is the only type to suffer from BSD (p. 281).

Generally speaking, each of us is qualified to name our own Enneagram Type, provided we have sufficient self-knowledge and sufficient knowledge of the Enneagram. The Enneagram was unknown to Merton, and we cannot know which Enneagram Type Merton might have claimed. Riso and Hudson (1996), however, have correlated Carl Jung's (1921/1971) eight psychological types with eight of the nine Enneagram Types. We do know which Jungian psychological type Merton claimed. After reading Jung's (1921/1971) *Psychological Types* one day, Merton (1995) recorded in his journal that he thought he was an *extraverted sensation* type (p. 96). According to Riso and Hudson (1996), the extraverted sensation type correlates to Enneagram Type Seven (pp. 262-263, 442). The *introverted intuitive* type, they say, correlates to Enneagram Type Four (Riso & Hudson, 1996, p. 147, 442).

The Childhood Pattern

If Merton is Enneagram Type Seven, Riso and Hudson (2000) would expect to find him having had frustrated object relations with his maternal figure but not frustrated object relations with his paternal figure (pp. 67-70). That is in fact the case. Merton's official biographer, Michael Mott (1984), tells us there was no one Merton loved more than his father (p. 182).

To explain a Seven's frustration with the maternal figure, Riso and Hudson (1999) would expect to find early evidence of the Seven's being cut off from the maternal figure's nurturance. They give as examples the birth of another child and the mother's absence due to illness (pp. 264-65). In Merton's case, both are true. His brother, John Paul, was born when Merton was around three and a half years old. We are told Merton now "had tantrums enough for any number of children" and his mother's "discipline grew harsher" (Mott, 1984, p. 17). Compounding the frustration occasioned by his sibling's birth is the fact that Merton's mother suffered from stomach cancer and died when Merton was only six. Clearly, Merton fits the childhood pattern for the Seven.

Merton's Depressions

Following his mother's death, what was likely Merton's first episode of major depression sounds crushing for one so young (Merton, 1948/1998, p. 16). His grief, he says:

...was not the grief of a child, with pangs of sorrow and many tears. It had something of the heavy perplexity and gloom of adult grief, and was therefore all the more of a burden because it was to that extent, unnatural. (Merton, 1948/1998, p. 16)

The little family split up, with John Paul remaining in the States with the maternal grandparents and Merton's father, a landscape painter, taking Merton along on his painting travels. The traveling life was no doubt chaotic for the young child Merton was, but he seems to remember it with at least some fondness (Merton, 1948/1998, pp. 20-21).

At age eleven, however, Merton's father sent him to a Lycèe (boarding school) in France and Merton experienced another likely period of depression. Merton (1948/1998) tells us he felt "pangs of desolation and emptiness and abandonment" for the first several months, during which he "plead[ed] with [his] Father to let [him] out of the miserable school" (pp. 54-55). His father's death when Merton was 15 was yet another occasion for major depression in Merton's young life. Although Merton only admits to being depressed for a month or two (Merton, 1948/1998, p. 94), it is more likely his depression lingered, causing the period of acting out, particularly at Cambridge University, that Merton tells us lasted for five or six years after his father's death (Merton, 1948/1998, p. 94). These are the first of many episodes of depression Merton suffered throughout his life, which may have given some the impression that he was Enneagram Type

Four. As Riso and Hudson (2000) have noted, however, Sevens can suffer from depression as much as any Type (p. 228).

At the beginning of his second year at Columbia, Merton experienced what sounds like a manic period in his life. He tells us that:

The energy of that golden October [1935] and the stimulation of the cold, bright winter days when the wind swept down as sharp as knives from the shining Palisades kept driving me through the year in what seemed to be fine condition. I had never done so many different things at the same time or with such apparent success. I had discovered in myself something of a capacity for work and for activity and for enjoyment that I had never dreamed of. And everything began to come easy...

It was not that I was really studying hard or working hard: but all of a sudden I had fallen into a kind of mysterious knack of keeping a hundred different interests going in the air at the same time. It was a kind of stupendous juggling act, a tour-de-force, and what surprised me most was that I managed to keep it up without collapsing. (Merton, 1948/1998, pp. 169-70)

By the Fall of 1936, however, Merton (1948/1998) "had begun to feel ill" (p. 178). Then, in short order, his maternal grandparents died and what was left of his family "really practically dissolved" (p. 175, 178, 220). During this time, Merton experienced a "sudden collapse of all [his] physical energy" (Merton, 1948/1998, p. 206), and suffered what sounds like an intense panic attack that he supposed was "a sort of nervous breakdown" (Merton, 1948/1998, pp. 178-180). Merton (1948/1998) tells us his life now came to be dominated by "something [he] had never really [consciously] known before: fear" (p. 180). In a journal entry dated October 22, 1952, Merton (1996A) notes that "I have been having another one of those nervous breakdowns. The same old familiar business. I am getting used to it now—since the old days in 1936 when I thought I was going to crack up..., and the more recent one since ordination" (p. 20). In 1956, when Merton seemed to have lost his "usual ebullience and gaiety" (Mott, 1984, p. 290), his friends were concerned enough about him to arrange for him to see a psychiatrist (Mott, 1984, p. 291).

Merton the Writer

Helen Palmer (1988) tells us that a lot of writers are Enneagram Type Seven (p. 300). Merton's output of writing at Gethsemani was prodigious, to say the least, as one would expect of a healthy Seven writer. He wrote on such a broad range of topics it is difficult to believe one person capable of writing them all. Mott (1984) tells us "the range of material...was equaled only by the range of magazines themselves—from scholarly monastic reviews to mimeographed underground newspapers" (p. 490). The fact is, Merton had the reputation among editors that he could write on almost any subject (Mott, 1984, p. 354), to the point that even Merton exclaimed "Great God, what have I done to make everyone believe I excrete articles like perspiration!" (Mott, 1984, p. 354; see also Merton, 1966, p. 49). Editors likely thought so because Merton continually "took on new interests without abandoning old ones" (Mott, 1984, p. 353), and threw himself into new topics with gusto. Although Merton would periodically make resolutions not to write so many articles or accept so many commissions, he would break them in the end (Mott, 1984, p. 354), having become too enthusiastic about the topics to let go.

Merton the Mystic

Some may be tempted to think that mystics are to be found only among those of introverted temperament, such as Enneagram Type Fours. If Merton was a mystic, some might argue he cannot be Enneagram Type Seven. Merton (1961) himself addresses this issue in *New Seeds of Contemplation*. He says, "...contemplation is not just the affair of a passive and quiet temperament" (p. 9). Rather:

> Contemplative intuition has nothing to do with temperament. Though it sometimes happens that a man of quiet temperament becomes a contemplative, it may also happen that the very passivity of his character keeps him from suffering the inner struggle and the crisis through which one generally comes to a deeper spiritual awakening.
>
> On the other hand, it can happen that an active and passionate man awakens to contemplation, and perhaps suddenly, without too much struggle. But it must be said, as a rule, that certain active types are not disposed to contemplation and never come to it except with great difficulty. (Merton, 1961, pp. 9-10)

As Merton notes (1961), "It is not [in any event] we who choose to awaken ourselves, but God Who chooses to awaken us" (p. 10).

Merton the Generalist

Besides being a talented and highly prolific writer on a wide variety of topics, Merton was exceptionally good at languages, a skill in which Sevens excel (Riso & Hudson, 1996, p. 269). In addition to having a command of Latin and Greek, Merton knew French, Spanish, German, Italian, and Portuguese, and often served as translator when French Cistercian superiors came on visitation to Gethsemani. He even taught himself some Russian, perhaps in order to communicate better with the writer, Boris Pasternak (Mott, 1984, p. 324), with whom he corresponded, and translated a Chinese text with the help of an eminent Chinese scholar (Mott, 1984, pp. 372, 382, 400, 406, 413).

Merton was a teacher even before he became Master of Scholastics and Master of Novices at Gethsemani, having taught composition at Columbia and English Literature at St. Bonaventure (Merton, 1948/1998, p. 298; Mott, 1984, p. 160). He was as well a great reader and lover of books. He liked nothing better than diving into a stack of recently-arrived books on his latest enthusiasms. The first entry in his *Asian Journal* contains this "lesson: not to travel with so many books. I bought more yesterday, unable to resist the bookstores of San Francisco" (Merton, 1973, p. 4).

Merton also knew how to have fun. There was, Laughlin (1984) tells us, a "wonderful gaiety" (p. 5) in Merton not only about his vocation, but also about his life. For example, Merton played the hand drums at Columbia (Harford, 2006, pp. 26-27) and later had two sets of bongo drums in his Gethsemani hermitage (Mott, 1984, p. 474). According to Jinny Burton, a friend from his Columbia days, Merton played the piano almost well enough to be a jazz pianist (Mott, 1984, p. 138) and his college dancing at clubs was "almost professional" (Mott, 1984, p. 138). Even after he is at Gethsemani, he sneaks the occasional visit to a jazz club to listen to the music he loves (Mott, 1984, pp. 345, 510). He drew cartoons and line drawings for publication while at Columbia (Mott, 1984, p. 163) and black and white calligraphic drawings at his Gethsemani hermitage (Mott, 1984, pp. 400, 409), the latter being exhibited and offered for sale (Mott, 1984, p. 407). Merton became adept as well at black and white photography (Mott, 1984, pp. 343, 409). All of these qualities speak of the generalist Seven, the Renaissance people of the Enneagram.

Merton's Greener Grass

Riso and Hudson (1999) tell us that

Sevens' characteristic temptation is the tendency to become dissatisfied with whatever they are doing or currently experiencing. The grass is always greener somewhere else, and so they begin to look forward to the future, as if another event or activity will be the solution to their problems....If Sevens...[get] distracted by the possibilities of the next moment rather than being fully in the present one—they will begin moving in a wrong direction. (p. 269)

As I interpret Merton, his ultimately unconquerable temptation to leave Gethsemani in quest of an order or monastery or hermitage more suited to his perceived needs is Sevenish in the highest degree. He continues to fall prey to his desire for what he calls perfect solitude—a solitary existence in which God would be the whole content of his life. His perfect solitude, however, is always somewhere else in geography, someplace other than he happens to be at the present moment. The restlessness overtakes him again and again. It is only at times that Merton recognizes his "strong desire" (Merton, 1953, p. 26) or "poisonous urge" (Merton, 1953, p. 76) for perfect solitude as the "movement of disordered appetite" (Merton, 1953, p. 20) that for him it was. The times he feels he has finally "arrived" at the home he has been so long searching for are the most telling. He forgets he has "arrived" before. He fails to realize that all his searching is for a place he cannot ever arrive at because he is already there. Perfect solitude can only be found within himself.

Merton's Gluttony

Gluttony is Type Seven's characteristic vice. Literally the desire to stuff oneself with food, gluttony needs to be thought of more broadly, particularly in Merton's case. Although "Sevens can be guilty of overeating and overdrinking, just as they can overdo all physical gratifications" (Riso & Hudson, 1999, p. 272), gluttony is really "the attempt to fill up inner emptiness with things and experiences" (Riso & Hudson, 1999, p. 272). It is the "attempt [by Sevens] to escape from anxiety by distracting themselves" (Riso & Hudson, 1999, pp. 272-73) as well as an "attachment to consumption....a need to be constantly taking something in" (Maitri, 2000, p. 239). As Sandra Maitri (2000) says, the glutton's "voracious appetite could be for ideas, stories, books, drugs, food, drink, or anything else that turns him on" (p. 238). But it is more than this. "Gaps in stimuli bring up anxiety..., the anxiety that signals [the glutton's] inner hunger is threatening to arise in consciousness" (Maitri, 2000, p. 239).

Before he entered Gethsemani, Merton certainly had an "unquenchable thirst for experience, intellectual stimulation, pleasure, and also for meaning—the one quality of life that seemed to elude him as he indulged his other desires" (Wilkes, 1984, p. xv). At times, Merton recognized his "intellectual gluttony" and the "excitement" reading brought him (Mott, 1984, p. 475). Merton (1953) himself speaks of his "sin of over-activity" (p. 256), his "constant gravitation away from solitude" (p. 253). He wonders "why I read so much, why I write so much, why I talk so much, and why I get so excited about the things that only affect the surface of my life....[to the extent that] I am worn out with activity" (Merton, 1953, p. 252). He speaks, too, of his "voracious appetite to know, to enjoy, to achieve, to get tangible results, and taste the immediate reward of my own efforts" (Merton, 1996B, p. 45). He chastises himself for "reading too widely about everything, trying to write too much...trying to set myself up as an authority on everything" (Merton, 1996C, p. 22). "Why must I make my head so full of things?" Merton (1996B) asks (p. 87). "Even when I am not writing," he (1996B) tells us, "I get distracted at prayer—anything will distract me. My mind is too active" (p. 45).

At times Merton recognized his gluttony for alcohol. "I have not always been temperate," he tells us at age 48, "and if I go to town and someone pours me a drink, I don't resist another or even a third. And I have sometimes gone beyond [the perfect third]" (Merton, 1996C, p. 324). At times he resolves to show more reserve and restraint (Mott, 1984, p. 485) only to recognize that aiming at moderation does not "work" for him (Mott, 1984, p. 514).

Before he entered Gethsemani, we find many occasions of drunkenness—following his graduation from prep school (Merton, 1948/1998, p. 114) and during his time at Columbia, where he suffered "prodigious hangovers" (Mott, 1984, p. 96). Even after his conversion, he drank and smoked so much it could take several days to recover (Mott, 1984, pp. 118-19). Presumably, while he was cloistered at Gethsemani, his opportunities for drinking or drunkenness were few and far between. After he had his hermitage, however, we hear story after story of Merton getting drunk, whether it was with visitors or in the company of friends in the area. He did not appear to be able to stop himself (Mott, 1984, p. 345; Baez, 1984, p. 42; Forest, 1984, p. 60; Harford, 2006, p. 149). Mott (1984) tells us that after Merton got his hermitage, friends learned to bring him a case of beer and a bottle of bourbon (p. 446).

Merton's Wing Type

If Merton is an Enneagram Type Seven, his Wing Type is certainly Six. In this Wing Type, "The adventurous search for experience in the Seven combines with the desire for security through connection in the Six wing" (Riso & Hudson, 1996, p. 292). Riso and Hudson (1996) describe healthy Sevens with a Six Wing as "highly productive individuals" who can "utilize the Six's discipline, cooperative spirit, and organizational abilities to accomplish a great deal" (p. 292). They can also be "highly creative and entertaining" (p. 292), both evident in Merton, who had the timing of a professional entertainer (Mott, 1984, p. 135) and was known to "bring down the [Gethsemani] house in laughter" (Burns, 1984, p. 104).

Riso and Hudson (1996) also say that "While they are essentially assertive, [healthy Sevens with a Six Wing] also want others to like and accept them....They are a kaleidoscope of contrasting traits—ingratiating and sassy, vulnerable and resilient, spontaneous and dependable, adult and childlike" (p. 292). To his friends, Merton was all this and more, great company, a cheerful, funny raconteur and stimulating conversationalist, so articulate, so well read. Merton was "excited by new ideas," "witty and engaging," and could show a child-like "hyperenthusiasm" for new people and new areas of interest (Riso & Hudson, 1999, pp. 266-67). "To the extent Sevens with a Six wing are insecure," Riso and Hudson (1999) tell us, "there can be a revved-up, manic, nervous quality to them" (p. 266). As Flavian Burns (1984) noted, Merton showed this quality as well (p. 105).

Conclusion

Thomas Merton was many things to many people. Although he has been thought to be an Enneagram Type Four, the evidence presented in this article make such an assertion doubtful. When Merton's life is considered as a whole, we see instead the rhythms and motivations of an ebullient Enneagram Type Seven who suffered from recurrent depression.

To date, Enneagram diagnoses of those in the public eye typically have been presented without supporting evidence. This article utilizes a case study model and extensive evidence supporting the contention that Thomas Merton is an Enneagram Type Seven. I recommend that all typing of exemplars follow this kind of case study, evidentiary approach.

References

Baez, J. (1984) Joan Baez. In P. Wilkes (Ed.) *Merton by Those Who Knew Him Best.* San Francisco: Harper & Row. (pp. 41-45)

Bamberger, J. E. (1983) The monk. In P. Hart (Ed.) *Thomas Merton/ Monk*. Kalamazoo, Michigan: Cistercian Publications. (pp. 37-58)

Bamberger, J. E. (1984) John Eudes Bamberger. In P. Wilkes (Ed.) *Merton by Those Who Knew Him Best*. San Francisco: Harper & Row. (pp. 113-124)

Burns, F. (1984) Flavian Burns. In P. Wilkes (Ed.) *Merton by Those Who Knew Him Best*. San Francisco: Harper & Row. (pp. 103-111)

Forest, J. (1984) James Forest. In P. Wilkes (Ed.) *Merton by Those Who Knew Him Best*. San Francisco: Harper & Row. (pp. 47-61)

Fox, J. (1983) The spiritual son. In P. Hart (Ed.). *Thomas Merton/ Monk*. Kalamazoo, Michigan: Cistercian Publications. (pp. 141-159)

Harford, J. (2006) *Merton & friends*. New York: Continuum.

Hart, P. (1983) Prologue. In P. Hart (Ed.). *Thomas Merton/ Monk*. Kalamazoo, Michigan: Cistercian Publications. (pp. 15-17)

Jamison, K. R. (1993) *Touched with fire*. New York: Simon & Schuster.

Jung, C. G. (1971) Psychological Types. In H. Read et al. (Eds.), H. G. Baynes (Trans.), and R. F. C. Hull (rev. Trans.). *Collected Works of C. G. Jung*, (Vol. 6). Princeton, NJ: Princeton University Press. (Original work published 1921)

Kelty, M. (1983) The man. In P. Hart (Ed.). *Thomas Merton / Monk*. Kalamazoo, Michigan: Cistercian Publications. (pp. 19-35)

Laughlin, J. (1984) James Laughlin. In P. Wilkes (Ed.). *Merton by Those Who Knew Him Best*. San Francisco: Harper & Row. (pp. 3-13)

Maitri, S. (2000) *The Spiritual Dimension of the Enneagram*. New York: Jeremy P. Tarcher/Putnam.

Merton, T. (1953) *The Sign of Jonas*. New York: Harcourt Brace.

Merton, T. (1961) *New Seeds of Contemplation*. New York: New Directions.

Merton, T. (1966) *Conjectures of a Guilty Bystander*. New York: Doubleday.

Merton, T. (1973) *The Asian journal of Thomas Merton*. New York: New Directions.

Merton, T. (1995) *Run to the Mountain: The story of a vocation*. New York: HarperCollins.

Merton, T. (1996A) *A Search for Solitude: Pursuing the monk's true life*. New York: HarperCollins.

Merton, T. (1996B) *Entering the Silence: Becoming a monk & writer*. New York: HarperCollins.

Merton, T. (1996C) *Turning Toward the World*: *The pivotal years*. New York: HarperCollins.

Merton, T. (1998) *The Seven Storey Mountain* (fiftieth anniversary edition). New York: Harcourt. (Original work published 1948)

Mott, M. (1984) *The Seven Mountains of Thomas Merton*. New York: Harcourt Brace.

Palmer, H. (1988) *The Enneagram*. San Francisco: HarperSanFrancisco.

Riso, D. R. & Hudson, R. (1996) *Personality types* (revised edition). Boston: Houghton Mifflin.

Riso, D. R. & Hudson, R. (1999) *The Wisdom of the Enneagram*. New York: Bantam.

Riso, D. R. & Hudson, R. (2000) *Understanding the Enneagram*. Boston: Houghton Mifflin.

Riso, D. R. & Hudson, R. (2003) *Discovering your Personality Type* (revised edition). Boston: Houghton Mifflin.

Rohr, R. & Ebert, A. (2001) *The Enneagram: A Christian perspective*. New York: Crossroad.

Shannon, W. H. & Bochen, C. M. (Eds.). (2008) *Thomas Merton: A life in letters: The essential collection.* New York: HarperCollins.

Wilkes, P. (Ed.). (1984) *Merton by those who knew him best*. San Francisco: Harper & Row.

Zuercher, S. (1996) *Merton: An Enneagram profile*. Notre Dame, ID: Ave Maria Press.

A NEW OLD SCHOOL OF HUMAN GROWTH AND PERMANENT REEDUCATION

Professor Alaor Passos and Dr. Claudio Naranjo

Editor's note: This article is actually two articles. The first is a personal history by Prof. Alaor Passos on his fascinating experiences and journey of self-discovery in Chile and his native Brazil in the 1960s and 70s as he navigated the political currents of the time. The second is by Dr. Claudio Naranjo, who should need no introduction to readers of The Enneagram Journal, on his hopes for the future of education.

The purpose of this article is to discuss a hope, a personal experience, and a proposal for educational change. It comprises two parts. The first mentions hope, and intends to contribute to changing education to change the world[1], starting with the educator and emphasizing the experience of the personal path. The second part outlines the framework of the proposal for a new, humanistic, and true education for the 21st Century.

I belong to a generation who wanted to change the word with bullets, and I was once devoted to doing so. I believed in it and suffered when I got frustrated with it. But I learned lessons that I deem precious

I have never denied the fairness and the correctness of the cause that inspired my generation. I would do it all over if the same situation were to take place again. However, I learned firsthand that despite the fact that the cause remains fair and that many times we were guided by the feeling of having "certainty ahead and History in the hand"[2], for many of us the dream became a nightmare because we were motivated by misassumptions. Like Nasrudin[3], inebriated by illusiveness, we were looking for the key in the place where we thought we could see more light, and not in the place where the key had been lost. In our ammunition we carried defiance and loathing that concealed the aim at love, which is what we aspired to.

I was part of a group of young sociologists recruited by professor Darcy Ribeiro to study for a Masters at the then emerging UnB (University of Brasilia), and simultaneously carry out the role of teachers, unfolding lectures delivered by the field's senior professor at the Great Hall. Friar Mateus Rocha was the

---

[1] A reference to the title of the renowned book by Claudio Naranjo, *Cambiar la Educación para Cambiar el Mundo,* Ediciones La Llave, Vitoria, 3ª edition, 2007.

[2] A line by Geraldo Vandré, in the song *Para não dizer que não falei das flores (Caminhando e Cantando).*

[3] *Histórias de Nasrudin,* Dervish Collection, Rio de Janeiro.

Principal in office at the time. My experience didn't last long. The military coup, which dominated the country for over two decades, had just torn the Federal Constitution to pieces, invaded universities, revoked academic independence, and monitored schools with the police force.

UnB was one of the first and most toughly patrolled of all Brazilian education institutions. I remember the principal getting into the police van, in voluntary replacement for a group of teachers who were cornered by the police while chatting at the Campus. I remember policemen in uniforms or disguised in civilian clothes "attending" our classes[4].

I also remember May 10 1964, when I left Brazil on my way to Chile, with "uncertainty ahead and History on the ground". Today I am thankful for the blessing that I received during that "flight," which was more like despair but ended up opening the gates to the world and to the soul.

This is how it all started. I have no intention of going into the details of memories, be them pleasant or cruel, but I can't help mentioning some of them. My existence is a component of the message of hope that I bear. Throughout the way I learned things, and I am grateful to many people particularly Friar Mateus Rocha who, in addition to representing an important master in my youth, was also a very dear friend. From him, I keep many good lessons and memories[5].

At the time, I was still a young sociologist, but also convincingly arrogant. I thought I dominated the "science" of society (quotes were added recently). I was crowded with sophisticated theories, and proud to think that I could alternate same with what we then called *"praxis"*. I looked down on those "illiterate blind right-wing ideologists" in a state of terminal agony. This is how I arrived in FLACSO (*Facultad Latinoamericana de Ciencias Sociales*) to study for my masters, subsequent to being awarded with a scholarship by UNESCO (May 1964).

---

[4] During exile, I was with Darcy Ribeiro only once, in Santiago, in an informal lunch that gathered exiled from several Latin-American countries. That day he said to me: "The Brazilian military government cannot manage and is not interested in implementing the UnB according to the model it was created. Notwithstanding, soon, and inevitably that University will be among the country's and the world's top." I think the prediction is coming true.

[5] I can't help mentioning two brief pieces of wise advice, with which he used to flood me: "- ...Boy, if not even Christ was Christian, or Marx was Marxist, why should you be distressed with labeling options such as these? What truly matters is humanism, wherever it may be"; "- ... Unrest like yours is equivalent to what I have been associating to Dostoyevsky, whom I call 'God's demon' when he refers to Sonia, the Christian prostitute (...) similar to what Glauber Rocha calls *'Deus e o Diabo na Terra do Sol'*; Betinho (Herbert de Souza) understands as the 'invisible revealing itself in the visible'; Juscelino, 'to make the impossible possible' and; Niemeyer, 'the functional showing itself in the beautiful' are more tangible. Yourself (me), in your troubled rebellion, understand how 'Faith is not jumping into the dark, but committing to the Truth.'" (I did not even remember saying that to him).

I had excellent teachers at FLACSO, the greatest of all being Johan Galtung, Norwegian sociologist and professor of methodology in sociological research. He is imprinted in my memory for his human values and the merciless boldness that he used to crush intellectual prejudice. He made me "swallow" the slide rule (today it would be a computer) as the main instrument of the sociological *praxis*. What was not possible to measure was not a sociological phenomenon, but rather ideology, abstract embellishment, or simply well-spoken verbiage arising from the bad habit of creating conceptual words conveying that one is discussing "social realities." And that bad habit contaminated a good number of my generation's sociologists, especially in Brazil.

I often had shocking experiences during my first years in Chile. The first time was when I almost immediately went to see [future Brazilian president] Fernando Henrique, who had arrived in Santiago only three days prior to my arrival and was already employed by the UN. Until then I only knew him as a prestigious benchmark to sociological intellectuality, in addition to having attended two or three of his lectures/classes. He didn't know me. In fact, he didn't even know I existed. He received me with friendly and sympathetic kindness in his office. As if between equals he told me something like this: "The wheel of the Brazilian history has lost one gear tooth and rotated backwards. We must wait until the normal movement is restored. It is time for studying and observing quietly. The spirit of the Brazilian solidarity is a solid cultural value and we should conserve it. Those of us who have a job here will help those who will be arriving, and watch over everyone's dignity until we are all able to support ourselves. Should you need anything, including cash, do not hesitate to ask."[6] He taught me a lot, both the human and the professional practice, and later on I was hired to work at CEPAL, where he was already member of staff.

The second great shock took place while I was reading a text that came to my hands by accident. It was a Xerox copy of the chapter *"Los Insulares"* of the book by Idries Shah, *"Los Sufis."* I read it and reread it without being able to understand a thing. The epistemological parameters of the Marxist dialectics that I had managed to successfully use in any situation were of no service to me then. I felt like the literate idiot in person. Not even the trick of invalidating the author seemed suitable, since I couldn't even guess right what the text was all about. Other shocks came in this same line as I discovered the books by Gurdjieff, Ouspensky, and other of the kind.

The third shock resulted from a lecture that I attended at CEPAL delivered by Felipe Herrera, exponent from UNESCO who was broadly exposed at the time. He must have talked about very interesting subjects, which I never really succeeded to understand. But one in particular remained in my mind because it addressed

---

[6] Since then I have had concrete reasons to disagree from the fame that he acquired as "stingy" when he became President of Brazil. It is true that his wife, Ruth, frequently patched his socks while talking to a visitor before dinner was served. We all saw that as ordinary informality and an act of conjugal care, but never as stinginess.

the need to set up and improve the practice of *Permanent Reeducation*. At first I understood it very simple-mindedly, and translated it into the need for recycling, being updated for renewal and all that kind of cliché. However, in my inner self something told me over the decades that this was not all the man meant. But what would it be then? My academic vocabulary did not accuse any similar entry, but my human unrest grew increasingly. I confess that not until much later I started to understand what exactly it meant, when more recently Edgar Morin and others drafted the synthesis of UNESCO recommendations for current education.

Other shocks hit me later. I watched a video tape come from California of a "crazy little old man" named Fritz Perls, who was doing gestalt-therapy with a group of people. I went to the Arica Institute in Santiago, Chile, and there I found powerful ministers of the then Chilean government engaged around a circle of younger people, deeply interested in something that to me sounded madly absurd and outdated. They talked about musical scale, cosmic scale, numerical scale, and they talked about a certain Gurdjieff, who told the Tales of Beelzebub to His Grandson, encouraged the development of real life within people, and was insolent enough to make references to anonymous characters such as Famous Men who he had met during his life. Besides, he was Belorussian, a fugitive from Bolshevism who talked about God, conferred on same the status of the Absolute within a cosmic scale that mentioned creation, planets, and galaxies, in addition to other theological insanities that did not resemble anything like the "sacred" postulates of the Revolution that my sociological beliefs validated.

I went crazy! Or almost, and maybe I was just starting to restore my mental health. In addition to all that a certain Oscar Ichazo, Bolivian philosopher/psychologist (Bolivian to top it up!), appeared claiming to hold an old wisdom similar to what Ouspensky, prominent follower of Gurdjieff, called "Fragments of an Unknown Teaching – In Search of the Miraculous," which impressed me enough. Firstly because deep in my heart I knew it addressed something valuable, and secondly because throughout my scholar life I had never heard anyone mention any of those philosophers.

I decided to have therapy. At the first Gestalt marathon that I attended, I met several colleagues from the UN, as well as other exiled, each one trying to hide from each other and from me, and I from them. The final result was a huge positive shock. On the second day, I literally beat up the therapist who dared to provoke my emotions totally repressed or unknown until then.

And in that context I heard about a certain Claudio Naranjo, psychiatrist, follower of Fritz Perls, and Oscar Ichazo's roaming buddy. He lived in California, was a friend of Carlos Castaneda and used to deliver distance lessons/guidance to a bunch of "weirdoes" that increasingly aroused my curiosity.

It was 1967. The leftist guerilla movement popped everywhere inspired particularly by the heroic Cuban experience, victorious since 1959, when I was still a freshman at UFMG (Federal University of Minas Gerais). This was almost simultaneous with the time when I was doing my civic duty in the "glorious"

Brazilian army as a candidate for Cavalry Official (reservist) and I passed on the war knowledge that I acquired there to a group of sociology students that was thinking of setting up the guerrilla fight in the Brazil when Jango (Joao Goulart) was disqualified to take office as Constitutional President. This daringness awarded me my first arrest until the first Parliamentary release was negotiated. It was 1961/62, and the training stage was my father's farm in the hinterland of Minas Gerais.

The previous paragraph is intended to explaining the reason why, at the end of the 60's, I was still feverishly infected by the guerrilla idealism virus, despite the abovementioned "intellectually shocking" experiences. The doors to my world were already opened to other unrests, but I was still teaching "Sociología del Desarrollo" at the University of Chile (as deputy professor), performed research and supplied consulting services to Latin America's left-wing governments. I also had bonds with exiled groups come from many countries and gathered in Chile. The juvenile "heroism" in me was still burning and the dream remained vivid.

In 1967 I was my true self. I *"chickened out"* by the time I was to participate in the guerrilla movement in Bolivia to fight alongside with Che Guevara[7].

Instead of going to Bolivia I decided to go to London to study for my doctorate. I actively participated in the University Revolution (May 1968). We did the first 100,000-person march (today that would be equivalent to the march of millions) against the Vietnam War. I went to Norway for a few months as *visiting scholar* at the *Peace Research Institute* invited by Galtung, the same one who had made me "swallow" the slide rule and taught me to perform empirical research. Afterward I passed through Mexico (doing research on Latin America's Business Leaderships, directed by Fernando Henrique) and after sometime I went back to Chile. It was the time of the rise and fall of Salvador Allende, democratically elected Socialist President.

---

[7] I was contacted by a Peruvian journalist who came from Paris and introduced himself by the name of "Señor Chan." Discrete, he didn't waste words; he confirmed that Che was in Bolivia and gave me instructions as to where I could find him. I should travel with him the week after to Peru, where we would meet up with Hugo Blanco, who would take us undercover to the Bolivian forest where Che was. It would be a one way trip: either victory (which at the time seemed possible), or death. A little more than one year later I cried in the streets of London when I saw the photograph of Che Guevara on the front page of the newspapers, murdered together with the last two fighters arrested with him on the previous day. They were the loyal fellow Willy, a Cuban, and the valiant El Chino, from Peru, whom I had met as "Señor Chan". I made a secrete vow (luckily not kept) that, on returning to Latin America, I would dedicate the rest of my days to find and kill the wicked Colonel Garrido and revenge the cold murder when he machine-gunned Che, prisoner and unarmed. I dreamed of the details of the execution at the final minutes. Unlike Che who died chin up pronouncing the famous last words: "shoot, coward! You are only going to kill a Man!" his infamous murderer would die knelt-down, listening to the words: "That is how cowards die!"

Those new times in Chile were troubled; a lot of heat, enthusiasm, and a brutal blow on the ideals of change. I was able to enjoy immunity as a UN employee, and acquired weapons, trained guerrilla war with a group of Tupamaros exiled from Uruguay, and provided protection to fugitive guerrilla fighters from many countries, including Brazil. During the bloody blow I used my UN car with white diplomatic plates to take more than twenty people who were being chased by the political police to the safety of embassies. Ultimately, the dream was reignited with passion. Alongside with Geraldo Vandré, severely afflicted by homesickness, we drafted heroic strategies washed down with good wine, and spent many nights of ballads, confident that we "knew what we wanted," which was to topple the dictatorship in Brazil. But the timing was wrong[8].

I couldn't stay in Chile any longer. The Brazilian police started to chase me in Santiago. The Chilean army invaded my house and shot down the goats on my farm[9]. I came to Brazil with *Laissez Passer* from the UN and was arrested in Rio

---

[8] Observing the final demand by the army, as broadcasted by the Chilean Official Radio, at 9 a.m. of September 11, 1973, the Air Force bombed the Palacio de la Moneda at 11 a.m. sharp, leaving no stone unturned, and soon after the Infantry shredded Allende to pieces while he was seated at his presidential desk with a pen in one hand, and, in the other, a machine gun he had received from Fidel Castro who had been in an official visit to Chile a few days before. Almost at that same time, Geraldo Vandré was getting off a plane at Galeão airport, without knowing what had just happened in Chile. He had left Chile at dawn that same day, before the revolt started. He travelled to start the execution of a plan to invade Brazil through Bolivia and Paraguay, in order to set up the ***República do Bemvirá*** in the Mid-West of Brazil, an area known as *Planalto Central*, the very seat of all three branches of the Brazilian Government. He was coming ahead to make false statements to divert the attention of the Brazilian army. Forthwith, the **"occupation troop"**, formed by us, a group of half a dozen idealists, bravely maddened, would follow. At the same time Vandré was making rehearsed statements to the Brazilian army men to confuse them – which ended by being labeled an "ill-famed treason," since the rest of the plan had to be aborted—the Chilean army invaded and wrecked the house where he lived without knowing he was no longer there.

[9] It was a gross retaliation. The diplomatic status that I was granted by the UN prevented my arrest on Chilean soil. But I was quite well-known to the Chilean police, in addition to being closely watched by the Brazilian police that headed the torture of the prisoners who were being piled up in the National Stadium. They had already murdered Vitor Jara (the Chilean Vandré) after cutting off his hands with a hatchet because he had dared to play his guitar to the crowd of prisoners. Shooting down a flock of goats meant "warning" and vengeance, because a few months earlier I had rented a huge farm (22 thousand hectares) on the Andes mountain range; inhospitable land that spread from Santiago to the border with Argentina next to Mendoza. I used to raise goats on the farm as an excuse. In fact, the farm was used as a secret route for the exiled and guerrilla fighters of the South Cone during Allende's administration. I made myself available to the *Tupamaros* for guerrilla training. Sometimes I followed them to camps and exercises. Discipline, the warlike eagerness and the shooting, they produced at those times were remarkable; almost

international airport, Galeão. With the intervention of the UN, I was released after one week and a lot of spanking. Before my release I went through grilling for over three hours. I was the only man able to see the face of his interrogator as they allowed me to take the hood off. At the very end, our talk was like what follows; he said: "We have been observing you and decided to bet on your innocence, unless you are very well trained to feign. If we meet again, it won't be so easy for you." I tried to answer sarcastically: "Don't you worry colonel. If we ever meet again, it will be with bullets!" He answered cynically calm: "There is no such a possibility. You will never know where you have been or who I am. My patent is false, my name is not this one you read, my car plates are cold, and should one day you recognize me in the street my security guards would never allow you to get nearer to me". He kindly served me a cup of coffee, offered me a cigarette and ordered his guards to take me, hooded, to my mother-in-law's house in downtown Rio.

I returned to Chile determined not to stay there. I imported a latest generation Mercedes Benz, crossed Argentina and left it via Paso de los Libres. I was arrested in Uruguaiana together with two Chileans who were fleeing from Pinochet, and whom I brought with me to live in Brazil. In addition to political reasons, I had to "explain" why I was carrying a tin of pot with seeds and three flasks of LSD. Everything was nicely packed together with an illegal record by the Tupamaros.

I left prison the next day, "by the work and grace" of the Holy Spirit, I think. It was Thursday night and one of the Chilean guys told me in the cell the Story of Mushkil Gusha, whom Sufis claim to be that who removes all difficulties, and I heard it for the first time. The next day, the policeman from Minas Gerais who was escorting me to testimony refused to handcuff me for the simple fact that he had been informed that I was also from Minas. He protected me, testified on my behalf, fetched my car (which had been kept at the Argentinean border), and convinced the commander to set me free in the middle of the night, saying that he would take responsibility. The commander returned the marijuana seeds,[10] swore at my mother and told me to leave.

Believe it or not, that is how it all happened. I looked hard at the commander, and told him in a tone between respectful and imperative: "If I am being set free, it means that nothing in my current behavior incriminates me. So I think it would be suitable that you returned to me everything that was confiscated at the moment I was arrested." He fired more offences against my mother, but ordered his aid-de-camp to return everything including the marijuana and the LSD. I learned later when I arrived in Rio de Janeiro that on the night of my arrest my then mother-in-law and my wife had been worried because I had not called them

---

deafening by the blast muffled by the hills. One would have the impression of a true war, live and in color.

[10] In those days it was possible to buy marijuana seeds in the Chilean supermarkets to feed birds.

since I had left Chile. They had then decided to go to a *terreiro*, as Candomble temples are known in Brazil, to find peace. The spirit of *Caboclo Girassol*–a Brazilian native called Sunflower—"came down" to the temple, informing them that I had been arrested by the Brazilian army. He promised he would take care of my case and would immediately appoint a "good spirit" to stay by my side. That "entity" never introduced himself to me, but I have the feeling that the policeman from Minas, come from nowhere and extremely efficient when it came down to making decisions, had something to do with the generous promise by *Caboclo Girassol.* Some time later I met this same Native when I was returning from India. At entering his temple a medium who spoke on his behalf came to me. She quickly knelt down, kissed my feet, stood up with dignity and elegance, looked in my eyes and said something like that: "Now you are ready! You will have the opportunity to begin and to take care of many people. It won't take long now. A closure. To do so you will have to spend seven days alone in the forest meditating and waiting." Needless to say, I did so, although shivering from fear and full of fantasizing expectations. But I did go! For seven days nothing coherent with my expectations happened, but I must say that the Native's prophecy has consistently come true ever since, and I never stopped planting sunflowers in my gardens and farms, following the Native's recommendation.

I stayed in Brazil semi-clandestine for sometime, and dedicated myself to taking care of "cattle and people," farms, buying, selling etc. I carried on with therapy, once again with Claudio Naranjo's close associates who came from Chile with my assistance.

Then I decided to go to the United States to be directly with Naranjo. I had with me a recommendation letter that I never gave him. After months, I finally met him in a Buddhist Meditation retreat lead by a monk from Cambodia, master in Vipassana, and we meditated together for twenty days. At the end of that experience I told him I had the introduction letter at home and asked him if I could take it to his house. He answered simply: *"No es necesario, ya estás presente!" (It is not necessary, you are already introduced!).* I got home and read the letter. It had only one phrase: "I deliver Alaor to you. He is coming out of a very dark hole." I tore the letter as it would not be of any use, and the following week I had an amazing surprise; the doorbell rang, and when I went to see who was at the door I bumped into the Naranjo himself who asked if he could come in. He didn't stay long. He only asked me a few questions as to my plans, indicated some places and people whom I should look for in Berkeley, recommended reading material, said good-bye and left.

A good friend whom I had met in California introduced me to Claudio during the Vipassana retreat; his name was Ron Kane, a Reichian psychologist who initiated and accompanied me at cracking Carlos Castaneda's *fantastic realism,* then at its peak. When we parted he said something that took me a while to understand. Something like "I have been playing with you the same role as Don Juan played with Castaneda. But as of now, your benefactor – Don Genaro will be Don Claudio Naranjo".

I only met again with Naranjo months later at a farewell party that some friends threw before I left to India, where I stayed with Swami Muktananda for some months. I didn't ask anything, and Naranjo told me about Sida Yoga and Muktananda, whom he had introduced in the United States. He advised me to stay with Tarthang Tulku Rinpoche. He mentioned the Sufi tradition, recommended reading material by Idries Shah, wished me good luck, said farewell and disappeared.

Needless to say that I did everything as recommended. I only met him again ten years later during another trip that I made to California. I was more mature, and the Amnesty Bill had been passed in Brazil. I had founded a *Research and Human Growth Institute*, in Belo Horizonte, after working in Rio de Janeiro for sometime. I had joined the local Sufi group, travelled to Turkey and Mexico in a kind of pilgrimage with the Master. I told Naranjo all that and invited him to come and teach in Brazil through my institute in partnership with Suzana Stroke.

He accepted the invitation, and we have been working together ever since. His first trip to Brazil was in 1984. He has come every year ever since. I organized a group of 29 people to whom he taught the Psychology of the Enneatypes through experience. Several of those people remain with us to this date. At that time, that was a subject *totally* unknown in Brazil.

Naranjo's teachings were spread throughout the world. His SAT Institute was no longer just a seekers' catalyzing agent. It evolved among a considerable international group of Gestalt followers, Fritz Perls' heirs, via Naranjo, the former's immediate substitute in Esalen. A solid group was gathered in Europe, where Naranjo's most prominent disciples and collaborators were from. The International SAT School was created and, in the last decade, a third comprehensive and ambitious work line emerged; no more and no less than the bearer of the initiative and the hope to Change the World by changing the educator[11] oriented, nourished, and dedicated to a new Humanistic and True Education for the 21st Century[12].

The core of the question comprises a proposal to make changes to the Educational System. The changes typically advocated by education-reform technical paladins who insist on giving "more of the same" to increase education are dismissed.

The SAT School intends to provide different things, devising new parameters. The way that could lead to changes cannot be found by reforming curricula and adding new subjects. It is necessary to change the attitude, the message, the

---

[11] That word is used here in its most strict sense. But it also encompasses a broader sense, a wide range of health professionals. Among the doctors who I better know, I would like to point out the studies by Dr. Silvana Moreira Benatti who developed the Unicist Homeopathy thesis in light of the Psychology of Enneatypes.

[12] The subject of a lecture delivered by Claudio Naranjo at UnB, in 1999, invited by me and Professor Thérèse Hofmann, then dean of the art department.

guidance, and the human quality of educators and students[13].

Synthesis of my apprenticeship with Naranjo

Saying that I *learned* with him is only a way of speaking. I am still learning. Maybe I have only just started learning; or only just started *learning how to learn*. For someone who before knowing Naranjo thought that he knew a lot is already learning in itself. But other aspects could be mentioned.

Firstly I should recognize that I learned, without being aware that I was learning, the tangible reality of what to me before was only a repetitive cliché, with scholars' snobbery: "There is more between heaven and earth than dreamt of in your philosophy;" the famous phrase that Shakespeare put in Hamlet's lips. I experienced and absorbed some of those things. And I am aware they are still irrelevant compared to what they can be in the future.

Secondly I learned to accept, sometimes without understanding, the beauty of the *Human Condition* where I exist. I learned to value it and I recognize its potentials, which now inspire my goals.

I should confess that writing like this sounds a bit strange and arrogant to me. But looking "inward," I confirm that what I have just stated on the above paragraphs is true, and therefore I allow myself to continue on the same track. I will not mention the extremely valuable scholarly, technical, and intellectual things I learned, which are inlaid in the Psychology of Enneatypes, in the meditation practice, in therapeutic techniques, etc. I will only mention my personal gains as an individual, a human being. I will not mention the "how" of the learning either, but I will rather provide a summary of some results.

Among these results the following stand out: I became more real, more present, more tolerant, and less conceited. I gained flexibility and *Inner Freedom*. I think that is the most relevant of all gains as it unfolds into many outcomes. One of them, just to mention a tiny example, is reflected on the fact of writing what I have written so far. In other times this would have been an impossible task. Shame and fear of what others would think of me and the shy and proud self-criticism prevented me from exposing myself honestly to whoever it might be beyond the "safe" intimacy of a small group of friends. Another obvious gain

---

[13] In my chair—*"Special Topics in Education and Cultural Diversity"*—I have been using films and videos, particularly those inspired by the book by Evânia Reichert, *"Infância, a Idade Sagrada"*, Vale do Ser Editora, RS, 2008, as well as by the tales of oral tradition teachings gathered by Nícia Grillo in *"Histórias da Tradição Sufi"*, Edições Dervish, RJ, 1993. In *"Project 3"*, I have included in the list of offers an experience program, created by Naranjo as known as SAT-Education (Education to BE), being adapted and applied. That Project was put into practice in Rondônia (Municipal Secretariat) with a group of government school teachers, and is in effect in some places in Mexico, Italy and Spain, all inspired by the Psychology of Enneatypes. To encourage creativity, I use the short stories of the book *"Histórias Mágicas"*, by Amina Passos and Laila Karina Passos, two children writing for children, Thesaurus Editors, Brasília, 2002. These are *tales of enchantment*, according to the terminology proposed by Câmara Cascudo.

therefore can be found in honesty, followed by spontaneity and the ability to build intimate relations.

Now I can say whatever I want, or allow myself not to say anything. In both cases, due to conscientious choice and not external pressure. Additionally I became a religious man without being a follower of any religion. I rediscovered Plato and understood that what my "philosophical enthusiasm" invalidated as platonic idealism was nothing but a symptom of my spiritual illiteracy. I realized that Socrates remains as alive an educator as when he internalized the "know thyself" from the Oracle of Delphos, and that psychology, even having developed as a separated branch of philosophy, owes him what is has that is most significant. The powerful Greeks were right when they condemned Socrates to drink hemlock, since without them knowing Socrates was truly a corrupting threat who would cause the youth to inject deadly poison in the then-ruling system.

I revisited the Divine Comedy, this time for real, going well beyond the simple enjoyment of the literary beauty. Simultaneously I understood that the splendor of each one's inner *Pieta* could only truly emerge after removing the excess of crude rock that covers human nature, a job inherent to a loving and patient artist.

Ultimately, I also acquired the freedom of thinking, breaking the parameters of logical reasoning settled in the prejudices that insist on putting straitjackets on reality, be they moral, theoretical, religious, ideological or simply abstract.

As a synthesis of all the above, it is worthy of mention that I learned to treat Christ with reverence, in Buddhism, in Hinduism, in Sufism, in Islamism, in Yoga, in Marxist Humanism and even in Christianity; that being the most difficult one, as a matter of fact. It is true that this learning started with Friar Mateus still in my youth. However that process only matured during the following decades.

As chaotic as the content of this summary may sound, I name it the *rescue of Love*. I am aware this is almost like paraphrasing Castaneda when he mentions "navigate the paths of the heart, any path that has a heart"[14]. It is simple but it does not address a simple duplication, let alone a simple quote. It is simple because simplicity is natural, and to me it became a corollary of the learning of cultivating Presence, another gain that I should mention.

It should be clear that before arriving at the synthesis there was a long process roamed about in phases. In one of them, I was convinced that I knew a lot, and I was defeated by the irresistible desire of teaching. Luckily it worked out. People used to say that they learned from me and I was encouraged and carried on teaching, feeling increasingly gratified, until I learned that I know nothing, and therefore I have nothing to teach. But at reaching that point things got complicated, since the number of those who said they learned from me increased. I was very impressed by that and started to pay attention, trying to understand what and how they learned. Sometimes I learned too. I especially

---

[14] Carlos Castaneda's complete works, from *The Teachings of Don Juan* to *The Fire from Within*, were best sellers as of the Sixties.

confirmed the certainty that I know nothing and realized that those who say they learn are those who already knew, without being aware that they knew. Therefore, in my opinion, the learning that they recognize is authentic. Hence, it does not bother me when they say they have learned from me, nor does it affect my belief that I teach nothing. All that is nothing but an apparent paradox that confirms the basic simplicity of actual things; since in fact there are those who are able to learn what they already knew. The condition required for that to happen is not to resign to stagnation and be too excited with what they learn. Knowledge seems to lie in the equidistant balance of these two extremes. At least it seems that it is one of its favorite dwellings.

Translating on behalf of simplicity, we arrive at what many are aware of; that in fact there is an invisible assistance that facilitates the perception of true knowledge. That assistance lies on the development of **A**ttention, together with the correct **I**ntention and with the corresponding **D**edication. With these elements, the right people will find the right place and the right time to share true learning events. One should not think that is an easy task. But I can testify that it is a feasible target although it requires more than just intellectual insight. And that is enough for now. Something in the back of my mind tells me that it is time to stop not to run the risk of going beyond the necessary, at this time. That is, if I haven't already.

On the next pages, Naranjo will speak for himself, through extracts of chapters of books still unpublished in Portuguese at the time of this writing[15]. It is just a summary of the ideas that he has been proposing in his many books[16], where he ratifies the view and guidance that arises from his contribution as educator, besides philosopher, thinker, sociologist, psychiatrist, gestalt therapist and transpersonal therapist, whose great credit lies in building a bridge where the traffic flows between Western Science and Eastern Wisdom. As to the

---

[15] Claudio Naranjo, *A Civilização Moribunda* and *O Ego Patriarcal*, soon to be published by Esfera Editora, São Paulo, in addition to an extract of the chapter *Things that I Come Saying (Coisas que venho dizendo)*, by the same publishers, 2008.

[16] In addition to the already mentioned *Cambiar la Educación para Cambiar el Mundo*, some stand out among others:
- *Cosas que Vengo Diciendo. Sobre el Amor la Conciencia lo Terapeutico y la Solucion al Problema del Mundo. (Things that I Come Saying)*, Kier, Buenos Aires, 2005.
- *The Enneagram of Society: Healing the soul to heal the world,* Gateways Books, Nevada City, 2004.
- *The End of Patriarchy and the Dawning of a Tri-une Society,* Amber Lotus, Oakland, 1994.
- *Autoconocimiento Transformador*, Ediciones La Llave, Victoria, Espanha, 1997.
- *On the Psychology of Meditation,* Penguin Books, New York, 1976.
- *Entre Meditación Y Psicoterapia*, Ediciones La Llave, Victoria, Espanha, 1999.
- *La Vieja y Novísima Gestalt*, Editorial Cuatro Vientos, Santiago, Chile, 2001.
- *Por una Gestalt Viva*, Ediciones la Llave, Victoria, Espanha, 2007.
- *Character and Neurosis – An Integrative View*, Ed. Gateways, California, 1994.
- *Sanar la Civilización*, Ediciones la Llave, Victoria, Espanha, 2009.

educational aspect, broadly speaking, what stands out here is what has been named the "Pedagogy of Love."

For Education Transcending Patriarchy[17]

Dr. Claudio Naranjo

As I grow older, I see things more clearly and I think that the world is the way it is thanks to not having an education that is more relevant to our actual needs. Insisting on "wanting more of the same" may seem noble and patriotic, and we do not hesitate in considering it an expression of our love. But we are in an obsolescence crisis, in which the diligence of the patriarchal and hegemonic spirit that has accompanied us since the beginning of civilization became potentially deadly. Instead of wanting to carry on with the same thing, it would be better to *aspire to something different* and higher than what is known so far.

The education model that currently predominates grew with the start of the industrial era and is widely based on an implicit curriculum that teaches people to respect their superiors, to remain quiet and to be patient with repetitive tasks. But what we increasingly and more urgently need is an education that incites the development of individuals – not only physical and intellectual, but also emotional and spiritual.

One day we will realize that our countless social problems – that today lead us to what seems the edge of a precipice – are not independent from one another, but they are rather related to a psycho-spiritual non-development problem. In other words, we should come to the agreement that the world is the way it is because we do not have an education other than the one that prevails today.

Some people think that the world would be better if we were more educated, and I must say that I do not agree with that. I don't think that it would help to have more of what we currently call education. I sympathize instead with a currently increasing movement, where parents choose to get their children out of school to guide them through a process of learning at home, and more broadly, in the world. I also like the idea of de-schooling, as proposed by Ivan Tillich, although I think that since we already have schools it would be better to use them for something truly significant.

If we take for granted the UNESCO recommendation of ensuring that people learn (among other things) how to live in society, we should be aware that that will not take place spontaneously through groups or communities' appropriate interactions; it rather requires the will to cure the individuals' emotional world. That is what underlies the relations with others and the relation of individuals

[17]Translator's note to the Portuguese text: the entire part attributed to Dr. Claudio Naranjo consists of sections or paragraphs from his writings that I (Alaor Passos) have recomposed on the basis of two books to be published for the first time in Brazil by Editora Esfera in Sao Paulo, or using short sections from *Coisas que Venho Dizendo*, which Editora Esfera published in 2008.

with themselves.

When I talk about curing our emotional world, I mean recovering our natural ability to love, which involves "unlearning" destructive behavior patterns acquired during our childhood in response to the families' psychological difficulties and setbacks of life.

The self-consciousness experience process, or self-knowledge, is one of the elements of the affective transformation that is in the core of psychotherapy. It is a kind of descent to hell and at the same time a process of purification; in other words, a process where the malfunctioning aspects of the emotional life are discontinued through understanding. But self-consciousness is not everything. There should also be a catharsis of emotions repressed during childhood, which should not only be revisited but fully perceived; that is experienced by diving deep into them. Therefore it is also necessary to unlearn the usual automatic behavior standards through which we express our "negative emotions".

There are several resources available in the field of psychotherapy and spirituality to educate the heart. But I don't think our ideal should be merely importing resources into the schools, but rather a more complex assimilation; an original integration in a new synthesis, a "technology transfer" meticulous enough to prevent the use of the visible terminology, or psychotherapy or traditional spiritual schools' formulas from becoming necessary.

The example that follows, extracted from a book where Rebecca Wild discusses her Pestalozzi school in Guayaquil, shows how a therapeutic undertaking does not require any psychotherapy or language form:

"For example, there was a little girl – small, chubby and very spoilt – who did nothing in kindergarten for three months but sweeping and mopping floors and washing dishes. One day, her very distinguished and elegant father, with a serious expression on his face, asked me: 'Could you tell me what you have been doing to my daughter here?'

I had little experience and felt insecure – cornered, one could say – and tried to deliver a lesson to the gentleman as to the Montessori Method. But he shook his head and said he wasn't interested in that.

'You see', he explained, 'before my daughter came here, she couldn't care less about me, and now she loves me. I just wanted to know how you did that[18] .'"

The feat was nothing but the result of trusting the child's choice, and that outcome tells us that the basic elements that make such educational action possible are not techniques or expertise, but a serious understanding of certain things that in turn will require that teachers of the future gain therapeutic and spiritual experience and insight through of first-hand immersion in those fields. I suppose however that in addition to future teachers' creativity, together with the simple ideas proposed, it would be useful to create a therapeutic laboratory with the specific purpose of encouraging a generation that will be kinder, more

---

[18] "Raising Curious, Creative Confident Kids", from the Pestalozzi Experiment in ***Child – Based Education,*** by Rebecca Wild, Shambala, 2000, pages 17 and 18.

compassionate and happier than ours.

If those who teach would clearly understand how much the expression of a person's potential to love is key to his/her happiness, and a guarantee against the vampirism of the insatiable yearning for love, which is typical of a degenerated condition of the consciousness, they would certainly convey that conviction and would do their pupils a great favor and cause them to take an interest in the idea of a journey of love; in other words, the idea that love is something that can be cultivated through practice.

Becoming healthy does not only mean being aware of the disease and removing or exorcising it through techniques of expression. It also means recovering the health inherent to what we can call both the inner child and the inner animal. That recovery is the liberation from psycho-cultural handicaps, which can be described as a process of unlearning or getting rid of some kind of mental parasite. A change for the better would be, for our future educators, the understanding that health, like freedom, is not so much something acquired, but rather something that emerges by breaking out from the prison of situations from childhood that everyone experienced when growing up. By going aboard the adventure of self-knowledge, they learn to look beyond their walls!

The question of learning as an experience education must reckon with has been so thoroughly discussed by Edgar Morin that there is little for me to add here, beyond noting that understanding is much more important than mere information and wisdom more than mere knowledge. Since Morin diagnosed our educational system, and many others have scrutinized Western culture and modernity, *it is time to focus our aspirations on the reality of the inner world rather than just knowledge of the outside world.*

Traditional education has been remarkably blind to the wisdom of Socrates (as has civilization itself, for allowing this to happen). Perhaps the greatest educator in the history of the West, the wisdom of this great teacher of philosophers involved not only being aware of his own ignorance, but also mastering the high art of *maieutic dialogue*,[19] and living his life in accordance with the know-thyself imperative inscribed over the entrance to the Oracle of Delphos.

Society has built a great monument to Socrates in the cosmopolitan city of the modern mind, but we have never honored him by taking him seriously. Superficially, an education that is limited to transmitting the outside world may appear to be fruitful. But our not heeding the call to cultivate knowledge of the inner world is just part of the complicity between education and the political-economic system, which is best served by easily manipulated robots.

Rather than studying psychology, knowing thyself is more a matter of lived experience than most people think. It starts with lucid contact with our feelings and perceptions, evolving toward knowledge of our emotions, including abrupt

[19] Term related to the role of the midwife, which was subsequently applied to people who used words to assist the psychic birth of others.

consciousness of the thinking process, and may reach a transpersonal level that transcends the realm of thinking, feeling and desiring. It is a thirst for transcendence or truth that makes us "seekers" until, like Oedipus, we solve the "riddle of the Sphinx".

The oracle's repeated urging to "know thyself" has two senses. One of them is psychological and refers to contact with our immediate experience, to understanding our personality, our unconscious motivations, our relations with others and our lives. But there is also a sense that we call spiritual, transpersonal, philosophical or mystical, which relates to the quest for understanding our innermost nature—the depths of consciousness we usually call "self" or "ego," a kind of more profound identity beyond our psychological identity, and similarly beyond the conceptual definition

These two aspects of self-knowledge are worthy of emphasis in the educational endeavor, but both are noticeably absent from today's institutionalized education.

Currently there is a much talk of integral or holistic education. UNESCO proclaimed a holistic ideal by recognizing the importance of not only learning to do and learning to learn, but also learning to live together and learning to be. However, confusion apparently reigns between rhetoric and reality. It is precisely the crisis of education that shows we are persisting—despite UNESCO's wise proposal—in the irrelevance and obsolescence of our efforts to transmit mainly information, whereas what young people need is the sort of education that will help them grow as human beings primarily, rather than forcing an alienating system on them.

My proposal is "tri-focal" education that takes into account the harmonious development of three aspects of the brain related to thinking, feeling, and wanting that harmonizes our inner nuclear family of father, mother, and child. Undoubtedly, traditional education not only prioritizes intellect, but also systematically turns against the instinctiveness and affectivity of our animal nature, vilifying it and prompting systematic self-rejection. Moreover, it is no less obvious that despite the current rhetoric about reviving values, our educational system not only fails to assist affective development, but also delays or obstructs it.

After many years heading a school that has been commonly referred to, among other things, as a "school of love," and now starting to get involved with education, people talk about my "pedagogy of love." However, since I work more with adults than young people and have described my work in books, at this point all I will say is that there is much more potential than we think, since we are able how to combine certain little-known and neglected—but powerful—resources.

I must add to this framework that I am posing in relation to education by briefly alluding to the fact that the human brain may be described as "three-fold". Neurophysiologists have very clearly shown that we have a reptilian brain that is instinctive; a mammal brain that is loving, in which the nexus characteristic of the mother-child relationship comes into play as the foundation for benevolent love;

and the human brain as such, the neocortex, which looks more to the sky than the ground, because it is capable of conceiving ideals and loving transpersonal values such as justice, truth, beauty, life, and divinity.

Since we have tripartite brains - one instinctive, one predominantly emotional, and the other intellectual - we ought to be able to achieve equilibrium between our three faculties. However, patriarchal society has notoriously led to the dominance of rationality over emotion, exploration over cultivation, and aggression over affection.

If the fundamental collective evil is the patriarchal organization of our minds and our society, and we are thus educating one of our brains rather than all three, then we will be able to pursue our health and plenitude by learning to become harmonious and whole tricerebrate beings. We are steering the boat of our collective life as a society by following orders or opinions from economists and other experts. But perhaps the level of complexity of life in society does not lend itself to this kind of knowledge. We are in the situation we are in because we are who we are. So we must also see that the world is the way it is because we have only the education we have.

Moreover, I would say that there is nothing utopian about my proposal for correcting this state of affairs by developing our less evolved faculties. Among our "three inner persons", the paternal subpersonality has eclipsed the expression of our maternal side and our inner child. Nevertheless, therapeutic experience has shown us that there are many ways of dealing with this issue.

Although not part of its usual language, psychotherapy does work with variations on emancipation of the inner child. Interventions are based on Freud's original proposal of releasing instinctive feelings and overcoming a generalized psychological situation in which the pleasure principle has implicitly been demonized.

We are well aware that Freud himself, the driving force behind psychotherapy, was no optimist. His last book argued that the conflict between instinct and civilization is an impasse, whereas his followers—such as Reich and Fromm—spoke of intrinsic goodness of human beings, which is now the prevailing notion in today's humanist environment. Although Freud did not believe this, they proclaimed psychotherapy a liberating activity and specifically a process of emancipation of the Dionysian spirit.

I love revisiting Nietzsche's proposal in this respect. As a great critic of society, Nietzsche may be seen as an apostle of Dionysius for his eloquent insistence on the need to revive the latter's spirit as an antidote to the fossilization of Christian society in the West.

Max Weber showed that all religious movements in history went through an initial charismatic stage, then a bureaucratic phase, moving from their spring to reach—over time—their winter stage. Nietzsche was implicitly referring to Christianity in its decadent stage, and the core of his apologia for Dionysius was the need to "de-demonize" spontaneity.

Dionysus, the god born of a woman, who dies and is reborn, is also the god of dance, madness and wine. Of course, wine is still the core of the main sacrament of this civilization that calls itself Christian but has become increasingly secular. Nevertheless, our *ethos* of exerting control over nature—both external and internal—has little to do with what wine originally represented: being dissolved into something bigger, surrendering control of the "small mind" over the mysterious profundity of life, transcending the known to enter into consonance with a spiritual reality beyond our control. The Dionysian way is one of abandonment and philosophy of letting go of control; this was the key to mysticism beyond cultural boundaries, from ancient prophecy and shamanism to Islam.

Thus we would have to revive our archaic reptilian brain, which has been culturally demonized. The image of the devil himself, with its horns and goat's legs, was copied from that of Dionysus. Both allude to animality, but a holy animality that we can only understand after centuries denigrating the body, and a denigration that is not intrinsic to spirituality, but the result of cultural contamination. The society in which Christianity was implanted eventually dragged the Christian spirit toward this misunderstanding of asceticism, which was originally an effective spiritual practice rather than a moral value, much less denial of the healthy animal that is part of our nature. It seems that we wanted to fly too high, and as Nietzsche's Zarathustra rightly said, we are so concerned with not sinning against heaven that we do not realize how much we are sinning against earth.

Let us now consider what a crushing impact the aggressive patriarchal spirit has had for our maternal side, which is no less in need of emancipation. If instinctive freedom is part of mental health and therefore of individual happiness, the ability to love—closely related to the inner brain—is crucial to the health of society and a contented social life. However, love is no priority for a power-oriented rationalist society, and is always ultimately eclipsed, even when it comes to formulating the highest ideals in relation to society or education. It has to be admitted that the word "love" is a real taboo—a term that may be used in art, literature or religion, but not in science—which the academic world looks up to as the criterion of truth. Of course it would be ridiculous to banish the word "love" from Christian language, since we are all familiar with the central commandment of Christianity, but psychology prefers to speak of things such as "positive reinforcement" or "need for relationship," and I think we are so immersed in a world controlled by the intellect that we do not realize that human life involves the betrayal of love with every step we take.

This betrayal goes right back to birthing, when women were assisted by midwives who did their job very well. Of all births, only one-half of one percent or so pose real problems that obviously need doctors to intervene with hospital resources, if there are many complications. But did you know that more than half of all babies in most civilized countries are delivered by Caesarean section? Why so? For the same reason, there are no more midwives and women are almost forced to give birth in highly technological hospital environments: because the powerful cash nexus so ordains. The fact that children are born between 9am and 3pm (when its suits doctors) implies that drugs are involved—both anesthetics and stimulants. There is no respect for the natural rhythm of birth, in which the fetus' adrenaline warns the mother that it is time to produce the corresponding hormones. This fact alone introduces major disruption at every step in the process of childbirth.

But more important than all this is the insensitivity of "scientific" medicine, which is shown by the practice of cutting the umbilical cord too soon, for example. The cord contains enough blood to supply the baby with oxygen until it begins to breastfeed, even before breathing. Cutting it too soon produces anoxia[20] and the anguish of anoxia may be the most terrible emotion we ever experience: death-anguish that we bear in our psychic substrate as a debilitating factor, birth trauma caused by anoxia. Moreover the immediate consequence of this oxygen debt is that the newborn's breathing has to be stimulated by slapping its back. Until recently, a certain percentage of deaths within a few days of birth were ascribed to unknown causes. But now we know that these deaths are the result of microscopic spinal hemorrhages caused by slapping. In the United States, black newborns are slapped more than whites, clearly proving that this practice leads to unconscious expression of aggression, as shown in the case of electric-shock treatment for psychotics in mental hospitals.

In saying that betrayal of love begins at birth, a key point is that in the scientific and commercial environment of a hospital, newborns are callously separated from their mothers, thus spoiling the formation of the bonding determining an individual's ability to be loving and caring in subsequent life. Although the importance of the mother-child bond for emotional development is widely recognized—particularly after the work of Bowlby, or more recently Marshall Klaus in the United States—I know of no more impressive proof of this than the point noted by Joseph Chilton Pearce in relation to the social deterioration of the Afro-American population in the United States. What struck me most was the deterioration of the previously strong social values of the black community there in relation to this loving care (reflected in literature in the figure of the ideal wet-nurse in *Gone with the Wind*).

That changed after the Second World War, or more recently, when the black community started to resource hospitals due to increasing poverty (although the world is getting wealthier, we know that the distance between the poor and the rich is growing). Since then all types of problems have been emerging in that community that is such a good example of it; they are shooting each other dead, and mothers reject their children. Social reality therefore "experimentally" validates the consequences (that we normally do not note or measure) of something that science arrogantly destroys with its technological "invasiveness" at the service of greed.

---

[20]Translator's Note to the Portuguese text: Diminished or suppressed tissue oxygenation.

Another piece of information that also came to my knowledge through J. C. Pearce is that when physicians were able to analyze milk they found out that women's milk is poorer in fats and proteins than that of other animals; they decided then that they should feed children with bottles of cow's milk. Nowadays we are more informed on the subject and we understand that nature has "planed" for humans to be breastfed much more regularly, because the most important thing is the contact: the cultural fact of maternity communication that starts so early with that heart to heart contact, especially on the left breast where the child's heart is in tune with the mother's heart.

Well, whatever starts that way continues in school, so much so that for some reason, we talk of the "fatherland" rather than the "motherland" (although in Spain may be called *la madre patria*, literally "mother-fatherland"). In noting that civilized countries have done away with the role of the midwife, and made natural birth so difficult, I am posing this fact as a monstrous symptom of how the patriarchal system oppresses the maternal spirit, and asking whether something similar may be taking place in education.

Educators often have a maternal vocation. Men or women, what motivates them is something like a prolongation of the maternal spirit. But even if educational activity is a form of "motherhood," its path is subject above all to the decisions of educational politicians—usually international and male—who have no first-hand knowledge of what is really going on: lacking the vocation or sensitivity of the true educator, they think of income and future economic benefits, and use computers more than their intuitive sensibilities. So here we find a betrayal of the spirit of true education, a betrayal of its "motherly" vocation, say, in which love is submitted to the model of Singapore, for example, where they were reportedly getting better results in terms of good grades; they were squeezing more out of individuals, their system being basically a police state where people may be whipped for spitting in the street or jailed for a minor infraction. So now pupils are kept busy sixteen hours a day passing exams in what we are prompted to see as "education of the future".

I reiterate that what is taking place today is a great tragedy for education: we are crushing the human spirit and profoundly ignorant of what we are doing. If we want to change the world, we must transform people and we cannot expect this to be done just through religion or psychotherapy, which are for minorities and based on the assumption that people feel a great desire for change and will make the great sacrifices involved in transformation. Swimming against the stream, or cleansing one's soul, and organizing one's inner world, are difficult propositions involving so much effort that few will reach the end of the road, or even halfway. The current economic situation means that all this is becoming even more difficult.

Discussing consciousness is to discuss the unification of our fragmented psyche and the understanding, which current neurology provides us with regard to interior conflicts, typical of neurosis (important concept, although it is not suitable to forget the old term), that goes beyond the Freudian concept of the tripartite brain. A notion that has now been clearly established was prophetically formulated in the early 20th century by Gurdjieff, with whose school I had contact in my youth. In a sort of science-fiction novel entitled *Meetings with Remarkable Men (All and Everything)* or *Beelzebub's Tales to His Grandson*, Gurdjieff was already writing of the "tripartite brain".

Beelzebub is on his return trip from the Absolute Centre of the universe, since he has concluded his mission (and horns are already growing on his forehead as a sign that he has reached maturity), and he explains to his grandson how sad it was to watch those creatures from a distant solar system, that such dark place in the universe... where, in this small planet called Earth, miserable tripartite-brained beings live and suffer because they cannot get their three brains to agree. It is a book with more than three thousand pages, I think, and it was one of the most important books of my life. When for the first time Gurdjieff created an institute, in Turkey, at the time he emigrated from Russia during the Bolshevik revolution, he named it after that concept: "Institute for Man's Harmonious Development".

Holism is fashionable nowadays. We know that our brain is a functionally tripartite embryological organ and Gurdjieff was quite right in his proposal to balance the emotions, intellect, and instincts. In my opinion, this is what psychology does implicitly, and this is what education should be setting out to achieve. Enunciating it is all it takes to realize that to achieve it we ought to give more relevance to a loving education; not just to emotional awareness but to removing obstacles to the expression of our innermost being whose intrinsic kindness is jeopardized by all sorts of "inner demons". It takes an interior war against the ego to achieve that, destroying the conditioned personality and being against everything that is usual and familiar. In my opinion that, which psychotherapy allowed us to understand, can only be preventively and massively implanted by the education of the future.

The education of the future ought to stop using authoritarian practices and start cultivating children's interests and feelings. From a young age they would develop the self-esteem that is so often talked about but so rarely found in the real world. How can they have self-esteem if the aim is to "get some sense into their heads" or if we still have this spirit of the "school of hard knocks." Children are no longer being whipped, but in psychological terms it is disdain that prevails, and classrooms are extremely unsmiling and disciplinarian places. Such is the funnel through which schools attempt to pour information without offering young people the experience of being heard and appreciated, or taking their preferences into account. My proposal is education having an element similar to "client-centered" Rogerian therapy, meaning child-centered education taking into account their interests rather than stamping out spontaneity, or punishing curiosity, thus preserving eagerness to learn. Everything that is "gotten into their heads" will later fall by the wayside; it will be useful for a while, but then it will prevent true learning. Learning is change. Education is not about reading, writing, or arithmetic—these are the means rather than ends of education.

I believe that often parents make a mistake in that, because many times there are true educators here and there, schools that want to innovate, and not only institutions or central bureaucracy of the different countries interfere in the priorities of development with their examination requirements, but it is community itself, the social inertia of the environment, that represses the reform required. Some parents say "but they don't teach my children the important things. Still they don't do it right, since the children don't get good marks in basic subjects and are already being distracted by sophisticated things."

What is required is not simply an education that has this or that extra branch, like a scenario or a sign of upgrading, but rather an education that has a solid basis, one that takes into account the fact that educating is to assist the full development of the human being; and that means change based on education. Educating complete beings is to educate to BE, rather than just to do. And to BE is an experience that only a whole person can have. I believe that all our malaises emerge from our incompleteness and all psychoses can be reinterpreted on the basis of the lack of being.

Freud saw neurosis as the repression of drives, or impulses. I believe the existential interpretation is more profound: there is a desire to fill some emptiness, the feeling of a void, recognized only because the culture has no name for it, which might be named "metaphysical anxiety." People do not realize this so they fill their voids with all manner of substitutes: some doing drugs and rock & roll, or riding motorbikes and living dangerously. Others filling the void with a thirst for knowledge and becoming very learned; yet others yearning for applause, and some developing dependence on love. However, none of these waters will quench their thirst: they are just ways of attempting to fill the central void that cannot be filled except by feeling and becoming conscious of existence itself.

However, "I am" is not something that can be said by an isolated part of our brain. Only the whole being can say it, and at the time he says it, something greater than the very human being echoes. When Moses asks God what he should answer when people ask him "Who sends you", God identifies Himself with the consciousness of the being by telling him to answer: "I AM sends me."

I believe that a satisfactory educational proposal must particularly include this human potential: the ability to awaken the spirit, to go beyond thinking and even beyond emotions: this contemplative dimension that touches the experience of being, initially recognizing its fundamental basis that is "not of this world," then of going through a process of dis-identification in relation to our personality itself—our apparent self or ego—which we must transcend just as the butterfly grows out of its cocoon.

If we propose something like that—which is almost like saying "pay attention to the kingdom of heaven and you will be given everything else"—people will certainly think we are eccentric, because everything that is concrete and visibly practical is fashionable; like the old English saying "Take care of the pennies and the pounds will take care of themselves" conveys, which is the same as saying "take care of the pennies and you will be rich" or "take care of the details and concrete things before anything else". Such is the trend in these times of globalization and privatization, where the quality of education is valued as an investment and it is eccentric to take care of something as vague as human depth, or whatever they call it.

If we pose the idea of an education for the being, we will certainly be in trouble. Since the proposal presumes primarily loving education, some will fear that it is too close to a therapeutic approach. However, in traditional education, an implicit taboo rules: educators do not wish therapy to be part of their sphere; it would be easy to picture that, for example, if children started to talk at school about things that happen at home, parents would not appreciate to see their "dirty linen washed in public," nor would teachers know how to handle it. And if they were invited to be more honest, who would be able to face that honesty in order to prevent it from leading to chaos? Psychotherapy culture would be required, in addition to overcoming that taboo by recognizing how deeply important emotional health is for education. And it would be necessary to do something like a technology transfer from therapy to education, even if things would not be given the same name.

There is also spiritual taboo, or religious taboo. Since the times when the State and the Church separated due to issues that submission to the ecclesiastic authority brought about, not only ecclesiastic authority was discarded but so were spirituality and the concept that education has to meet people's core needs.

In that case it would be necessary to reimport the spiritual, although no longer in a sectarian way—or Christian, or Muslim, or any specific religion—but in an intercultural transsystemic way; a spirituality where all pupils get acquainted with the basic thinking of each of the world's great religious genius. How did Confucius think? What was Buddha's view of life? And what was Lao Tse's message? And in the same way one goes to places to taste wine and chooses which one to take home, in my opinion school should be a place where one could test the basic spiritual exercises of the different traditions, in order to allow students different ways of working on their own spiritual development. Of course that is not so compatible with the policy of religions that aspire to recruit souls from the moment they are born, although I believe it would be quite praiseworthy. Some years ago, I heard Bishop Myers, in California, say at the San Francisco Cathedral: "We are going through times where it is up to us to become heirs of history's full legacy." And I agree that it is not convenient to carry on being so isolated.

However, there is one more problem; when these obstacles are overcome, there is still the economic problem. That proposal of changing the course of education is too big a proposition that also includes reeducating educators. It is true that in education, like in everything else, there are people with a true call and talent (and even heroes who manage to do wonders swimming against the current), however a proposal for a legitimate education reform based on the development of whole beings goes well beyond the power of a body of professors trained to supply information.

However when people say that the issue will be impossible to manage, I could answer to that with the actual subject of my conference to which everything I stated so far was an introduction.

I think I have good news to share: I am sure one can do all this economically, simply because I have done so myself.

After many years training therapists, I devised a program and successively honed the scale needed to implement it until finally reaching what I believe is unprecedented transformative efficiency. I shall now attempt to convey some idea of this in few words, since I have used so many words to get this far.

I would not exactly say this is of my own invention, but rather something I have followed through in a natural evolutionary process, which originated from an inspiration that was at the same time an improvisation. The first phase was with a group of searchers in Berkeley, which gave rise to the SAT Institute, and I worked with them for about three years. The second was a program for training psychotherapists in Europe (announced as a "personal and professional education program"), which was similar to the first group, but in the intensive form of a month-long meeting each year for three consecutive years. I then continued refining and compressing the proposal, making it more economical, paring all excess until the theoretical part was no more than smuggled in alongside the practical exercises. I was able to develop a certain art of doing theory without doing theory, helping people realize how the most important things can be learned through a few sentences delivered at the right time in contact with the pertinent living experience.

And as computers get smaller with time and do not lose memory, but rather gain more power and possibilities, what I have been doing has similarly been getting smaller, so much that currently I can do it in approximately 10 days per year. And not only have many therapists gone through the program but so has a considerable number of educators and other professionals.

Chilean psychologists held an event in my honor at the University of Chile a few years ago, and I had an opportunity to explain my "Transpersonal Integrative Program for Training Agents of Change" without referring specifically to therapists or educators. However, I also called it a "curriculum for self-knowledge, interpersonal re-education, and spiritual cultivation." So powerful is the outcome of this program, so emotive the experience of those who go through the process, and so strong the impact I have seen it make on people's lives over the years, that I have sometimes referred to it as "an ego crushing machine." Again, people have often referred to it as a "school of love" or a "school of humanization." When one of them is asked "what have you learned?" the answer is often "I feel more myself."

In the course of several years working in different countries, having repeatedly found that my school (I say " school" because it is more than just a program, since there has to be a person able to put it into practice) can have a really transformative impact in such a short time, which led me to think it could be a resource of great transformative value for tomorrow's education. If I am not mistaken in thinking that it may be useful to supplement the training of educators, without enormous expense, then the right thing to do is to convey the formula and the corresponding training to others. I think we would all agree that just as life can only come from life, so consciousness only comes from consciousness, so education does not come from books or curriculums, but is spread by contagion. Therefore, we have to provide supplementary education for educators so that they can convey this consciousness (which in turn is a higher way and life) to young people; their minds have not crystallized and are much easier to cure and emancipate than those of adults.

I now move in the world as someone whose tree of life has yielded its fruit, which has ripened and fallen on the ground, and it contains many things I learned from my pilgrimage as a seeker, that have been integrated, and converged in a particular synthesis. However, I think that this yield has to be planted in lands far from its country of origin, far from the tree that yielded the fruit. I come from the world of therapy and spirituality, in terms of both the specialty of my teachers and my own past activities. Education became conscious for me because it came knocking at my door, so to speak. Providentially, I was there to engage with it, without having chosen it.

That started as soon as I arrived in the United States. The Education Policy Research Center, of the prestigious Stanford Research Institute – SRI, hired me to draw up a report on the techniques used at the level of the so-called Human Potential Movement, which could be applied to education. At the same time, I was privileged to be able to collaborate with the Esalen Institute, which George Leonard (in his book *Education and Ecstasy*) claimed to be the most daring experiment in loving education. More recently, invitations for several congresses on education allowed me to realize both the critical status of education and the relevance of my own professional experience gathered in a different subject.

In my opinion, the more I become aware, the more I understand what goes on in the world, and I am naturally driven to contribute to improving it. During a good part of my life, I lived in an ivory tower, extremely introverted, and interested in science and art. I went to medical school because science colleges did not exist then, and later I was about to drop out of it thinking that I would find in physics something more compatible with my philosophical call. However, I ended up discovering Jung's world and I thought that being a psychiatrist I could also quench my thirst for research and knowledge. And I remained in that, getting to like psychotherapy little by little, developing my personal creativity, and integrating same to my experience in the spiritual journey. Nevertheless I never thought I would eventually contribute to education, let alone fight for its cause. My militancy alone is what has encouraged me in recent years, and I am speaking on behalf of it; that of contributing for changing the world through the crucially important change in education.

And without really seeking it, I realize that I discovered something socially useful. I find myself with this new resource—this program and process—in the hands, so to speak, and now I say: "here it is;" this time directing attention to the relevance, and the hope, that the view of *possible and urgent change in education* is disseminated, since I particularly do not know anything that can be compared to the institutional inertia in the world of education.

There is institutional inertia in all large organizations: the bigger the bureaucratic system, the more difficult it is to change. But education is a very special case. By definition, education must mean the advancement of consciousness and culture; however, it appears to be the slowest and most obsolete of our institutions. I believe that we really have is an anti-educational institution, since its interference with the educational potential of life overrides what it contributes. In have much sympathy with the position of Ivan Illich, who proposed de-schooling, but with one important difference: I think it is worth making use of existing schools, putting new wine in old bottles.

I am past the age of talking for the sake of it. I hope that what I am saying will have an effect. The idea I would like to convey to you is this: not only is the world in a bad state, but our current malaise is just the crisis of an evil that is as old as civilization itself. We need to change course; we need healthier and wiser human beings, and nothing could contribute more than profoundly reshaping the aims and forms of education. In our period, the age-old patriarchal system has been wrecked, the boat is sinking and lifeboats are being manned. The salvage operation will consist mainly of educating human beings to be more conscious and better individuals, thus able to find a better way of living in society.

The level of unfairness and violence in today's world is so high that it is easy to feel helpless in face of the idea of contributing to a better state of things. But despite the fact that many roads are closed, I believe we have a bridge to a better future; education is the bridge to hope. And if that view is spread and communicated to the authorities, it will be widespread among parents who have children in school, and in the schools themselves it will help one to come face to face with the dreadful institutional inertia that paralyzes education; and that may seem mysterious, but it surely complies with political and economical pressures that come from beyond governments.

It is my belief that the underpaid and under-appreciated teaching profession contains redeeming potential greater than that of religions or psychotherapy, which can only help isolated individuals but not attain change on the scale required to transform society. However, for this potential of education to become effective, it will have to incorporate resources that have been developed by therapeutic activity and spiritual traditions. My work is a contribution to this incorporation or integration, and I hope it may provide encouragement for the great task I am proposing: that of giving back education its meaning as stimulus for human development, both individually and collectively.

Curing Educators to Transform Education

It is one thing to formulate an educational ideal and quite another to embody the ideal of transforming education. Just asking how such a transformation could be carried out is enough to realize that mere formulations of educational policies and curriculum reforms are insufficient. As I said before, life can only originate from life, and consciousness can only proceed from consciousness. Such is the subject of this section too: the idea that the key to renewing education is a new way of educating educators.

All it takes for considering that proposal is appreciating what happened recently in the field of the education of values that seemed to be the logical response to the growing impoverishment of culture in terms of virtues and ideas. Until recently, the law in several South-American countries, as well as in Spain, proposed an education that would merge an explicit "vertical" curriculum with a "horizontal" curriculum of values, in such a way as to allow, for example, a Biology or History teacher to seek at the same time to contributing to communicate to their pupils an approach of solidarity, peace, or freedom.

That was a noble proposal that for some time, in certain people's opinion, was the right solution to the lack of concern for the human in education. However, it did not take into account that to be able to convey values it is necessary to have much more than just courses on the alleged "education of values." Would it be possible for a non-sympathetic person to convey a sympathetic spirit? Or would a person who is not free be able to deliver education based on freedom? "Values" such as solidarity, freedom, peace, or authenticity are features of a mind that has matured, and not just subjects that one knows how unfold after having heard or read certain things, including those that are communicated in courses on "education of values". Or it addresses aspects of a change to character that leads the individual from some sort of worm condition—which is his ordinary condition—to a potential state of health and fullness that relies more on the soaring aim at transcending the ego, allowing thus the emancipation of the essential being, than on specific learning.

Fortunately, the world of educators' needs are the same as their own needs—something they are not aware of—and either due to pressure or to the fact that they are used to courses that contribute little or nothing to their wellbeing, or true development, they doubt what the institution offers them.

In most countries of the Eastern world teachers are depressed, and many suffer from psychosomatic diseases, but they are particularly unmotivated. I am certain that to be able to assist them to recover their essential will one needs to nurture their emotional life[21]. That is the reason why the "specialization courses"

[21]When I revisit this subject, I would like to note something crucial, although little recognized: educators' malaise that not even they can explain, similarly to their students', is due to the fact that they have to sell themselves to an activity that does not have true value to their students. We all need to feel useful and however much we make mistakes

they need are not those known so far in the core of traditional pedagogy; it would be better to have activities through which wisdom traditions are conveyed and psychotherapists are educated. It is crucial for them to have a predominantly experiential school that shows the work necessary to overcome destructive emotions and develop higher emotions and virtues; a school for self-knowledge and dissociation from the untrue character, opening them up to discover their true being. What is crucial is to have something similar to an intensive version of the educational ideal that I have been proposing as necessary to all, as an experience supplementary to the scientific and humanistic curriculum. Or a curriculum of self-knowledge, interpersonal cure, and experiential spiritual culture, free of dogmatism.

I hope that those who are interested in finding that method to educate educators rejoice to know that is exactly what I have to offer, after an ongoing investigation of approximately four decades.

Currently the "SAT Program" consists of three modules of approximately ten days each—one a year—and saying that the results are unheard of would not be an overstatement. If anyone who reads this statement were to ask how it is possible to expect so much from ten-day programs, I would answer that it is due, in part, to the fortunate combination of psychotherapy with selected of spiritual traditions and, in part, to the fact that a significant mosaic is more than the addition of its parts, and also, in part, to the integration of powerful resources till now underestimated by the scholar world (like Buddhist meditation, the Enneatypes Psychology, the word with parental relations inspired by Hoffman, the legitimate movement, an original form of therapeutic theater, etc.). The results from the "SAT process" would not be imaginable if it addressed a mere curriculum or a bunch of ideas and resources. Its implementation is supported by the ever growing experience lived by their scholars.

The SAT school activities intend to develop a way of living that is more human and truthful. For many, it means finding the spiritual side of life. Many leave old ways of feeling and seeing things behind, and feel that their lives take a new course. In brief, for most participants it means the gateway to the transformation journey. Those who are more dedicated travel a considerable part of the way.

A significant aspect of the "SAT Program" has a psychosocial feature. The group of participants becomes a real team where everyone can show what they are like, explore alternative behaviors, and find out that they are accepted and dear regardless of their usual roles. But the "SAT process" is not just a process where people feel they are accepted and validated. There is also a strong opposing element in it that provides a balance between the nurturing aspect and the declaration of a "holy war against the ego."

Once I organized a panel with a group of colleagues with the purpose of

---

defeated by a systemic mistake, we are unmotivated when we realize that our lives need some sense.

discussing what the "SAT experience" had been like for them. I was impressed by seeing them emphasize what a gift it had been for participants to have had the company of so many scholars who "worked on themselves" rather than hiding behind their professional role.

Nowadays it is broadly recognized that psychotherapy relies more on relations and insights rather than technique. That is equivalent to saying that it is the therapist benevolence that allows for "controlling" patients better than their parents managed. Less broadly recognized is the therapeutic value of dependability, although that seems to me a crucial element of this living school.

Observation has continually proved to us that the therapeutic practice provided in the SAT Program is of interest and service to both the highly experienced therapists and new participants, and that every course is "almost like a miracle", considering the large amount of situations that take place and things that are learned. I think it is really like this, and I consider that success to be an experimental confirmation of my inspiring conviction. I mean, to be able to help others we do not need lengthy studies, but the experience of one's own inner journey through self-knowledge and the appropriate efforts. Three things are relevant; practical/experiential training, a clear view of certain crucial things, and the ability to get through to the patient. Due to the prominence of the latter in the educational practice I organized, we say that "cure by way of truth" happens often.

I would say that the SAT experience has already produced many people who, subsequent to having seen the light, continue on the same course, fully aware of how much they lack to embody the consciousness of which they saw a sign, and that sets them apart from impostors. I can hardly say that I produce fully enlightened people, since not even I have arrived at the end of my journey, but it seems that our work has been "protected by the gods." It mirrors not only the value of my collaborators and those who work hard on themselves, but also support of other factors, from those providential and unique to the group's magic to that of a true community, and the blessing of several spiritual lineages. I believe the SAT has not only helped a lot of people to grow, but also managed to become a living school where its group of teachers knows what to do not just intellectually but also through the mastery of their fields by experience. I say that the "SAT process," rather than just a mere program is a true experience of initiation that opens people to the unknown. Or an experience that does not only place people on a pre-established track, but in a process of change that becomes irresistible as one understands its sense.

Again, I reiterate my belief that our sick and crisis-ridden world needs the encouragement of individual transformation, since a healthy society is inconceivable without healthy individuals, and we cannot expect the need for self-realization to be filled by the traditional means alone. What is needed is something akin to a democratization of psychotherapy, and this could be done if education were to show people how to work on themselves, spiritually and psychologically, and to help each other. This is one characteristic achievement of the SAT process, which transcends its integral curriculum and living "experientialism."

I fear that describing my own work as capable of providing a master key for the transformation of education and thus curing our collective malaise, sounding like a blatant sales pitch, particularly in this era of business and advertising. Yet people who know me well are well aware that I have never sold anything in my life, and that I would not be doing so now. What urges me on is a sense of responsibility for my work, like a father's feelings for his child. In this case, the feeling of responsibility is inspired by the profound conviction that "it has worked." Responses from hundreds of participants in my programs, year after year, have persuaded me that I have started something that does hold great pro-life potential, and specifically something that really could change society by educating educators. So I just think this justifies sharing the good news.

Now I am ready to move on. As Cervantes said at the beginning of *Persiles,* I have one foot in the stirrup. Others will carry on the work I started. At a recent event in Madrid (sponsored by the Tomillo Foundation) I said that I felt like a fairy-tale character who came across a magical plant in the backyard of his own home, and its sap had the power of weakening a dragon that had been tormenting the district. In the course of my customary work, after many years, apparently accidentally, I realized that my findings, which appeared to be only for the benefit of the participants (and indirectly their patients in the world of psychotherapy), could be a key component for the transformation of education, on which I believe our collective destiny depends so critically. Despite feeling that I was in possession of a public asset, I have not yet gotten to feel that my task has been accomplished: what is a seed before it is planted?

In light of that, I have been dedicated to providing information about my view of the tragically wasted potential of education and about my contribution to the education of teachers. As a result of private conversations and conferences, I managed to attract the interest of some institutions, governments, and educators, some of which are gathering in groups in several countries and creating organizations based on promotion and financing programs to equip basic and intermediary school teachers, as a supplement to university studies or in a contest of ongoing education. For example, in the book "Changing Education to Change the World" I communicate the excellent results of two modules of the SAT Program offered to 30 teachers' educators called by Mariana Aylwin at the time she was the head of the Ministry of Education in Chile[22]. More recently a Foundation was created in Barcelona named after me, thanks to the initiative of friends and enthusiasts for the idea, as sometimes I say paraphrasing H. G. Wells: *"the future is a race between education change and catastrophe."*

---

[22] In Brazil, the excellent result of the three modules of the SAT program delivered to more than fifty teachers of the municipal network of Porto Velho, Rondonia, to be soon disclosed, is sponsored by the local SEMED – Municipal Secretariat of Education (Translator's Note to the Portuguese text).

TOWARDS AN INTEGRAL ENNEAGRAM

Peter McNab

Abstract

In this article I consider how mistyping can happen by looking at the issue through the lenses of Ken Wilber's Integral Model of A.Q.A.L.A.L.A.S.A.T. (All Quadrants, All Levels, All Lines, All States, All Types). Recognizing that the best that any model can be is "true and partial", and thus all models should be held lightly, I briefly describe the Integral Model before moving on to the All Quadrant aspect of it. There follow sections on the "monological gaze vs. duological gaze", "introversion vs. extraversion", and "individual vs. collective" in which I point out that unless we consider all of these aspects when working with others there is a strong possibility that we might mistype others. There follows a brief introduction to NLP (Neuro Linguistic Programming) leading into a section on the Meta Model, which is a tool to help us with the category errors that we might make while considering Quadrants. There are examples of how two of the thirteen patterns from the Meta Model can be used, Modal Operators and Nominalizations. The final section explores the "All Levels" aspect of Wilber's model by introducing Clare Graves' work on world-views and how it might relate to mistyping.

1 Introduction

For as long as I can remember I have loved magic and out of that love came a thirst for knowing how the magic works. For me, the "trick" becomes even more magical once I know how it works, but although I am not alone in this, there are also many people who don't want to know how "tricks" work; they want to hold on to the "magic". Once I know how things work, however, I have a much better chance of replicating them. As I explored further, one of the main things that I have learned is that even the best magic, the most magical of "tricks", has, at its heart, the simplest of principles. Once you understand the principles you realize how simple it is; suddenly, it makes total sense.

My favourite "trick" at the moment is one where the magician riffles through a deck of cards and asks someone to say, "Stop," and in doing so chooses a card that only she and other participants see. She puts it back anywhere into the deck and it is now her job to find the card that she chose. The magician deals out the cards into six piles, turning the remaining four cards face up, and, of course, the chosen card isn't one of them. Our participant then has an entirely free choice in discarding five of the piles and as the piles are discarded they are turned face upward. Once there is only one pile left, the remaining eight cards are dealt out with the last two being discarded face up. The participant then has an entirely free choice in discarding the cards one by one until there is only one left; when it is turned over it is revealed to be the chosen card.

If you really think about it, there is only one way that this trick could possibly work but not one person, including magicians, has been able to tell me how it does. We are programmed to work with what we see, and if there are any gaps we fill them in. What we fill the gaps with seems to matter less than the fact that they are filled in, and that is how this "trick" works. The eyes see things, not the whole picture, of course, but enough that the mind can fill in the gaps.

This is not just true of magic. In other situations, maybe at an unconscious level, we fill in gaps, we interpret, we make assumptions, we make inferences. There are very good evolutionary reasons for us to be hard-wired in this way. Our ancestors were far more likely to survive on the African plains if they responded instinctively to the slightest movement in the grass; it might be a predator and not to run at that point would not be the best option, even if they were wrong. Those who did not run were more likely to take their genes out of the gene pool. The best option in those circumstances is to run, even if ninety nine per cent of the time you are wrong.

Wilber puts all of this into context for me when he writes that any model that has been created can only ever be *"true but partial"* (Wilber, 2000a, p.140).

"In this Theory of Everything, I have one major rule: Everybody *is right. More specifically, everybody – including me – has some important pieces of truth, and all of those pieces need to be honored, cherished, and included in a more gracious, spacious, and compassionate embrace, a genuine T.O.E."* (Wilber, 2000a, ibid.)

It is for this reason that I try to hold models like the Enneagram lightly. Each model we use to look at a situation will offer some truths, but it will not offer the whole truth, and that is why I use other models while I am using the Enneagram. I happen to believe that it is one of the best typologies around at the moment; this does not stop it from being "true and partial".

This article is an attempt to move towards a more robust Enneagram, a more Integral Enneagram. It is informed by extensive reading and attending many workshops, but more importantly it is based on over twenty years of running workshops and coaching in a wide variety of organizations in the public sector, the private sector and not-for-profit. I have set forth some of my thoughts in the hope that this will be the start of a dialogue and I would welcome feedback and comments, because this article can only be "true and partial".

1.1 1995

1995 was a magical year for me. I had been learning and then teaching NLP for six years when in 1995 I qualified as an INLPTA Master Trainer (which meant that I could certify NLP trainers), certified as a MBTI Practitioner, discovered the Enneagram, was introduced to Clare Graves' Model (a year later to become known as Spiral Dynamics), and started reading about Ken Wilber's AQAL Model. It was also the year that "Sex, Ecology, Spiritually" was published and went on to become the best-selling textbook in the US.

Initially, I kept these models apart. Over the years I realized that not only was this futile, it was also detrimental to my work, as each of them offer different perspectives of the same situations. Integrating them allowed me to gain a richer view for me and for my clients. Since then I have been working towards integrating them to create the richest model that I have experienced up to this point (while recognizing that there is much further to go).

2 Integral

The word, "Integral" has been creeping inexorably into the Enneagram world, the NLP world, and the Spiral Dynamics world. As someone at home in each of these different worlds, I have been pleased to observe this and also to be a small part of this development, because I believe that the concept has the potential to enhance each of those worlds.

2.1 So What?

The more practical of you may be asking *why* you should be interested in the Integral Model and *how* it intersects with the Enneagram world. My work, and the work of many others that I have trained and worked with, has become more efficient: in my workshops, in my training programmes, in my teambuilding work, in my coaching, and in my writing. We are now able to ask better questions, give better homework, and achieve better results, faster. We find it easier to work out what's behind the tricky questions that our clients ask us. In fact, in any situation where it is important to understand another person, the Integral Model offers a deeper and richer perspective, and it is this that I'd like to share with you.

But we need to take a step back and explain these models briefly before we can explore how we can use them.

2.2 The Integral Model

Since publishing his first book, *The Spectrum of Consciousness* in 1967 (an expansion of his doctoral thesis), Ken Wilber has been trying to develop a model that is inclusive rather than exclusive as most others are. In all of the models of the world that he has studied, and he has listed hundreds in the vast appendices of *Integral Psychology* (Wilber 2000b), there were truths contained in each but he also noted that they are contradictory. How can this be? He realized that each of these models is "true" but it is also "partial". In other words, it describes and explains part of the picture.

This is problem because we seem to have a built-in need for simplicity making it much easier to believe one model rather than several, which is the Freudian-Behaviourist-Marxist-Jungian problem that I write about below.

I also feel that it is important to address the category errors that are made with the model by people who are conflating the different elements involved and thereby contaminating all of the models involved, be they "quadrants", "levels", "lines", "states" or "types". This also causes problems in taking this material into the "real world", giving the people we are trying to convince of the efficacy of what we do every reason to dismiss the models because they don't make sense when presented in this way.

As I mentioned above, the Integral Model itself also helps to explain why people try to conflate the models because the complexity necessary to understand and utilize them is beyond them. In terms of "levels", some people have not yet reached the point where they can comprehend such complexity.

In Wilber's words, the *"pre/trans fallacy"* kicks in here and the concept that simplicity lies at the other side of complexity not before it.

"The essence of the pre/trans fallacy is itself fairly simple: since both pre-rational states and trans-rational states are, in their own ways, non-rational, they appear similar or even identical to the untutored eye." (Wilber, 1995, p.211)

Once this has happened, argues Wilber, one of two fallacies occurs, either *"all higher and trans-rational states are reduced to lower and pre-rational states"* or *"if one is sympathetic with higher or mystical states, but one still confuses pre and trans, then one will elevate all pre-rational states to some sort of trans-rational glory".* (Wilber, 1995, ibid.)

2.3 AQALALASAT (All Quadrants, All Levels, All Lines, All States, All Types)

According to Wilber, if we are to fully understand any situation we need to pay attention to at least the five elements of *"quadrants"*, *"levels"*, *"lines"*, *"states"*, and *"types"*. Elsewhere I have written about how *"quadrants"* and *"levels"* intersect (McNab, 2005) and for this article aimed at an Enneagram audience, I want to add in *"types"*. I recognize that I need to add in the other two elements but believe that it will be easier to assimilate the three already mentioned and save *"lines"* and *"states"* for another time.

In short, paying attention to *"quadrants"* ensures that we have considered the internal and the external of the individual and of the collective, *"levels"* recognizes that each part of the *"quadrant"* may also be at different levels of consciousness, *"lines"* invites us to look at different skills that may be manifested in different quadrants and at different levels, *"states"* understand that we may manifest different states of consciousness at any level, and *"types"* show us that we may go through each and every part of this model in different ways depending on our particular typology.

If we are to have a truly Integral approach we need to be paying attention to all of these elements in any interaction with self and/or others. However, it can get very complicated to always address each and every part. This is what the Integral Art group of the Integral Institute came across when considering what an integral piece of art might look like. They decided, and Wilber agreed with them, that a piece of art can be *"integrally informed"* without necessarily having to contain all of the elements of the AQALALASAT. This makes sense to me when I am coaching and when I am in the training room; I am aware of the different elements as they appear and pay specific attention to the ones that will enable us to meet the specific needs arising in that moment. Like the integral piece of art, the intervention may be very simple but elegantly meets the needs manifesting.

3 All Quadrants

The idea of *"true and partial"* had been one that I had been considering for decades, without knowing the name for such a concept. During my teacher training in the 1970s and my social work training in the 1980s, I was introduced to a variety of models and perspectives. I found that each, not only had merit, but was also practical and useful. Freud started me on the road of exploring the internal world not only of myself but also of my pupils and my clients; Skinner showed me that helping people to change their habitual behaviours could really help them; Marx helped to deepen my understanding that sometimes it is deep-rooted societal issues that need to be addressed if the people we work with are to be helped; Jung was really useful in exploring some of the cultural nuances that affect us. I was attracted to each of these great thinkers but was told, basically, that one has to make a choice; one cannot be a Freudian-Behaviourist-Marxist-Jungian. In fact, each of these models looks at the world through a particular set of eyes that is different from the others.

Wilber describes in *Sex, Ecology, Spirituality* (1995) and *A Brief History of Everything* (1996) how he sat with the masses of different hierarchies that he had collected from a wide variety of philosophers, biologists, psychologists, and educators and tried to make some sense of them. How could each of these models be true and yet contradict one another? It was after two years of contemplation (Wilber is a self-confessed Enneagram Type Five and this shows just what it must be like for a Five to live in Seven for two years until suddenly all of the pieces coalesce into one) that he created the concept of *"quadrants"*.

The quadrants consist of four elements: the Interior and the Exterior, and the Individual and the Social or Collective. When we put these together we get the Individual Subjective or Upper Left, the Individual Objective or Upper Right, the Collective Subjective or Lower Left, and the Collective Objective or Lower Right.

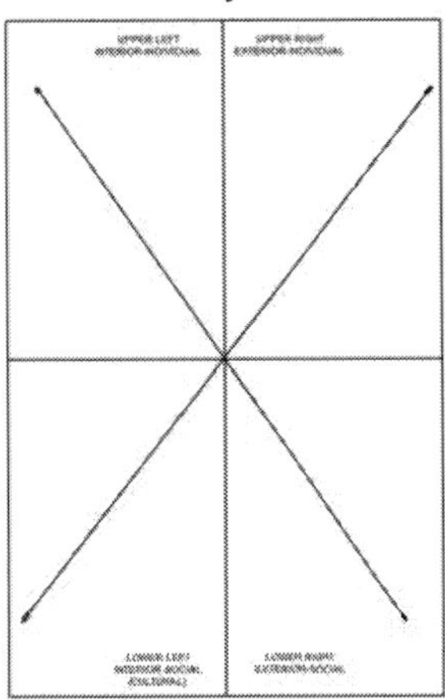

The Individual Interior or Upper Left includes what we think and feel and what we can see and touch.

The Individual Exterior or Upper Right includes our brain, our body and our behaviours.

The Social Exterior or Lower Right includes the external manifestations of our society such as buildings and societal structures.

The Social Interior or Lower Left includes the culture and belief structures of our society.

In other words, I am an individual with intentions that derive from my beliefs and values (Upper Left Quadrant) that I can bring into the real world by exhibiting behaviours (Upper Right

Quadrant) and that these can only exist within a culture that is the sum of my society's beliefs and values (Lower Left Quadrant) that have created a physical space and system of structures that reflect and affect the culture (Lower Right Quadrant).

One of the problems in describing this process is that we have to start somewhere and wherever we start can be assumed as the most important quadrant. In reality, each one is as important as the others and we could in actuality start anywhere.

If we go back to my own little dichotomy from teaching and social work days, Freud is predominantly looking at the world from the perspective of Upper Left Quadrant, Jung from Lower Left Quadrant, Skinner from Upper Right Quadrant, and Marx and Engels from Lower Right Quadrant. Each of these perspectives provides an equally valid way of looking at the world *but* each is true *and* partial.

If we approach the Quadrants with the understanding of only one model, there is a strong chance that we might conflate any models we meet subsequently with the one that we already know. For example, if someone only knows the Enneagram and then discovers the Quadrant Model then it is possible that we might think and argue that Sixes operate exclusively in the Lower Left Hand Quadrant. At first sight this appears valid because Sixes appear to be so heavily invested in what the culture around them is saying; it could explain why they have a tendency to defer to Authority. On the other hand, as all Enneagram aficionados know, Sixes also have issues with Authority and living exclusively in the Lower Left Hand Quadrant does not explain this. In fact, it is an understanding of the Quadrants that can help to us to explain this supposed dichotomy, as has been borne out by many of the Sixes that I have met.

If this imagined Six were operating exclusively from the Lower Left Hand Quadrant then there would only be conflict if the Six were living in a world where there were conflicting cultures, and this might explain some of what is going on. If we bring in the Upper Left Hand Quadrant, however, we can see that a much richer picture emerges. We know that Sixes tend to have a very strong set of beliefs and values tied in to a sense of moral obligation, and while this may have been learned from the culture that the Six grew up in, it is also likely that this will have been integrated at a deep level and probably have shifted up into the Upper Left Hand Quadrant. At times when these two sets of values are in conflict, it might be difficult for the Six to make a choice and the result will be an internalized sense of confusion as two sides of the Six's internal world fight it out.

If we were to leave it there, however, we would still have an incomplete version of what is going on for the Six. We need to add in the elements on the Right Hand Side. The Lower Right Hand side is how the Six checks out what is going on in the external world, the behaviours of others, and also the external representations of the internal culture and mores. The Upper Right hand side is the way in which the Six manifests the conflict, the words being spoken and the tone in which they are being spoken, plus the body language that accompanies it.

If I am to work with this particular Six then I need to use all of the elements in my attempts to understand them and make an intervention, and to show the Six that there is a much richer self-model to be developed when we use all aspects of our experience.

One of the problems is that we all have the propensity to consider just one or two of the Quadrants, not realising that a richer and potentially more useful version is available.

3.1 The Upper/Lower Split

One example of this that I studied at school was the situation in the United Kingdom in Victorian times. The Conservative Party in those days was very keen on keeping the status quo; change for them was a bad thing and they emphasized the Lower Left and the Lower Right to maintain this. What society thought and valued was far more important than the individual's right to do what he wanted to. The Victorian Age was really one of consolidation. It was the non-conformists who believed that individual freedoms were more important than maintaining a repressive status quo. If we jump a few decades, the position shifts and the Conservative Party (now led by Margaret Thatcher) has become the party of the individual and Thatcher once famously said that there is no such thing as society. If individuals are not doing so well or need a job then they are responsible. As Norman, now Lord, Tebbit, a senior Conservative politician in the UK in the 1980s famously said. *"I grew up in the '30s with an unemployed father. He didn't riot. He got on his bike and looked for work, and he kept looking 'til he found it."* At the same time in the UK, the Labour Party shifted from a universal belief in individual freedom to one that believed that individuals are not to blame for their own problems; it is society's responsibility to find them work. This rift between Upper and Lower Quadrants is still being fought today, although the battle lines are shifting, and this may be a realization by both that all Quadrants are needed; we need to look at Upper and Lower elements – private and public responsibility.

3.2 The Left/Right Split

The other way of splitting the quadrants also produces some interesting quandaries.

If we believe that all that really exists is the objective truth then we can try to deny the existence of the Left Hand Side, and Skinner famously did at one point in his career, when he asserted that we are *only* behaviours. A similar thing happens if we only believe that the Left Hand Side is correct and we deny any physical evidence that disagrees with our particular worldview.

What Wilber is saying is that in every situation there are all four elements of the Quadrants present. Although we may have our preferences, if we fall into the trap of believing that these preferences represent the whole picture we will reduce our understanding of the situation considerably. We must pay attention to all Four Quadrants.

3.3 Using The Quadrants

All that we can engage with when communicating with another is the body language that we see, the words that we hear, and the tone of voice in which those words are spoken. And yet, there is much to another than just mere body language, words and tone of voice; at the simplest level, there are the beliefs and the values that underlie the behaviours, and for some even these may be outside of conscious awareness. In order to get closer to the meanings underlying the internal processing of another we have to engage with them.

Habermas (1987) differentiates between the two "gazes" that we might put upon another, "monological" and "duological". The "monological" gaze is when we observe the other; the "duological" gaze is when we engage in dialogue with the other. Habermas seems to be saying that if we want a closer understanding of the other, we must use both gazes. This concept is deep at the heart of Wilber's Quadrant theory (Wilber, 1995) and the "monological" gaze is "looking" at the Right Hand Quadrants whereas the "duological" gaze is "looking" at the Left. There are, of course, proponents and champions of both and, depending on their Level, they may even deny the other side, and certainly its value. Complete rationalists will argue that we cannot truly know what is going on inside another (and even they may get this wrong or be in denial) and so it is best to ignore the Left hand Quadrants; this was the view of Skinner, a radical behaviourist, who at one point argued that there is no such thing as "mind", and that all solutions will come from changing behaviours. Complete relativists will go as far as denying the Right Hand Quadrants because they believe that we create our own reality and that everything in the world is merely a projection of our own thoughts. If this were the case there would be no need to bother with the material world.

(This has been an issue in the world of NLP where, because we can model excellent exemplars, the unnatural extension of this was twisted and took hold in some parts into the idea that if one person can do something then anyone else can. This radical denial of the Right Hand Quadrants was supposed to have emanated from the original developers of NLP, but, to his credit, it was certainly debunked by Richard Bandler. I was told many years ago that Bandler had been approached by one of his more incredulous participants who put forward this theory. Without batting an eye, Banlder took the participant right up to a wall and told him that the wall was only made of molecules and that he should be able to walk through it; he then rammed the participant's face into the wall. I am sure that this tale is apocryphal, but it surely makes the point that we have to pay attention to all four of the Quadrants so that we can get as much of the "picture" as we can.)

We need to be very careful, as there are many peculiar individual and cultural differences. The example that I give in my workshops is of folded arms that everybody knows means that the person is being defensive, and we all know how ridiculous that assertion is, for we have all had occasions when we have felt relaxed and crossed our arms, when we have felt cold and crossed our arms, when we have felt defensive and crossed our arms, when we have spilt coffee on our shirts and crossed our arms, etc., etc. What we need to pay attention to are the patterns for each individual; there will be patterns for each person and those patterns may mean something but it is only after being with that person for some time and talking with that person that we start to notice these patterns and they start to become useful, but we still have to be very careful in making judgments about them.

3.4 Introversion vs. Extraversion

An example of this that I can personally relate to is the difference between those tending to introversion and those tending towards extraversion within the MBTI model and which can lead to the mistyping of others if they don't understand the Quadrants.

If I use myself as an example, as an introverted (INFP) Three, my primary function is "feeling" and my secondary is "intuition". What this means is that in any situation the first thing that I do is to relate whatever is happening and my response to it to my values. I am asking myself if there is a fit or a mismatch, and this is of primary concern to me; all of this is processed internally in the Upper Left Quadrant (although I will in all probability refer to the values being espoused in the situation and in my culture and compare these to my own, which takes in the Lower Left Quadrant). However, what I externalize in words and behaviours is my secondary function of "intuition"; while I am internally processing in one way, I am externalizing something completely different, and the other person sees and hears lots of ideas and possibilities as concepts are connected. Internally, I "feel" like a Three; externally, I may look to others like a Seven. It is only other "introverts" that I have discussed this with who have understood and as we are in a minority of three to one this can explain why we feel that we are misunderstood (this is written about very eloquently in a new book by Susan Cain, *Quiet: The Power of Introverts in a World That Can't Stop Talking*).

Other examples I have met include an INTJ Eight (with Introverted Intuition as his primary function and Extraverted Thinking as his secondary) who is often mistyped as a Five, and ISTJ Five (with Introverted Sensing as her primary function and Extraverted Thinking as her secondary) who is often mistyped as a Seven.

When we are communicating with Introverts, I believe that it is even more important that we engage in dialogue with them, otherwise we shall be basing our intuitions on data that is important but maybe not paramount.

3.5 Individual vs. Collective

As someone from the UK who has spent a lot of time in other countries and on other continents, I have also found that the cultural aspect also affects the ways in which we manifest our Enneagram Type. Generally speaking, when we are "typing" others or helping them to type themselves, we are paying most attention to the Upper Right Quadrant; for reasons given above, it should now be clear that we need to pay attention to the Upper Left Quadrant too, but it also behooves us to look further than that. The Lower Quadrants also come into play, as anyone involved in coaching will know. It doesn't matter how much I help an individual to change and grow if we do not pay attention to the environment into which they are to return to exhibit these changes. If we do not help the person to consider this environment and to explore *how* they are going to ensure that these behaviours stick and they do not revert back to old habits and behaviours that are not useful. This is the domain of the Lower Quadrants and they are equally important when we consider Type.

As most of the Enneagram literature has been written from an American perspective and most of the research has been conducted in America, there has been an (unwritten and unacknowledged) assumption that Type is universal without any variance depending on culture.

When I raised this with C.J. Fitzsimons, he e-mailed me the following:

Hoffmann et al (2004) offer evidence that this is not the case. While the book focuses on how cultural differences impact working together in international projects, the authors also explore how expression of Type is affected by culture.

Hofstede defined culture as the collective programming of the mind distinguishing the members of one group or category of people from others (Hofstede (1997)). He developed a five-dimensional model of culture based on an extensive survey of ca. 80,000 people in 76 countries. One of the dimensions is Power Distance, which expresses the degree to which the less powerful members of a society accept and expect that power is distributed unequally. One example in Hoffmann et al (2004, P. 195) illustrates the different responses of a Spanish (moderately high power distance culture, Type One) and a US American (lowish power distance, Type One) project manager during a team development workshop. Neither was able to tolerate flexible, undefined structure that their US American Type Seven boss was proposing to introduce to the department. Toward the end of the first day, the American Type One could no longer hide his irritation and demanded a clear definition of his role in the new structure. His Spanish colleague, who had a higher power distance differential to overcome only exploded on the third and final day of the workshop and demanded a clear and logical structure with well-defined responsibilities.

It has been my experience, and the experience of others I have spoken with from outside the US, that the way that type manifests is the same the world over; the Quadrants Model is a great way to explore and explain this. I have met many Threes, for example, who do not fit the American stereotype of a Three because it is not socially acceptable to behave in that way.

An example of this was when I was wandering around Copenhagen with two other Brits and an American when we came across a billboard advertising Carlsberg lager. Fellow Europeans will know that this particular lager has been advertised for many decades as "probably the best lager in the world"; the irony clearly works beyond Denmark and the slogan has been translated into many languages. Our American friend, however, was completely flabbergasted and could not understand why the "probably" was there. In Denmark there is a concept called "yendelaw". Very roughly translated, it means that people should not put themselves above others in their society as it is considered to be bad manners. The "probably" supports this as it would be bad form to advertise a lager as "the best in the world". This makes it difficult to act out as a Type Three in Denmark and other countries where there is some version of "yendelaw", or "tall poppy" syndrome.

In conclusion, if we are to engage with others in a meaningful way, we need to get beyond the external, we need to take the duological gaze and shift from Upper Right and get in touch with the Left Hand Quadrants, and we can only do this by asking questions. We know that every person and every situation contains the elements of all four Quadrants, so all of these must be revealed if we are to get the full picture.

While we are eliciting information from all four Quadrants, we also need to be aware of the different Levels. Most people will have a centre of gravity around one or two worldviews and we can discover this through dialogue but we must also be aware that people will revert to previous worldviews when stressed or talking about times when they were stressed.

Within all of this, each Type will exhibit both the Quadrants and the Levels in their own particular way. This makes any interaction incredibly complex and maybe too complex for some, and for most of these, they will tend to have a fallback position of just one element over-simplifying the situation too much. In our Enneagram world we have the tendency to mistype if we are not careful.

This is why, while all of these models are incredibly useful, it is also important that we hold them lightly and integrally.

3.6 Some Examples

Many people accuse Wilber of being too abstract and while I do not find him so, I can understand this; for me, he is a really good storyteller and his books read like the best page-turners. To try to overcome this perception, I'd like to give some examples of how useful the Quadrants can be from my own book, Towards An Integral Vision:

3.6.1 A Health Example

Let's listen in on a typical discussion about health:

"Health is all about fitness and diet – as long as I get those right I'll be O.K."

"No, no. What you need to do is get rid of those unhealthy emotions and say your affirmations – feel and think healthy and you'll be healthy."

"Actually, all you need to do is to join a therapy group where you can share all of your problems and emotions and you'll be fine."

"The real way to good health is to join a private health scheme because they have all of the latest technology – that'll get you well."

Each of these perspectives has something to add to Health but none of them will keep us healthy or get us well alone because each emphasises only one of the quadrants – in order, UR, UL, LL, LR.

You can exercise and diet as much as you like (UR) but if you break your leg you'll need a well-equipped surgery or hospital to help you (LR) but if as a society we don't believe in the value of health care for all (LL) then the hospital will be run down and there will be no individuals willing and able to have the motivation (UL) to train as doctors and nurses but it doesn't matter how much you believe in your own good health (UL) it won't work unless you do something about your physical health and watch what you eat (UR) but however healthy you are as an individual that won't make a difference if you live right in the centre of a polluted city (LR) ... and so we go around the quadrants ...

If we are to achieve maximum health for the greatest number of our citizens, we must ensure that any health service that we develop reflects all four of the quadrants equally. We now know that the mind-body connection is a powerful part of the healing process and that people working on their own beliefs and values in conjunction with the medical treatment delivered by the health service are more likely to heal themselves quicker than those who don't. This is not to say that we can heal ourselves *just* by saying affirmations and changing our beliefs about health. Nor is saying that *just* working with the physical body will work optimally either. We need to consider *all quadrants* every time.

Ironically, the problem that often arises from Ken's all-inclusive approach is that everyone feels attacked because he does not believe that their one approach is the best one. Rather than being flattered at being included in an integral map they tend to get annoyed at being knocked off their perch as the best approach to any situation.

3.6.2 A Business Example

That big speech the Boss made (UR) about us all needing to make sacrifices (LR) to save the company was received well and we all believed (LL) in his passion (UL) to work (UR) with us (LR). When he arrived the next day in his new company top-of-the-range Rolls Royce (UR) (LR) (LL), it became really hard for me to motivate (UR) (UL) (LL) my managers. They no longer believed (LL) in the messages we were trying to get through to the workforce ... and so we go around the quadrants ...

The message for business and organisations is that each of these quadrants is equally important to us and that each affects the others. Mission Statements may be developed by individuals (UL), but they need to be owned by the whole company (LL) if they are to affect our behaviours (UR). And they need to be reflected by the ways in which we structure our company and develop the business environment in which we work (LR).

In an organisation you need to make sure that all four quadrants are considered and especially during any change process. You need to make sure that every individual's thoughts, feelings and emotions are considered important (UL). You need to make sure that there are corporate values that everyone shares (LL). You need to make sure that each individual is enabled to behave in ways that allow them to feel congruent with their own and company's values (UR). You need to make sure that the structures and processes that are put in place to support the company and its workforce are in line with all of the above (LR). It is important to reiterate here that the order in which you consider these doesn't really matter because you need all of these elements to be in place simultaneously. Only when there is a fit between all of them can the organisation move onwards and upwards together.

3.7 Working With Individuals

The Quadrants is a really useful tool that I have in mind when coaching individuals too. As we start to set an outcome together I get the person I am coaching to consider the issue that we are exploring from all four angles (I also use *"levels"* and *"types* too but for simplicity's sake let's stick with just the Quadrants here). I ask them to consider all of their beliefs and values around the situation and we then check that these match what it is that they want in the situation. We need to ensure that the behaviours that they are going to exhibit in the new situation will not clash with their beliefs and values. As a lot of incongruence is often at an unconscious level, much of the work here is using questions and language patterns to bring these patterns to conscious awareness.

A simple example of this might be someone who lists "health" as a really highly regarded value, but when we explore their behaviour we discover that they get up incredibly early to drive for many hours to get to a meeting that lasts an hour and then repeats the stressful journey back home stopping only to grab a burger and a coke and a chocolate bar for an evening meal having already missed breakfast and lunch but filled up with coffee and cigarettes to stem the hunger. Most of us would agree that there is some incongruence between the stated values and the behaviours exhibited to achieve them.

This is not the full picture because we then have to take a look at the lower quadrants. Do the organisation's espoused values match those of the individual? And do they match the organisation's "behaviours"? There may be a perceived match between UL and LL but is this real. A common statement made to me when I am running workshops is that the organisation has a "blame-free" culture (an interesting use of language in the first place if we remember the purple alligator and the glass of milk; why do they use the word "blame-free" rather than "an enabling culture?). The important question is what happens if someone does take a risk or even make a mistake, what *behaviours* does the organisation manifest then? And so often in my experience, that is when organisations show the incongruence that really exists between LL and LR.

Once we have congruence between UL and UR, and I will use the Quadronics Language Patterns to ensure this, we need to move down to LL and LR.

In this exploration we are looking for the anomalies and the gaps in the map. If there are none then we know that the individual's UL and UR are in synch and that the organisation's LL and LR will actually support these. If this is not the case then the individual has to decide whether or not she or he is in a position to influence the organisation, if not then maybe it is time for the person to move on to another organisation. This has proved a very powerful tool in my work with individuals (and even more powerful when we add in levels and type).

4 Neuro Linguistic Programming

The three models so far discussed are really useful as descriptors but unless we have a technology to help us to change (or when we are working with others, to help them) they will remain as merely that. What NLP allows us to do is take the issues revealed by these models and apply specific tools and techniques to speed up the change. There are many books that describe these processes and I will not go into them now; suffice it to say that there are methods to help people to transform limiting beliefs into empowering ones, to relieve phobias and allergies, to resolve internal conflict, to gain better control over our emotional states, to take control over annoying habits and addictions, etc., etc. I would, however, like to share one of the first and most powerful tools from NLP.

4.1 The Meta Model

Like all of the processes in NLP, the Meta Model was modeled from an exemplar found by Richard Bandler and John Grinder in the mid-1970s as they were developing what became known as the field of NLP. Virginia Satir was a family therapist who had already started working with Systems Theory in her work with families when Bandler and Grinder discovered her work. Bandler was recording some of her workshops for her and was aware that something special was happening when Satir asked questions. He called in Grinder, a linguistics professor, who recognized some of the patterns from his understanding of transformational grammar but he also realized that there were other things going on (and indeed, Satir was successful for some of the other things that she was doing in her work with dysfunctional families).

The two of them started codifying her work and developed what they called the Meta Model, so called because it enables the person being questioned to go to the "meta" position of Observer to their own process ("meta" is ancient Greek for "aside", "beyond", "above").

4.2 Deletions, Generalisations & Distortions

The major patterns that Virginia Satir was challenging were the deletions, generalisations and distortions that her clients were making as they talked about their inner experience. In transformational grammar this is described as the distinction between the "surface structure" and the "deep structure", where the surface is what we can see and hear of the other's communication as they attempt to explain the deep structure that includes everything that happened in the experience. Inevitably, we will not explain everything that happened in any situation. For brevity's sake we delete information, we generalize about what happened and we distort what happened for a variety of reasons, good and bad. A large part of Virginia Satir's work was to help her clients to get closer to the deep structure of their experiences and also communicate as much of this as possible within their families. This is also one of the most powerful tools in any coach's toolbox.

You will have noticed, of course, that there is a strong correlation between the deep structure and Wilber's Left Hand Quadrants, and the surface structure and Wilber's Right Hand Quadrants. One of the best ways to reach from the Right Hand to the Left Hand is via the Meta Model.

Each of these major patterns has a different number of subsections. I do not have the time and space to explore these in great detail but I would like to share a couple that I have found to be the most useful in my coaching work; one will take us from the Surface Structure into the Deep Structure, while the other takes us from the Deep Structure into the Surface Structure.

4.3 Modal Operators

There are two types of Modal Operators: the Modal Operator of Necessity and the Modal Operator of Possibility. They both help us to make generalizations about the world and the way that it works. When we use them well, they help us to generate our beliefs about the world; when they are not working so well for us, we may find ourselves limited by our own beliefs and thought patterns.

The Modal Operator of Necessity reveals what the person believes that they *have* to do, what they *must* do, in order to stay in line with their own beliefs. The Modal Operator of Possibility reveals what the person believes they *ought* to do to stay in line, what they *should* do. The main difference between these two categories is where in time the cause of the belief lies; in the former it is in the past and in the latter, the future.

It is imperative to state at this point that many of the beliefs that we hold are useful to us, even the ones that we may feel are limiting us; for this reason, whilst it is useful to challenge these beliefs, we must do so with care and respect, and recognize that the person has some good reason for holding the belief even if they are not currently consciously aware of its positive intention for them. The Meta Model is a very powerful tool and has to be used judiciously.

In a coaching session, or even in general conversation, whenever I hear someone say, "I have to do this", I immediately become aware of the Modal Operator of Necessity. I know that there is a belief or a rule that the person has, maybe at the level of unconscious competence or unconscious incompetence. I will challenge the pattern if it seems to be limiting the person, and I am also aware that it could be generated from several different places.

Ones, Twos and Sixes all have heightened superegos that generate such beliefs or rules but they also come from different places in terms of Quadrants. Ones are more likely to have generated them in Upper Left, Sixes Lower Left, and Twos either of them. If I am to challenge the belief or rule (and this would only be appropriate if that is our "contract" and if a challenge will produce a more empowering position so that the person can transform the Upper Left or Lower Left and produce more useful behaviours in Upper Right to improve their situation in Lower Right), it makes a huge difference as to where the belief or rule was generated.

Generally speaking, Ones generate their "rules" internally and find it hard to explain why the "rule" is the case because it is at a gut level. As a belief is a generalisation made about the world, the best way to get the person to challenge is for them to find "counter examples" to the belief. As the One's generalisation has been made internally, it is necessary for the "counter examples" to be ones personal to the Ones, times when they have "broken" the rule and it worked for them or was appropriate to the situation. This may then generalize out into the world (Lower Left), but I have found that the starting point always has to be internal.

Generally speaking, Twos have picked up the "rules" from others and then internalised them. "Counter examples" that work for them can be found in the "real world" of Lower Left and Lower Right and this makes the work much easier because of the very fact that the "rules" are generalisations and there have to be "counter examples" to them as there are few "universal quantifiers" in the world.

Interestingly, Sixes generate their "laws" both internally and externally and flip between the two realms of Lower Left and Upper Left. Most of the Sixes I have met have an internal set of "laws" that they live by, their internal morality, that, if broken, causes them great internal turmoil. At the same time, however, they also hold strictly to the "laws" of the land, the "laws" of their society, the "laws" of the group that they have affiliated to. As all of these are "generalizations", they do not, in reality, always hold true all of the time and there will be times when fall down. Whether these are inconsistencies of the internal or the external "laws", they cause Sixes internal anguish. The problem is compounded for them, however, when there are inconsistencies *between* the internal and the external "laws", and this is the root cause of their ambiguous relationship with authority. When I am working with Sixes, I have to pay attention to the generalisations of both the internal and the external worlds, the Upper Left and the Lower Left, and how these affect and are affected by the concrete world of the Right Hand Quadrants.

On the other hand, however, the Modal Operator may come from an entirely different place; it may come from the Level or worldview that the person holds, and I'll comment on that in due course. For now, it is useful to know that the "rule" that lies behind the Modal Operator may be coming from a different Level which means that the most appropriate intervention will be different.

4.4 Nominalisations

For those of you who studied grammar at school, a "nominalisation" is an "abstract noun", and there is an easy test to check out whether you are looking at a noun or a nominalisation: can you put it into a wheelbarrow (assuming that said wheelbarrow is large enough)? Nominalisations cannot be put into wheelbarrows because they are not really nouns, they are verbs masquerading as nouns, and they are processes that have been nominalised. We have taken a whole series of experiences and generalized them to such an extent that they have now acquired a solidity that they did not originally have. This generalising process has its uses as it allows us to shorten our communication when talking of such concepts as the "Enneagram" and "Type". The cost, however, is that there will be a myriad of meanings that people make of such concepts (itself a nominalisation). When I teach this part of the Meta Model quite a few people get lost at this stage but I believe that this is merely the residue of poor teaching at school as the concept is both easy to understand and incredibly useful.

Some examples at this stage might prove useful. We could take the word "Enneagram" but I think that we'll consider that later. For now, consider the word "relationship". What does this word mean to you? When you think of a "relationship" or "relationships", what pictures do you see? When asked this question, most people report a picture or a series of pictures that are static, still, lacking movement, like a photograph or series of photographs, but as you reconsider your most significant relationship, can it really be summed up as a photograph or series of photographs?

Now, as you consider your most significant relationship again, think instead about how you are "relating" with the other or others (in linguistic terms, we have "denominalised" the abstract noun and turned it back into what it was originally, a verb). This time, most people tell me that they now see a movie or a series of movies.

Looked at through the lens of Wilber's Quadrants, you have probably taken something that you have internalized in the Upper Left Quadrant, and moved it back to where it happened, the Upper and Lower Right Quadrants. This has several effects: it releases energy as "relating" is more dynamic and includes the element of time. It also helps us to recognize that both parties had an effect and some degree of responsibility in the outcome of the encounter, and to realize that this is not the only time that we have been with this person, allowing us to compare and contrast different events. The end result is the release of something that was stuck, which helps both parties to be more resourceful the next time they meet.

The problem is, however, that the English language (and most of the others that I have encountered in twenty years of teaching this material) is stuffed full of nominalizations. Here are just a few that I hear on an almost daily basis:
beliefs, communication, competences, education, health, leadership, learning, management, morale, motivation, organization, politics, religion, skills, spirituality, team, values.

As I said above, these words are really useful to help us to shortcut our communication. The problem is that when we hear any one of these words, we have to go inside to make sense of it, but we do so based on our Deep Structure and not the Deep Structure of the of the person uttering the word.

What has this to do with mistyping? Hopefully, you have already realized the huge pitfalls that this concept produces in the Enneagram (nominalisation) Community (nominalisation) as we discuss Type (nominalisation) and whether we believe that someone is a Type (nominalisation) Three or a Type (nominalisation) Seven. If we do not engage with the other and ask them questions (nominalisation) about their understanding (nominalisation) of the concept (nominalisation) under discussion (nominalisation), we cannot understand the other in any real way, and as we are a Global Community (nominalisation) in communication (nominalisation) with one another in ways that are predominantly written, we really do need to be very careful with one another.

Interestingly, Gregory Bateson, the British anthropologist, on first reading Bandler and Grinder's *The Structure of Magic 1,* asked them: "Is 'I' a nominalisation?" Their answer was a resounding "No!" but certainly Grinder has had a change of mind (story quoted in DeLozier and Grinder, 1987, pp.195-6).

This is one of the reasons why I prefer to use the term "space" (still a nominalisation) rather than Type when introducing the Enneagram. If we are aware of this process of nominalising, however, and challenge it when appropriate, we are less likely to mistype one another and have a richer model as a consequence.

These are just two of the thirteen patterns modeled from Virginia Satir's work and I would highly encourage you to look out for one of the many NLP books on the subject (my favourite is still Lewis & Pucelik's even though it was written as long ago as 1982).

5 Levels of Development

It is fairly clear thats we engage with people that they are at different Levels of development. At its simplest, children are not as developed as adults. Their worldviews are not as complex and they are unable to work with or accept the same levels of complexity as the adults around them. There are many ways in which we can look at these different Levels and Wilber lists over 200 in the appendices of *Integral Psychology* (Wilber, 2000b). I have found through experience that Clare Graves' version is both easy for people to understand within organizations and also quickly useful; at the same time, it also bears much deeper study and in my experience this often follows after a brief introduction. In my work with a large scientific civil service organisation in the UK, it has become a really useful lingua franca when exploring difficult interpersonal and organizational issues.

(It is also important to state here that the levels that I will be discussing are different from the Riso/Hudson Levels of Development, which are levels within type; the Levels that are under discussion here lie outside Type. Once we have looked at both models, we can start to explore how different Types move through the Levels and/or how the Levels manifest differently in each Type. It is important however to emphasise how important it is to differentiate between the different ways of looking at any relationship or intervention before we start to consider integrating the different models; the cost of not doing so is to over-simplify things and to fall into another version of the "pre/trans fallacy".)

Many of you will be familiar with the work of Abraham Maslow (1998) renowned as the first psychologist to produce a book based on his work with psychologically healthy people. A friend and colleague of his, Dr. Clare Graves, was a little concerned by how little research Maslow had done before producing his theory of the Hierarchy of Needs At almost the same time Graves was going through his own personal crisis. Working as a psychology professor in upstate New York, he was becoming quite disillusioned with his work. He was becoming increasingly bored by his students constantly asking him what a psychologically healthy person was and why there were so many different views on this amongst the "experts". This mirrors Ken Wilber's own "dark night of the soul" when he was considering over two hundred hierarchies and which led to his Quadrant theory.

Dr. Clare Graves' solution to these conundrums was ingenious as he turned them on their heads. Every semester for a couple of decades he started his series of lectures by asking his students the question first. Their prime concern for the rest of the semester was to answer the question: *"What is a psychologically healthy person?"* With another stroke of genius, at the end of each semester he gave the papers that his students turned in to his colleagues and asked them if they could "grade" them in any way.

Although Graves was always very tentative about the results of his research, and he studied over a thousand students over a semester for several decades, and even more tentative about going public with them (and his one book was not finished or published until long after his death), significant and consistent patterns started to emerge.

The first thing that he noticed was whether his students considered psychologically healthy people to be "expressing self" or "sacrificing self for others" (this primary attention on Self or Other[s] has strong correlations to the Upper and Lower Quadrants of Wilber's Model but more of that later).

These two were also broken down into sub-sets: *"Express self for self gain but calculatedly and rationally"* and *"Express self with concern for others but not at the expense of others"*, and *"Deny/sacrifice self now for later reward"* and *"Deny/sacrifice self now to get acceptance now"*.

Graves conducted his research over several decades and when he had the opportunity to interview his students again after a break of several years, he noticed another interesting pattern that started to emerge; if people changed their worldview, there was a specific direction in which they all moved. Whilst in particular circumstances it might be more appropriate to recognize a "lower" worldview, the trend when people are "healthy" and growing was in one direction. As the general centre of gravity clustered around a particular worldview, Graves could predict the next worldview that would emerge. For example, if someone was moving away from Blue, it would be towards Orange, and while for some time both worldviews could be observed, the general shift would be into Orange unless the world circumstances changed and a drop back into Blue was more appropriate. This might be the case in terms of behaviour, but, once tasted, the Orange worldview would prove more attractive in the long run.

Due to affirmative action programmes, Graves also started to notice a worldview he hadn't seen before: *"Express self impulsively at any cost"*. When asked about this worldview, Graves' students gave a consistent and completely understandable answer, *"You don't understand, Doctor Graves, it's a jungle out there; you'd be a fool, or dead, to respond in any other way!"*

This brings us to another really important aspect to Graves' Model. He posited that it is our environment that influences our responses, which in turn transforms our responses, which in turn changes the environment, which in turn ... and so on. He used the newly discovered concept of DNA to describe this process and came up with his "double helix" theory where one strand is the environment and the other the human response; while this is not the same as Wilber's Quadrants, there is some similarity to the Upper and Lower Quadrants. He eventually called his model, *The Emergent Cyclic Double Helix Model Of Mature Adult Biopsychosocial Behaviour*, and although this is a mouthful, it does elegantly describe what he had discovered.

The final thing that we need to draw attention to is the concept of First Tier and Second Tier thinking about which Graves was even more tentative (and he did speculate that he may only have seen the shift from FS [Green] to A^1N^1 [Yellow] as a major leap because he was operating from ER [Orange]).

AN	1	Beige
BO	2	Purple
CP	3	Red
DQ	4	Blue
ER	5	Orange
FS	6	Green
GT (A^1N^1)	7	Yellow
HU (B^1O^1)	8	Turquoise

He noticed that with the first six worldviews of AN, BO, CP, DQ, ER, and FS, people not only held that worldview, but also believed that that was the way that world was and that everybody either held that view or ought to. Anyone who did not was not just different but wrong. When people reach the Second Tier, however, they get to a point where they can see that the world is a much more complex place and that not only do people hold different worldviews but that this is appropriate for them and that this complexity needs to be worked with if we are to achieve results. In organizational terms, this is often a major breakthrough for many of the clients that I work with as they realize that not only do organizations consist of different worldviews but that this diversity makes it a healthier organization when these differing worldviews are welcomed and valued when they emerge in the appropriate places.

This is not the place to describe the different worldviews in massive detail and my hope is that I shall have piqued your interest enough to go to the source material, given in the bibliography, for more information *A Theory of Everything* (Wilber, 2000a) is a good starting point (and I have also been told that my own book is a useful introduction).

But before I give short descriptions of the worldviews, a little about the names. As above, Graves first used letters to describe them. He started at the beginning of the alphabet for the environments and then the middle of the alphabet for the human response to it; hence, AN, BO, CP, etc.

It is important that we use both letters to emphasise the point that we are looking at four very different aspects of a situation; the human and the physical, the internal and the external. Interestingly, this precedes Wilber's Quadrants, although there are similarities, and probably explains why Ken picked up on the Graves' Model when I introduced it to him. It also provides a useful shorthand in my coaching when people realize that they may be operating in an environment where the centre of gravity is different from their own.

This has given some the idea that Graves thought that there were only thirteen potential worldviews and in the mid-1990s it was possible to travel to the US to learn the thirteenth level; this is a complete misunderstanding of what Graves was sharing. He described the model as "emergent", recognizing that the worldviews emerge from the constant interplay of environment and humans. In fact, one of the problems that Graves had with Maslow was that his model had an end in sight, "self-actualization". Part of Graves' research project was to find out if there was an end point or if we were in states of constant change; the difference between "self-actualization" (nominalization) and "self-actualizing" (process) that we shall explore further below.

Back to the letters, as you can imagine it is conceptually quite difficult to talk with others about the differences between BO and ER, and the similarities between DQ and FS; Graves knew that he needed a better way to describe them. He started giving them numbers and AN became 1, BO became 2, CP became 3, etc., but he became concerned that, whilst there is a hierarchy to the Levels, no one of them is any *better* than any other, as each response is context-dependent.

He reverted back to the letters and uses them in his book (Graves, 2005). He also used A^1N^1 and B^1O^1 for the 7th and 8th Levels not only in to differentiate between First Tier and Second Tier but also to recognize his speculation that A^1N^1 revisits the issues of AN, and B^1O^1 revisits the issues of BO, but at a global level.

Two students of Beck and Cowan, who were amongst the first to bring Graves' work to the attention of the public, gave Graves' theory the name that it is generally known as, *Spiral Dynamics* (Beck and Cowan, 1996), although the theory had been written about as early as the late 1980's (Lynch and Cordis, 1988; James and Woodsmall, 1988). They started using colours as an easier way to remember the different worldviews. Although the colours do have some resonance with political parties in some countries, they do not seem to contain the same hierarchical value judgments as numbers.

There is a lot of speculation about where the colours come from and some have decided that they relate to the "chakras" or "colour therapy". The truth is much more prosaic. Chris Cowan told me that he was sitting down in a hotel room going through his overheads the night before giving a presentation and thinking how dull they looked. He started colouring them in trying to find the most appropriate colour for each worldview.

"Express self impulsively at any cost"
"Deny/sacrifice self now for later reward"
"Express self for self gain but calculatedly and rationally"
"Deny/sacrifice self now to get acceptance now"
"Express self with concern for others but not at the expense of others"
"Deny/sacrifice self to existential realities"

5.1 The Emergent Cyclic Double Helix Model Of Mature Adult Biopsychosocial Behaviour

As mentioned above, I am not going into great detail here about the different worldviews as there are plenty of better places to go to get better descriptions than I could give (see bibliography). What I would encourage you to do is to notice where you recognize yourself most and also how you might mistake your Level for your Type as it is my conjecture that when we type others, this might just be what we are doing.

As with Wilber's Quadrants, there is a tendency for people to try to squash Type and Level together and this is just as much of a mistake here. In reality, all of the Types can and do go through all of the Levels but will manifest them in different ways. You will notice, however, that you may be drawn to a particular Level because of your Type and because you feel comfortable there, the temptation may be to stay at that Level. The encouragement, however, is to "transcend and include" the Levels as you move on, remembering that each Level is the accumulation of everything that has preceded it *plus.*

The worldviews shift between two basic needs – "to express self" and "to sacrifice self for the greater good". This is something that we all go through all of the time, we have a need to be our own unique person *and* we have a need to be part of the group, and we constantly shift between these two depending on the situation that we find ourselves in. The switch between the different worldviews appears to mirror that tension. In evolutionary terms, this makes complete sense. It is important for me to survive but it is also important that my family, my tribe, my species, also survive. I need to look after myself but I also need to look after others so that I can survive so that the tribe can survive, and so on.

This shifting emphasis on Self and Other is one way that some people immediately jump to Type to explain as some Types are more self-oriented and other Types more other-oriented. But when we really consider it, both are about survival. If I do not survive, then future generations will not survive in which case I shan't survive. As with the Quadrants, we need all elements to survive; it is just that the emphasis shifts depending on which worldview predominates.

To illustrate some of these differences between the Levels, I now outline the Red, Blue, Orange and Green Levels.

5.2 Red

It is important that Graves believed that each of these worldviews emerges from the particular environment in which it finds itself and from this develops what feels like an appropriate response to it. At its roots, Red believes that it is living in a world in which there are limited resources and so it is a survival imperative to go out and get what it needs; not only that, but anyone who didn't do this is foolish. It follows that in such a world power and strength are what is needed to survive. This is a world in which "might is right", "strength is all".

It would be easy, and simplistic, to mistake this behaviour for that of an Eight, or even an unhealthy Two, and it is true that this would be correct for some Eights and some Twos. Someone who supposedly tramples over others to get what they want disregarding others' wants and needs would also make sense for any of the other Types *when* they are living within this worldview or believe that they are; it is behaviour that makes total sense if one is living in a world in which there are limited resources. It is less acceptable, while still fully understandable, when mainstream society has moved on from this need as resources become more easily accessible to the majority. There will still be pockets of Red, however, if resources are not shared equitably, and so it still seems to Red that there are limited resources. People will also revert back to this behaviour if they find themselves in a Red environment again, or believe that this is the case. We must also remember that every human being goes through each of these stages as we develop and grow; something that every parent will be fully aware of when toddlers believe that there aren't enough toys to go around and discover that the strongest one will get the teddy (even if that is Mummy or Daddy intervening).

As with all of these Levels, we have to identify the motivation behind the behaviour before we can know if it is Type or Level that we are seeing and hearing, as the behaviours may appear the same.

5.3 Blue

Blue is the antidote to Red, which is why each of these Levels emerges, to pull back from the excesses of the previous worldview. Taken to its extreme Red will eventually destroy the world that it inhabits and everyone in it, such anarchy must be controlled and what controls strength is a greater strength, a greater power, a greater authority. In the new Blue world I am willing to subsume my own needs because in doing so Blue will control Red and produce a world that is safer for me and mine. The compact that I am willing to make is that if I do this I will be rewarded later. In an organizational setting, this might take the form of promotion or a good pension when I retire; societally, it might give us entrance into heaven.

In this world, I can relax knowing that there is a right thing to do and I do the right thing I certainly won't be punished and I may be rewarded. I can put my own ego to one side and a much larger superego than mine can take its place. This is a much easier world to live in for many. If we use Riso's and Hudson's framework, this sounds very much like the Hornevian Earners, Ones, Twos and Sixes, and maybe even Nines, who seem to be the obvious candidates for Blue, but only if we use the simplistic viewfinder of Type. The truth is that we all know Ones, Two, Sixes and Nines who do not conform to this stereotype. For example, Ones may take their "knowingness" from society but I have met far more whose "knowingness is totally unique to them – if you like, these are the Ones who are more driven by the Upper Left Quadrant rather than the Lower Left. The same is true of counter-phobic Sixes who very definitely have issues with "authority", and would be considered the anti-thesis of Blue. At the same time, I have Threes, Fours, Fives and Eights who can operate very easily within an authoritarian Blue environment, but they do so in their own way.

5.4 Orange

Although Orange is similar to Red in some ways, it is very different in that it can defer its gratification and its needs; Graves described it as "express self calculatedly" rather than "express self now". This is because in the Orange world (according to Orange anyway) there are actually unlimited resources and so there isn't the scarcity mentality that exists in the Red world. Orange has also got to the stage where it has developed lots of technology to resolve the problems that it sees in the world. It has developed out of Blue because the "sacrifice self" side tends towards atrophy and inertia and Orange wants to redress this balance to achieve, to streamline, to make things happen, to achieve goals and objectives, and as it has technology and there are unlimited resources, what is to stop it? "If you want to join in on the Orange adventure, fine, come along with me; if not, fine, but don't come whining to me". Unlike Blue that respects authority and tradition, Orange only really measure things against its own experience and has no truck with anything that is outside of this.

Those of us who teach the Enneagram (or the Graves Model or NLP) will recognize these participants who remain cynics unless and until they have checked out what you are saying for themselves. This happens on a regular basis on my four-day NLP Business Certificate; the first two days of input are considered very skeptically and then the participants have three or four weeks to try the material out in their own lives. When they return, they are either converts and become my best advocates in the organization, or they remain skeptics; it all depends on their experience and what has happened as they try out what they have learned.

Does all of this remind you of anybody? If you are not careful, you may have typed Orange incorrectly as a Three or a Seven or an Eight. Stereotypically, Threes will be primarily those who operate from Orange (and even more so, American Threes living in a predominantly Orange culture), as they are the ones who will thrive the best in such a culture and also be highly prized there. There are even those who type whole countries and I have heard the US typed as a Three culture (although how you can type a whole culture is beyond me – except where I type it according to Level). It is true, however, that what we *see* of American culture is predominantly Orange (although there are clearly elements of it which are more likely to be fundamentalist Blue). Hopefully, my message is by now clear, which is that we need to look below the surface and can only do so by engaging with individuals and cultures at a much deeper level.

5.5 Green

Green is needed to address the extremes of Orange. The immediate problem that Orange has failed to notice is that there are not unlimited resources, that they will eventually run out and that a more appropriate response might be to start preserving them. Green's presupposition is not just that this is dangerous but that it could even presage the end of society as we know it; apocalyptic indeed. Green also recognizes that not everyone can succeed in the Orange world; it is inevitable that people will get left behind and this is not "fair", and fairness is important to Green that believes that everyone deserves a place at the table. This is not just because of the fairness issue, but also recognition that there are skills and attributes that are needed to sustain a healthy society that Orange just cannot see. Green has a facilitative style and needs to ensure that in decision-making consensus is reached because everyone has something to offer. At its best, Green includes everyone; at its worst, nothing happens because so much time is taken up in including everyone. As with all of the "sacrifice" worldviews there is a tendency towards consolidation, which can lead to inertia. Do you recognize any personality traits in this description? I think that you'll agree that the most obvious contender is Nine but we can also see elements of Two and Six and even Five. As with previous worldviews, such stereotyping would be a mistake as all Types can reach Green and beyond. But imagine what a Green One, or Three, or Eight would look like; nothing like the usual picture of such

Types but no less true for these types as for others in experiencing the world from this point of view.

Graves, and later Beck and Cowan, and Wilber, have written about this as a tremendous shift in consciousness, but we need to take a step back for a moment.

Ken Wilber differentiates between "translation" and "transformation"; simplistically put, the former is growth within a Level whereas the latter is growth to another Level. He has written about this concept in several places, but nowhere more compellingly, I believe, than in the journal that he kept in 1997 and later published, *One Taste* (Wilber, 1999).

"With translation, the self is simply given a new way to think or feel about reality. The self is given a new belief – perhaps holistic instead of atomistic, perhaps forgiveness instead blame, perhaps relational instead of analytic. The self then learns to translate its world and its being in the terms of this new belief or new language or new paradigm, and this new and enchanting translation acts, at least temporarily, to alleviate or diminish the terror inherent in the heart of the separate self.

"But with transformation, the very process of translation itself is challenged, witnessed, undermined, and eventually dismantled. With typical *translation*, the self (or subject) is given a new way to think about the world (or objects); but with radical *transformation*, the self itself is inquired into, looked into, grabbed by its throat, and literally throttled to death." (Wilber, 1999, pp. 27-28)

This is certainly something that I recognize in myself when I first discovered both NLP and The Enneagram; *translation* was achievable with both of these technologies, but the change felt both shallow and temporary. This was also borne out in my training work and in my coaching; it feels as though *transformation* is something very different and much rarer. Looking back, those times when either I was shifting from one Gravesian world-view to another, or watching as others made this shift, it felt and looked very much more like what Wilber describes as *transformation*.

Given all of this, Graves noticed an even bigger shift in his students when they transformed from FS (or World-view 6 or Green) to GT (or World-view 7 or Yellow). According to Graves, there is such a massive change in consciousness that he called the next level the beginning of the "second tier".

(I think that it is also worth noting a conversation that I had with Chris Cowan some years ago when he told me that Graves thought that he was operating predominantly from Orange and that what he saw as a major shift in consciousness might only have appeared so because of where he was looking at it from.)

The biggest difference that he noted in his students was that whereas the worldviews in the "first tier" were self-contained, in the "second tier" there was an ability to see and to understand and truly communicate with the different worldviews. For example, when someone is operating from Blue, not only do they consider that to be the only worldview for them, they cannot imagine that anyone else would consider operating from any worldview other than Blue. From the Second Tier, the values of Blue can be seen and also how useful and necessary this worldview can be, but also the limitations of such a worldview. Second Tier is also able to establish and maintain rapport with Blue, and, in fact, with any of the other worldviews. Although Blue will find Second Tier a bit different and maybe even eccentric, it will get on with it and also quite like it, whereas Blue may have big problems with other worldviews (actually, most often with the worldview that it is heading for, Orange, and the same is true of Orange which does not really get on with Green).

Second Tier is much more able to see things from a more systemic perspective, recognizing that all of the worldviews offer something to a situation but that no single view offers the whole picture; as always, it may "true" but it is also "partial".

5.6 Fear

In addition to the shift into second tier Graves noted something else quite fundamental in that shift, as people reach Yellow fear drops away. And once again we can recognize similarities to the fears of types again explaining how and why we can mistype when we mistake Level for Type.

According to Graves,

- Beige is afraid that it will not find food.
- Purple is afraid that it will not have shelter.
- Red is afraid of those stronger than itself.
- Blue is afraid of god.
- Orange is afraid that it does not have status.
- Green is afraid of social rejection.

At the risk of stereotyping, Purple might be mistaken as the fear of Sixes, Red as the fear of Fives and Eights, Blue as the fear of Ones and Sixes, Orange as the fear of Threes and Sevens, and Green as the fear of Twos, Fours, Sixes and Nines.

5.7 Yellow

Yellow emerges from the inertia of Green in which, although it is good at including people, potentially little is decided and little happens. The issues that have been emerging are not being dealt with as the problems of Beige re-emerge at a global level. A new way of exploring issues and problems is needed; a systems approach is needed as the different worldviews interact. When Graves put "yellow" students in groups he found that they were much more flexible and creative and would come up with as many as ten times the solutions to problems he set them as all of the other worldviews put together. The motivation in Yellow is also very different, as it wants to engage with issues that are complex and interesting. It has resolved the fears of the previous six previous worldviews, has enough material things, and the ability to earn the money it needs, isn't bothered about status and doesn't really care about what others think or feel. What it does recognize and celebrate is knowledge and skills and expertise. Rather than accept leaders and authorities that Purple, Blue and Green will but only those based on the above criteria plus fun and engagement and being interested and the ability to make a difference to the system and at a larger scale, the world. Although not all Fives and Sevens are operating from Yellow and above, they do look like them, don't they?

Yellow also does not recognize hierarchy in the same way that others do and bases its operations around which part of the system has the skills and the competences and the knowledge for any specific project. For this reason it is happy not to be in charge and likes to see leadership shift around as is appropriate for the situation. Yellow does not like to feel restricted and gets involved in projects where it feels that it can make a contribution and where it can feel engaged in something intellectually and learn from it.

As it has gone through the previous stages many of its needs have either been met or else fallen by the wayside and for this reason Yellow can easily survive on very little in terms of the material things that the previous worldviews seem to "need". In my experience, Yellow can find organizations restrictive and often operate outside of them, dipping in as needed and as appropriate.

It should now be clear that any Type can achieve Yellow but in terms of the Enneagram Sevens seem to be the obvious candidate for mistyping here, with Fives and Eights following closely behind.

Graves also posited that it might be the case that when we reach Second Tier we are in fact revisiting the issues that we faced earlier, that Yellow was in fact "second tier" Beige except that now the issue was about the systems rather than the individuals which is why he also called Yellow A^1N^1.

Yellow emerges from the inertia of Green which, although it is good at including people, because of this potentially little is decided and little happens. The issues that have been emerging are not being dealt with as the problems of Beige re-emerge at a global level. A new way of exploring issues and problems is needed, a systems approach is needed as the different worldviews interact. The motivation in Yellow is also very different, as it wants to engage with issues that are complex and interesting. It has resolved the fears of the previous six worldviews, has enough material things, and the ability to earn the money it needs. What it does recognize and celebrate is knowledge and skills and expertise.

With the same caveats that I gave when looking at the Meta Model, some of the Level Look-alikes that I have noticed:

- Purple can look like Four or Nine
- Red can look like Two or Eight
- Blue can look like One, Five or Six
- Orange can look like Three or Eight
- Green can look like Two or Nine
- Yellow can look like Five or Seven

5.8 An Example

In my experience, lots of people assume that understanding these models is an esoteric affair, but, as someone who has always been a pragmatist, I am only interested in models that I can use. I'd like to finish with an example from my own coaching work that demonstrates how useful these models are.

Several years ago I coached a very successful businesswoman. She and her surgeon husband had a beautiful house in the best part of town. She had led an organization from near bankruptcy to profitable success in very difficult times during the 1990s. She had been rewarded by her industry and by the city that she had lived in all of her life in a variety of ways. I had not long known about the Enneagram and immediately typed her as a Three and having predominantly an Orange world-view. Our sessions progressed based on that assumption and we had some degree of success. Looking back now, I believe that it was probably at the level of *translation;* there was some change and she was happy that we were working well together. We both knew that something was missing from our work.

One of the things that I like about NLP is that it is future-oriented and a concept that I use a lot in my coaching is that of "Present State" plus "Resources" leads to "Desired State". In most cases this works, but sometimes it becomes necessary to explore the past as well, and this always means shifting the emphasis from the Right Hand Quadrants to the Left Hand Quadrants. As we delved deeper and deeper it became clear that I had mistyped her in several ways. Although she talked a lot about her successes, and they were clearly important to her, that wasn't what motivated her.

One of the things that I started to notice was that whenever I was with her I got her full attention, unless and until someone of authority entered the room; at which point I was quickly dropped and full attention shifted to the other person. This was disconcerting and also a little annoying. As I watched her, I began to see that this behaviour wasn't just aimed at me, it happened to others too. When I asked about this, she was mortified that I had noticed and also wanted to know how this affected me. As we talked more and more, it transpired that she had been very ill when she was a child and had become very fearful as she spent less and less time with her family. She told me that she didn't feel that she belonged and that this was a terrifying thought. As we tracked back, she became even more aware of this trait; it was vital for her for her safety that she belonged to as many groups as she could. She sought out the influential people and groups and started joining them. If necessary, she would work really hard to get the qualifications needed to join the group. What looked like Three Achievement behaviour was in reality Six Belonging behaviour, but I only found this out when I started to dig deeper. It was the same with what appeared to be Orange behaviour emanating from an Orange world-view; it was in fact Blue behaviour as she did the "right" things to gain the acceptance of the "authority". Our work from that point on had a very different quality as she relaxed into her "Blue" "Sixness".

6 "Putting It Together"

If I were reading this article, I would be asking how one brings all of the above together and puts it into practice, and that it what I would like to finish with. As I mentioned earlier, it is very difficult to pay attention to all aspects of the Integral Model all of the time and it is more important to be "integrally informed". When I am working with someone, I have all of these models and tools and techniques to draw upon and tend to find that the most appropriate ones surface as and when they are needed during an intervention with another individual. It is also worth noting that the other person does not need to have an understanding of any of the models, although I prefer to share these with them at some stage.

For as long as I can remember I have loved magic and although I can manage a little sleight of hand and read people's minds, the best magic that I perform is when I am working with someone using the Core Transformation™ process; actually, the process is more akin to alchemy as it helps people to transform the problems and issues and symptoms of today into the pure gold of "Core States". I have been using the process for over twenty years but my success with it has changed over the years as I have added more and more elements of the Integral Model.

6.1 Core Transformation

I first learnt the Core Transformation process from its developer when I was assisting her in 1991 at her only UK workshop. The genesis of the process is interesting in itself. Despite having a vast array of NLP tools and techniques at her disposal, Connirae Andreas set herself the challenge of working with clients for three months using anything but them. When she and her husband Steve unpacked what she had been doing, two major new NLP processes fell out of the modeling exercise: Aligning Perceptual Positions and the Core Transformation process which includes Parental Timeline Reimprinting.

Since 1991 I have taken hundreds of people through the process and taught many more how to use it with others. It sometimes feels as though there is no issue that cannot be improved by the process but here are just a few examples: people with phobias, allergies, and addictions; people trapped in the world of their own limiting beliefs who are ready for personal growth and development; people working in organizations who feel blocked in some way in aim to become more efficient, including Board Members and even Teams; sportswomen and sportsmen wanting to raise their game to a higher standard (including an Enneagram Type One who worked her way up from Number Ten in the world in her sport to her current position of Number Three in less than twelve months).

The Core Transformation process is elegant and simple and gently paces each individual's model of the world. Taking a person through the whole process takes between an hour and two, and the vast majority report that it is one of the best experiences that they have ever had, with many experienced meditators telling me that the process has taken them to places even deeper than those achieved with their usual practice.

6.2 An Abridged Version of the Process

The basic presupposition of the Core Transformation process is that the symptoms that we experience, be they physical or mental, are self-generated and that some part of us has created them in order to remind us of a need that is not being met. If we communicate with this part it will eventually let us know what this need is. This might seem a little twee or esoteric but the metaphor is reflected in our language and even the most rational of clients generally goes along with this. For example, when we have an internal conflict, such as that between fasting and binging, we say that a part of us wants one thing whereas another part of us wants something else; with the process we are pacing this metaphor.

Once rapport has been established with the "part", usually through a light trance, it is a simple matter of asking what it wants, what it's outcome is. The presupposition that we are working with, and that has proved the case every time I have taken someone through the process, is that as the "part" was created by the person, then it will have had a positive intent in doing so. This is what makes the process so invigorating to use, whatever the "symptom", whatever the initial problem, the end result is a "core state".

We ask how the person knows that it is an issue and this is useful information about Type. The most common answers are that it is a voice, either inside or just outside the head, it is a picture, or it a feeling or sensation inside or outside the body, in the head, or the chest area, or in the belly. Obviously, this is a metaphor but a useful one as it represents how the person perceives the issue.

Having established what the "part" wants, we keep asking it what it would get if it already had this, and repeating this with whatever response is given. Very often these are "positive" but sometimes they might be "negative" (*"I'll kill them all"*); all we do is to pace this, *"And if you did kill everyone, what would you get from killing them?"*. If we follow the process we eventually get to what Connirae Andreas started calling "core states" after discussing it with her clients.

There are several common shifts during the process, even if the "part" starts as a physical symptom (in the Upper Right Hand Quadrant) eventually the locus will move inwards (to the Upper Left Hand Quadrant). There may be shifts back to the Right Hand Quadrants (behviours) but these are usually manifestations of the consequences of the "outcome" on the "chain" rather than the "core state", what the "part" really wants. The length of the "outcome chain" can vary from one or two to over a dozen but we are aiming for the major physiological shift that occurs when the person achieves the "core state"; breathing becomes much deeper and slower, tension is released from the body and especially from the face, and it often looks as though people have lost five years. At this stage the "part" can often not respond verbally as words are beyond this experience which is not an emotion or feeling or behaviour but a state of being beyond all of these.

We grab for words but they seem like clichés when we read them later; words like "connectedness", "peace", "OK", "at one".

The "part" now needs to learn that the only way to achieve this state again is to just to step into it. Previously it has believed that it has needed to behave or think in the way suggested by the "outcome chain" but this has patently not helped the person to achieve the state. Once this has been accepted it is an easy thing to step into the "core state". We the reverse the "outcome chain" bringing the "core state" to the surface and then ensure that it does not just reside in the part of the body mentioned earlier but that it spreads throughout the whole of our being.

There are a few other things to do but basically we are making sure that the "core state" is fully present in the "now" with the realisation that this has always been the case, and there is a timeline exercise "giving" the "core state" from birth to the future that integrates the whole experience.

Whilst I recognise that this may sound a little "airy-fairy", I have taken the most hardened, scientific, cynics through this process with great success.

6.3 Towards An Integral Core Transformation

The Core Transformation process works beautifully on its own and does not *need* anything added to it to make it work, however, we can make it an even richer experience.

The first place that we start to see correlations with the Enneagram is when we ask where the "part" is located. As mentioned earlier, the most common places are the head (usually voices, pictures or pressure), the upper torso (usually a sensation but sometimes a voice), and the lower torso (also more usually a sensation). As with all information that I see or hear during any interaction, I hold this information lightly without making judgments too early, but I have found a strong correlation with the three centres of the Enneagram. The more useful place however is during the elicitation of the "outcome chain", the things that the "part" believes are necessary in order to attain the "core state"; if I do not already have some inkling about the person's Enneagram Type, it becomes clear now. The "outcome chain" often consists of behaviours that the "part" feels it "ought" or "must" do (which brings us back to the Modal Operators of the Meta Model), but there comes a point where the "part" gets stuck. For example, I have yet to work with an Enneagram Type Six who does not have "safety" and or "security" on the "chain" and it usually takes a while for the "part" to work out what it would get if it had this. The breakthrough, when it comes, is often into" peace", matching exactly the journey from Six to Nine. Another common example I have found is Enneagram Eights who want "power" or "to control them" who break through to "play", and this is often accompanied by a shift into a more childlike physiology. Threes usually have "success" or "achievement" on their "chain" and Ones "being right". This is really useful information when we work out what "homework" is needed before the next session as the real success measure of the process is the change in behaviour that accompanies the holding of the "core state" in everyday life.

While this is going on, I am also noting where in Wilber's Quadrants we are during the process and this is most easily noted through the use of personal pronouns. Twos and Sixes often start the process by using "you" and "we" a lot but by the end of the process they have more often than not shifted to "I", which is a lovely thing to see and hear. Eights and Fives have a tendency to the opposite and they shift from the Upper Right Hand Quadrants into a better appreciation of the Lower Quadrants using "we"; to hear a Five have as a "core state" "connectedness" is wonderful thing to share.

I have already mentioned the shift between the Quadrants during the process as an indicator of where we are in the process and that when I am hearing about behaviours and actions, we are either on the way to the "core state" or hearing the consequences of achieving it.

Throughout this process I am also aware of the "levels" that are manifesting during the process. When people come to me and we decide to do the Core Transformation process together it is usually because they are dissatisfied not just with the "unhealthy" side of their Enneagram Type but also the "level" that they are at:

- If at Blue, they are fed up with the status quo and want to move on and become more efficient or make more money.
- If at Orange, they are beginning to realize that there is more to life than material rewards, labels, and technology.
- If at Green, they realize that although they deeply care about others and the planet, if things are to change, they need to do something.

Remembering the "Self"/"Other" split that Graves discovered in his students, we can notice that the solutions to each of the above existential problems requires a shift from either self to other, or other to self, and as none of them have actually experienced the next worldview, they don't know what they are trying to achieve. I have found that the Core Transformation has the solution built into its structure. As we take the "part" on its journey to the "core state" it becomes apparent that there is a journey back in time (this becomes even clearer when we ask the "part" how old it; generally speaking, the answer is between three and seven). This means that some of the resources needed to move forward are already there in the "part's history".

- For Blue wanting move on to Orange, the resource will be the Red energy from the past.
- For Orange wanting move on to Green, the resource will be the Purple and Blue energy from the past.
- For Green wanting move on to Yellow, the resource will be the Red and Orange energy from the past.

It is an awareness of *all* these elements that can make our work more effective, more efficient, and more elegant.

And, of course, for me, that's magic.

Bibliography

Andreas, Connirae with Andreas, Tamara (1994) *Core Transformation: Reaching The Wellspring Within* Moab, Utah: Real People Press

Armour, Michael C. & Browning, Don (1995) (2nd. Ed. 2000) *Systems-Sensitive Leadership – Empowering Diversity Without Polarizing The Church,* Joplin, Missouri: College Press Publishing Company

Bandler, Richard & Grinder, John (1975) *The Structure of Magic 1: A Book about Language & Therapy,* Palo Alto: Science and Behavior Books.

Bandler, Richard & Grinder, John (Edited by Steve Andreas) (1979) *Frogs Into Princes: The Introduction to Neuro-Linguistic Programming,* Moab, Utah: Real People Press.

Bandler Richard (Edited by Connirae Andreas & Steve Andreas) (1985) *Using Your Brain for a Change,* Moab, Utah: Real People Press.

Beck, Don Edward & Cowan, Christopher C. (1996) *Spiral Dynamics: mastering values, leadership, and change,* Oxford: Blackwell Business

Cain, Susan (2012) *Quiet: The Power of Introverts in a World That Can't Stop Talking,* New York: Crown Publishers

DeLozier, Judith & Grinder, John (1987) *Turtles All The Way Down: Prerequisites to Personal Genius,* Scotts Valley, Ca: Grinder & Associates

Edwards, Mark G. (2010) *Organizational Transformation for Sustainability,* Abingdon, Oxon: Routledge

Gadamer, Hans-Georg (2004, Second, Revised Edition) *Truth and Method,* London: Continuum

Gebser, Jean (Reprint edition 1986) *The Ever-present Origin: The Foundations and Manifestations of the Aperspectival World,* Athens, OH: Ohio University Press

Graves, Dr. Clare W. (Edited & Compiled by Christopher C. Cowan & Natasha Todorovic) (2005) *The Never-Ending Quest: A Treatise on an Emergent cyclical conception of adult behavioral systems and their development,* Santa Barbara: ECLET Publishing

Habermas, Jurgen (1987) *The Philosophical Discourse of Modernity: Twelve Lectures"* (Translated by Frederick G. Lawrence), Cambridge: Polity Press

Hoffmann, H.-E., Schoper, Y.-G. and Fitzsimons, C.J. (2004) Internationales Projektmanagement – interkulturelle Zusammenarbeit in der Praxis Deutsche Taschenbuch Verlag

Hofstede, G. (1997) Cultures and Organizations: Software of the Mind. 1st edition, McGraw-Hill USA

James, Tad & Woodsmall, Wyatt (1988) *Time Line Therapy & The Basis Of Personality,* Cupertino, Ca: Meta Publications

Laborde, Genie Z. (1983) *Influencing with Integrity: Management Skills for Communication & Negotiation,* Palo Alto, Ca.: Syntony Press

Lee, William R. (Ed.) (2002) *Clare W. Graves: Levels Of Human Existence – Seminar at the Washington School Of Psychiatry, October 16 1971,* Santa Barbara, Ca.: ECLET Publishing

Lewis, Byron A. & Pucelik, Frank (1982) *Magic Demystified: A Pragmatic Guide to Communication and Change,* Portland, Oregon: Metamorphous Press

Lewis, Thomas, M.D., Armini, Fari, M.D., & Lannon, Richard, M.D. (2000) *A General Theory of Love,* New York: Vintage Books

Loevinger, Jane (Ed.) (1998) *Technical Foundations for Measuring Ego Development: The Washington University Sentence Completion Test,* Mahwah: Lawrence Erlbaum Associates

Lynch, Dudley & Kordis, Paul L. (1988) *Strategy Of The Dolphin – Winning Elegantly By Coping Powerfully In A World Of Turbulent Change,* London: Arrow Books

Macknik, Stephen, and Martinez-Conde, Susana, with Blakeslee, Sandra (2011) *Sleights of Mind: What the Neuroscience of Magic Reveals About Our Brains,* London: Profile Books

Marion, Jim (2000) *Putting On The Mind Of Christ – The Inner Work Of Christian Spirituality,* Charlottesville, VA: Hampton Roads Publishing Company, Inc.

Marion, Jim (2004) *The Death of the Mythic God: The Rise of Evolutionary Spirituality,* Charlottesville, VA: Hampton Roads Publishing Company, Inc.

Maslow, Abraham H. (1998) *Maslow on Management,* New York: John Wiley & Sons, Inc.

McNab, Peter (2005) *Towards An Integral Vision: Using NLP & Ken Wilber's AQAL Model To Enhance Communication,* Victoria, BC: Trafford Publishing

Miller, George A. (1963:81-97) *The Magical Number Seven, Plus or Minus Two: Some Limits on Our Capacity for Processing Information,* Psychological Review

Nardi, Dario (2011) *Neuroscience of Personality,* Los Angeles: Radiance House

O'Connor, Joseph & Seymour, John (1990) *Introducing NLP: The New Psychology of Personal Excellence,* London: Mandala

Tosey, Paul & Mathison, Jane (2009) *Neuro-Linguistic Programming: A Critical Appreciation for Managers and Developers,* Basingstoke: Palgrave Macmillan

Wade, Jenny (1996) *Changes Of Mind – A Holonomic Theory Of The Evolution Of Consciousness,* New York: State University Of New York Press

Wilber, Ken (1967) *The Spectrum of Consciousness*

Wilber, Ken (1995) *Sex, Ecology, Spirituality: The Spirit of Evolution,* Boston & London: Shambhala

Wilber, Ken (1996) *A Brief History of Everything,* Dublin: Newleaf

Wilber, Ken (1999) *One Taste: The Journals of Ken Wilber,* Boston: Shambhala

Wilber, Ken (2000a) *A Theory Of Everything – An Integral Vision for Business, Politics, Science, and Spirituality,* Boston: Shambhala

Wilber, Ken (2000b) *Integral Psychology: Consciousness, Spirit, Psychology, Therapy,* Boston & London: Shambhala

Wilber, Ken (2007) *The Integral Vision: A Very Short Introduction to the Revolutionary Integral Approach to Life, God, the Universe, and Everything,* Boston & London: Shambhala

THE ENNEAGRAM AND SCHULZ VON THUN'S PSYCHOLOGY OF DIFFERENTIAL COMMUNICATION

Sabine Elisabeth Gramm

Abstract

What would it mean to you if you were to realize that two different personality systems in different languages were independently developed at different times in different cultures? And that they came to very similar results about their archetypal insights. What would this mean as a confirmation for both typologies, that know nothing of each other and what might it mean for the verification of human typologies in the first place?

Introduction

In this article I want to invite you on a journey to two worlds that seem, at first glance, to be complete strangers: university-based communications science with Germanic roots and an orally transmitted middle-Eastern philosophy. The aim is to build a bridge between the psychology of differential communication developed by Prof. Schulz von Thun and the Enneagram. I was privileged to learn both systems almost simultaneously at the end of the last millennium and was from almost the first moment astounded by the similarities between the individual theories. A detailed comparison demanded many months during which I dove so deeply into both systems that my understanding went beyond simple terminology. This was necessary since, on the one hand, the mode of expression is very different in both systems, and on the other hand, sometimes the same term is defined quite differently in each system. For example, when one speaks in the psychology of differential communication (PDC) of a selfless person, one means literally a self-less person, i.e. no inner orientation, no backbone, no principles and – in the worst case – no self-confidence or opinion: someone who likes to be told what to do. In contrast, the Enneagram rather understands a selfless person as someone altruistic, who on their own initiative takes on responsibility, sometimes with self-sacrifice, helping others tirelessly while being in charge. That is why it was only possible to check the compatibility of the individual characters when we moved beyond terminology.PDC observes the person from the outside and makes deductions about their inner psychological state based on their communication. In contrast, the Enneagram looks from the inside out, by showing in a differentiated manner how previously defined inner weaknesses can show themselves in observable behavior towards others. In contrast, the Enneagram looks from the inside out, by showing which previously defined and distinguishable inner states exist and how these can show themselves in a nuanced manner in external behavior towards others.

As a reader of the Enneagram Journal, you are already familiar with the Enneagram, but perhaps the psychology of differential communication is not so familiar. Therefore, before undertaking a comparison of both systems, I would like to say something about PDC. It was developed by Prof. Friedemann Schulz von Thun, who was born in Soltau (Germany) in 1944. He is officially retired from his position at Hamburg University in 2010 and now concentrates on his Institute for Communication www.schulz-von-thun.de. Since the early 1980's he has published 14 books on communication, of which 11 were bestsellers and some of which have been translated in 8 languages. He has also co-authored or edited 15 books, written 10 introductions for other books and published 61 papers. He is recognized as the most important communications psychologist in the German-speaking countries. His main contribution is to clearly analyze deep, psychologically complex, interpersonal behavior, visualizing this using his own models and explaining it understandably. In addition to his best known model, the Square Communication, he has also developed the Vicious Circle, the Situational Model, the Inner Team and the Riemann-Thomann Model and the Values Square (based on Helwig's work). He published the eight communication styles of PDC in his book *Miteinander Reden 2* (*Let's Talk!*, Volume 2), first published in 1989.

Next, I would like to propose a schema for personality models so that it is possible to identify the main differences between the systems logically and visibly. For this I use a classification in three-component and four-component models, based on an idea of the TMS master trainer, Hartmut Wagner. I've diligently followed his ideas on how to classify models of personality and applied them to many models? While doing this I noticed that three-component models take a different approach to four-component models. This has to do with the view from within out into the world, i.e. from which perspective the world is observed, e.g. aesthetically or pragmatically. In contrast, four-component models view the person from the outside and attempt to draw conclusions about their inner state. Naturally these result in different emphases in purpose and usage, to which I shall return.. The Enneagram belongs to the three-component models, since it is based on the gut, heart and head centers. Schulz von Thun's psychology of differential communication belongs to the four-component models, since in its basic form it can be aligned with the four basic tendencies of Riemann-Thomann's model (Closeness—Distance—Steadiness—Change).

First, I would like to explain the essence of the three-component and four-component models and develop a deeper understanding of the main differences, before I bring the Enneagram and PDC face to face.

Three-Component Models

Since ancient times, Three represents a holy number and symbol of true unity[1]. It concerns itself with the inside of an outwardly appearing wholeness. Christians understand the one god to consist of a trinity of Father, Son and Holy

---

1 cf. Werner (2006), P. 106.

Spirit. In the Hindu tradition, the divinity is in the form of Brahma (the creator), Vishnu (preserver) and Shiva (destroyer). India's traditional medicine which takes a holistic view of person, nature and cosmos, comprises the three life-giving dimensions of Vata, Pitta and Kapha. Time comprises past, present and future. All good things come in threes. Popper's three-world teachings say that our reality consists of three linked and mutually influencing worlds: physical objects and events, mental objects and events, and objective knowledge[2]. From a biological perspective, a person develops from three cotyledons in the embryo and possesses, according to the neuroscientist Paul MacLean, a triune brain consisting of the reptilian complex, the limbic system and the neocortex[3]. A personality is generally agreed to comprise an integrated gestalt of body, soul and mind[4]. To illustrate the three-component view of the world, the following table contains a small selection of three-component models from different cultures and disciplines.

	Component 1	**Component 2**	**Component 3**
Ayurveda	Vata	Pitta	Kapha
Three Worlds (Popper)	physical objects and events	mental objects and events	objective knowledge
Brain research (MacLean)	reptilian complex	limbic system	neocortex
Primary Colors (Goethe)	yellow	red	blue
Hindu	Brahma	Vishnu	Shiva
Human biology (3 cavities)	stomach	chest	head
Catholicism	God the Father	God the Son	Holy Spirit
Sociology	father	mother	child
Physics	neutron	proton	electron
Corporate Development	organizational development	staff development	strategy development
Time	past	present	future
Egg	albumen	yolk	germinal disk
Person	body	soul	mind

Table 1: Three-Component Models

This trichotomy turns up in numerous models of personality: early in the last

2 cf. Hauk (2003), P. 319.

3 cf. Schirm (1997), P. 8 and Schanz (2000), p. 63–66.

4 cf. Rosenstiel and Regnet (2003), P. 105.

century Kretschmer[5] recognised three different body types—the athletic, the leptosomic and the pyknic[6] (a bold attribution of physical shapes to internal mental states, that shows the early days of typologies and is now generally accepted as outdated). Friedmann's[7] process-oriented psychology of personality (PPP) divides the human areas of life into thinking, feeling and acting[8] and developed from that the rational, relationship and action types[9]. This is a modern and elementary approach that is taught across Germany in numerous ILP schools Based on this, Friedmann's pupil Winkler developed a psychographic map that distinguishes 81 subtypes. Neuberger's[10] three leader archetypes are father, hero and healer, while Pitcher uses artists, craftsmen and technocrats[11]. In business, the widely used managerial GRID systems[12] distinguishes between the authoritarian, caring and analytical managerial styles. The structogram that results from a biostructural analysis distinguished between red, blue and green[13]. These three basic components are often refined, e.g. in the Enneagram which contains three character types per center. Table 2 lists a few three-component personality models.

	Component 1	**Component 2**	**Component 3**
Leader archetypes (Neuberger)	father	healer	hero
Biostructural anal.	green	red	blue
Enneagram	gut center	heart center	head center
GRID system	authoritarian	caring	analytical
Ontogram (Gramm)	matter	love	spirit
Pitcher	craftsman	artist	technocrat
Process-oriented psychology	action	feeling	thinking
Psychography (Friedmann/Winkler)	action	relationship	rational
Structural model of the psyche (Freud)	superego	id	ego
Transactional Analysis (Berne)	parent ego-state	child ego-state	adult ego-state

Table 2 Three-component models of personality

5 Ernst, German psychiatrist, 1888–1964.
6 cf. Wagner, in: Schimmel-Schloo and Seiwert (2002), P. 16.
7 Dietmar, German developer of psychotherapy, b. 1937.
8 cf. Friedmann (2000), P. 42–62 and Friedmann (2004), P. 22–86.
9 cf. Winkler (2001), P. 34–56.
10 Oswald, German psychologist, b. 1941.
11 Cf. Niederwieser (2002), P. 79–89.
12 cf. Wagner, in: Schimmel-Schloo and Seiwert (2002), P. 16.
13 cf. Schirm (1997), P. 63–75.

In short, across different cultures, religions and sciences we find similar trichotomies with rational, emotional, and active aspects. The three-component models of personality assume that each person carries three dimensions, one of which is preferred.

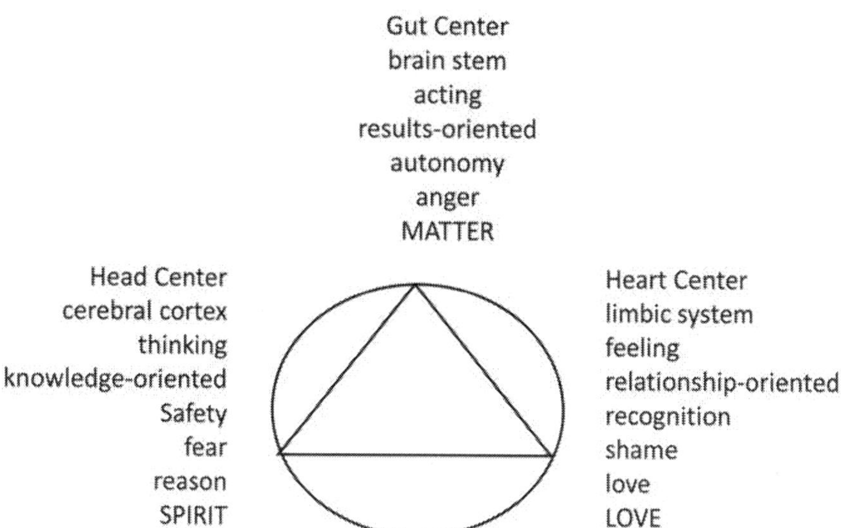

Figure 1: Ontogram (from Sabine Gramm)

In the Enneagram, the three basic components of gut, heart and head divide into three further types. Not all authors discuss this trichotomy, e.g. Goldberg, Gallen and Neidhardt, Hauser, and Harms, go directly to the description of the nine character types. Jaxon-Bear[14], Mächler[15], Palmer[16], and Rohr and Ebert[17] describe the qualities of the centers in detail: the brain stem automatically steers processes in the body that are required for survival (e.g. breathing, heart rate). The limbic system controls emotional responses in a given situation. The cerebral cortex is home to the ability to reflect and reason. These centers in the brain closely correspond to the psychological perspective of body – soul – mind, the bio-structure of the brain centers in the structogram, Winkler's psychography[18] and Friedmann's PPP[19]. The Enneagram authors Riso and Hudson[20], and Küstenmacher[21] make a direct link to neuroscience and the three centers of the

14 cf. Jaxon-Bear (2003), P. 60–64.
15 cf. Mächler (1998), P. 100–104.
16 cf. Palmer 2000/1, P. 63–65.
17 cf. Rohr and Ebert 2002, P. 40–46.
18 cf. Winkler (2001), P. 140.
19 cf. Friedmann (2000), P. 151–178.
20 cf. Riso and Hudson (2000), P. 77.
21 cf. Küstenmacher (1998), P. 20–24.

brain. Since the Enneagram symbol already possesses a trichotomy through the inner triangle and the analogy of these inner qualities is obvious, it is easy to connect the Enneagram to the structogram, which is based on brain research.

	Component 1	Component 2	Component 3
Leader archetypes (Neuberger)	father	healer	hero
Biostructural analysis	green	red	blue
Enneagram	gut center	heart center	head center
GRID system	authoritarian	caring	analytical
Ontogramm (Gramm)	matter	love	spirit
Pitcher	craftsman	artist	technocrat
Process-oriented psychology (Friedmann)	action	feeling	thinking
Psychography (Friedmann/Winkler)	action	relationship	rational
Structural model of the psyche (Freud)	superego	id	ego
Transactional Analysis (Berne)	parent ego-state	child ego-state	adult ego-state

Tab. 2: Three-component models of personality

In the Enneagram, development of personality is offered through activating the neighboring Types ("wings") and the "flow" and "stress" points that are derived from the lines in the symbol. From a present day perspective, I see this as an expanded static description of personality of the five Types with which a client is dealing (i.e. their own Type + two wings + flow point + stress point). I describe the activation of these slumbering areas of character as an unfolding of personality and use this as a tool in the further development of my coachees.

In my experience, this occurs when the unfolding is viewed as a cyclical process, as taught by the German personality researcher Dietmar Friedmann[22], who has worked extensively with the Enneagram. Through the process-oriented psychology of personality he uncovered at first six types. Through his Enneagram knowledge, he expanded this to nine types and adopted the numbering of the

---

22 Educator, b. 1937 in Pforzheim (Germany)

individual character types for his system.

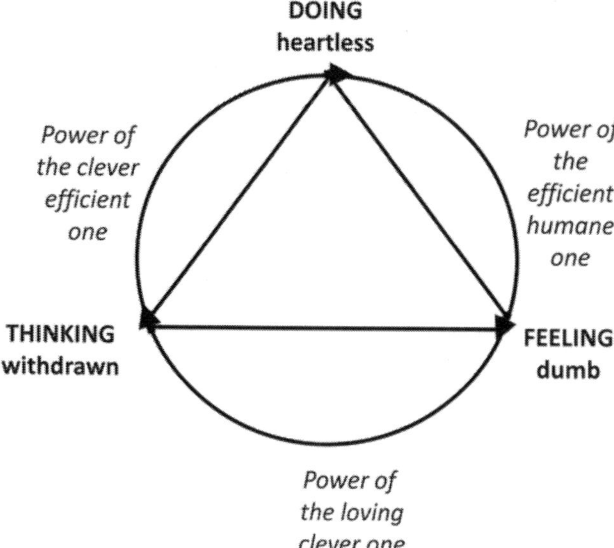

Figure 2: Development of personality, based on Friedmann's Integrated Solution-focused Psychology

In this approach, he does not use the flow and stress points ideas from the Enneagram, i.e. he didn't make use of the inner hexagram. Instead his model describes the development of each character type in clock-wise paths described by equilateral triangles that take the type through each of the other centers. For example, a representative of Type 9 (Gut) develops via the 3 (Heart) to 6 (Head); a representative of Type Four develops via the Seven to One, and a representative of Type Five develops via the Eight to Two[23].

Overall the three-component models give us a structured view of our inner life and indicate with which area of being I most strongly identify: doing, feeling or thinking. This influences our theoretical understanding and practical experience of the topics of self-knowledge and personality development, since nobody can look so deeply inside me as I myself. It is worthwhile to get to know all these different parts, since the more homogeneous one's inner life, the greater one's charisma, just like for a precious jewel.

Four-Component Models

According to Jewish beliefs God created the world according to laws of numbers. As it says in the Old Testament: "you have chosen to measure, count, and weigh everything you do"[24]. Pythagoras, the founder of numerology, assigned to four the meaning of the physical world — the visible phenomena in life[25]. "It is first the Four that grants pure spirit an appropriate form of appearance".[26] Four serves to orient people in the world. The four cardinal

23 cf. Friedmann 2000 und 2004, Darmstadt.

24 Die Bibel 1994, P. 717; Das Buch der Weisheit 11,20.

25 cf. Werner 2006, P. 11 - 17 und P. 113–117.

26 cf. Werner 2006, P. 115.

directions orient in space and the four seasons in time[27]. Empedocles (483 – 420 BC) recognized the four elements of fire, water, earth and air in all life forms; everything changes through the mixing and separating of these substances with each other. Nothing remains the same and still the sum of the energy stays constant; a viewpoint that is still valid today. The term element is due to Aristotle, who used the term to describe something that was not further divisible[28]. Here is a table with a small selection of four-component models from different areas.

	Component 1	Component 2	Component 3	Component 4
Elements (Empedocles)	earth	fire	air	water
Cardinal directions	East	South	West	North
Seasons	Spring	Summer	Autumn	Winter
Chemistry	solid	plasma	gas	liquid
Qualitative properties	hard	warm	moving	cold

Tab. 3: Four-component models

In the area of personality models, many systems show from the outside the person towards she strives to be and what she shows of herself. Before I explain the Riemann-Thomann Model, which I consider to be the basic model of the psychology of differential communication, I present a small selection of four-component models of personality in tabular form.

	Component 1	Component 2	Component 3	Component 4
C.G.Jung	feeling	sensing	intuition	thinking
DISC	dominance	inducement	submission	compliance
Galen's tempraments	choleric	melancholic	sanguine	phlegmatic
HBDI® (Hermann)	sequential	interpersonal	imaginative	analytic
Hippocrates' humors	yellow bile	black bile	blood	phlegm
INSIGHTS MDI®	Reformer Director	Coordinator Advisor	Motivator Inspirer	Observer Supporter
Kant (Anthrop.l Characteristics)	thick-blooded	warm-blooded	thin-blooded	cold-blooded

27 cf. ebenda, P. 113 f.
28 cf. Aristotle 1970, P. 116 f.

LIFO®	reason	performance	activity	cooperation
Macoby (Manager typology)	jungle fighter	company man	playmaker	expert
Mastenbroeck (behavioral styles in conflict)	analytic-aggressive	flexible-aggressive	flexible-compromising	ethical-convincing
MBTI®	feeling	sensing	intuiting	thinking
Reddin (3D-Program styles)	task	relationship	integration	process
Riemann	compulsive	depressive	hysterical	schizoid
Schulz von Thun	aggressive-devaluing, deciding-controlling	helping, needy-dependent	communicative dramatic, self-demonstrating	distanced, selfless
Thomann	Steadiness	closeness	change	distance
TMS (Margerison)	producing monitoring	organizing advising	innovating promoting	developing maintaining

Tab. 4: Four-component models (with no claim for completeness, as not all models are so oriented on axes)

Riemann-Thomann Model

In the 1960s the German psychologist Fritz Riemann distinguished four basic forms of fear that, in his opinion, present in different amounts in each person and which could either move or paralyze them:

1. Fear of self-sacrifice, experienced as a loss of self and independence.
2. Fear of self-realization, experienced as a lack of security or isolation.
3. Fear of change, experienced as transience or insecurity.
4. Fear of necessity, experienced as finality or lack of freedom.

He considered all possible fears to be variants of these four basic fears, which are in turn anchored in four basic human aspirations:

1. The aspiration towards self-preservation and isolation.
2. The aspiration towards self-sacrifice and belonging.
3. The aspiration towards continuity and safety.
4. The aspiration towards change and risk.

These accentuations of personality are normal, as long as they do not cross any boundaries through excessive one-sidedness; only when they are excessively and one-sidedly lived do they cross the boundary into the pathological areas of the four classical neuroses of clinical psychology: schizoid, depression, obsessive-compulsion and hysteria. Riemann said: "These neurotic personalities reflect in an exaggerated or extreme form general human existence, which we all know. Finally, it is about four different ways of being in the world"[29]. In the 1980s the Swiss psychologist Christoph Thomann further developed a "map of personality"[30] by translating the characteristics of the four human psychological cardinal points with the common terms distance, closeness, steadiness and change.

All people, some more than others, experience a need for

Closeness: familiar closeness, attachment, love, safety, harmony and empathy, to be there for others and to be needed, belonging.

Distance: Differentiation and to be oneself, self-realization, independence, privacy and individuality, intellectual knowledge, task orientation.

Steadiness: reliability, order, planning and foresight, constancy, law, system, control and power, outlasting the moment.

Change: magic of the new, daring, adventure, fantasy, playfulness and delight, spontaneity and passion, intensity of the moment, freedom[31].

If we transfer that to the star diagram (see below), human behaviors can be placed quite well. People appear to be spontaneous and flexible (Chance pole) or conservative and consistent (Steadiness), people-oriented (Closeness) or task-oriented (Distance). All of these are equally important and valuable, just different. Philosophically, they represent the coordinates of the two dimensions of space (Closeness – Distance) and time (Steadiness – Change) in which all life takes place[32 33].

To understand inter-personal interactions it is necessary to know, under-stand and be able to use the attributes of all four areas. Each person contains all four, just in different strengths. It is helpful when I recognize which pole my counterpart is currently using, so that I

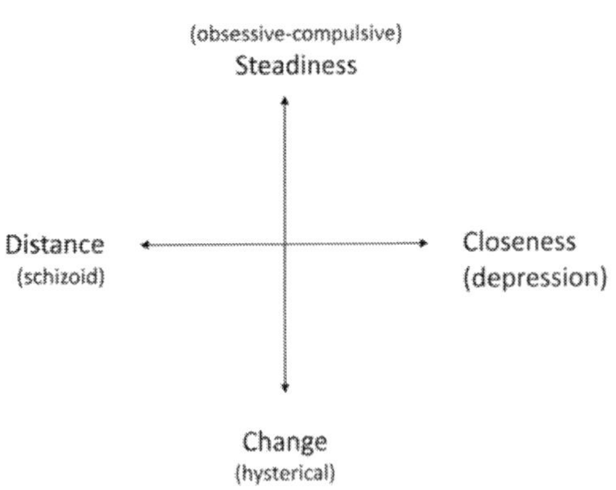

Figure 3: Thomann's four basic aspirations [33]

---

29 cf. Riemann 2002, P. 15 f.

30 cf. Thomann and Schulz von Thun 2006, P. 174.

31 cf. Thomann and Schulz von Thun 2006, P. 176 f.

32 Insight provided by the economist and yoga teacher, Bettina Wentzel (Ettlingen). *priv. comm.*

33 Based on Thomann and Schulz von Thun (2006), Fig. 7, P. 177.

can communicate with him appropriately. For example, if I meet someone with a lot of Distance, then I know that he is currently at home in the area of thought, where the rules of objectivity and logic are important. At this moment, it would not be helpful to attempt to convince him using emotional arguments. It is very important to remember that people are not just placed at one of the poles, but can display different behavioral preferences at different times and in different contexts. A classical example of this is someone who is quite distant at work and is more emotional with family and friends. What a person is currently displaying need not be congruent with his deepest self. The insight into human nature does not presume we can x-ray people in the same way that self-knowledge can. That would be stressful for both parties in a relationship. Therefore I believe that the three-component models are less useful here since they look inward. Here it is more about being able to recognize more clearly in which of the Riemann-Thomann bi-polar states my counterpart finds himself here and now, what he shows of himself and which values he represents in a particular topic. If someone shows himself as conservative on the topic of flexible working times, conformant with the Steadiness pole, where regularity and predictability are important, it does not mean that this person is in principle a conservative person. The same person could show a very relaxed and non-conformant attitude (more aligned with the Change pole) to the topic of behavior while driving. For a professional knowledge of human nature it is enough to know the laws and values of the four poles and be able to derive suitable arguments from this knowledge, as needed. More freedom for the individual would not be a valuable argument for a conservative counterpart in the case of flexible working times. However, if I can mention the increasing reliability and commitment for the private sphere that flexible working times would make possible, I would be addressing his values.

Naturally, everyone has their center of gravity, usually one of the poles, where she prefers to be. Or she rejects one of the poles and attempts to keep it at bay which can reduce vitality, flexibility and joy. Depending on which pole is preferred and which ignored, different psychograms and living realities result. This does not prevent someone from being at home in all four cardinal points so that they can meet a representative of any of the polarities in their element. One has been, so to speak, washed with all the waters and can use this to the advantage of both parties at any time in a cooperative manner. When I can understand and speak the language of my counterpart, the doors to interpersonal understanding are opened wide. Peace and success are thus more likely. Four component models show two contrary, opposing and viable realities. I have attempted to show here that this double dialectic view is especially useful for the areas of insight into human nature (the external view of people or how they show themselves) and conflict management (the juxtaposition of contrary values).

I would like to comment at this point that one could extend this systematic palette to include five-component models. This gives access to other sensory-physical models. Based on my current knowledge, six, seven, eight or even more component models can be assigned to one of the already described categories (three, four or five components).

Psychology of differential communication

In 1989 Schulz von Thun[34] published a typology with eight different communication styles. The model is based on Adler's individual psychology and characterology, Riemann's four forms of fear, Reich's analytical theory of personality, Berne's transactional analysis, as well as his experience as a trainer and communications therapist. In his own words, these communication phenotypes arose so: "that which I repeatedly encountered and seemed suitable as a starting point for a person's further development"[35].

This phenomenological approach views the person and her style of communication in a partially exaggerated dramatization, through which the essence comes more clearly to light as in the typical interactions with people. Here are the eight styles as he would present them:

The needily dependent style[36] aims to show herself as helpless and overwhelmed and to give the other person the feeling, they should jump in, help, decide and take responsibility – or else all would be lost.

The helping style[37] is the patient listener and advice giver who is always ready to step in confidently to help the weak and helpless, even beyond her own levels of exhaustion; she doesn't need anyone else herself.

The self-less style[38] senses the wishes and needs of others and serves them self-sacrificially and subserviently; feels herself as meaningless and valueless; overlooks herself.

The aggressive-devaluing style[39] is antagonistic towards others and treats them patronizingly, tends to provocation, humiliation and degradation of individuals and entire groups.

The self-demonstrating style[40] strives to position herself in a good light through techniques that impress and put on a good face; like to present herself as more perfect than she really is.

---

34 German Communications scientist (b. 1944).
35 Schulz von Thun 2006/1, Band 2, P. 60.
36 cf. Schulz von Thun 2006/1, Band 2, P. 61–75.
37 cf. Schulz von Thun 2006/1, Band 2, P. 76–92.
38 cf. Schulz von Thun 2006/1, Band 2, P. 93–114.
39 cf. Schulz von Thun 2006/1, Band 2, P. 115–152.
40 cf. Schulz von Thun 2006/1, Band 2, P. 153–169.

The determining and controlling style[41] wants to guide and correct events and people so that they remain under her control and thus proceed correctly; hates unpredictability, chaos and powerlessness.

The distant style[42] has an invisible wall around herself, so that nobody can come too near; communicates formally and impersonally, shows reserve and displays no emotions.

The talkative dramatizing style[43] enjoys being surrounded by people and to fascinate them through an exhibition of emotions; makes themselves the center of attention for the entertainment of all.

It is important to note that the communication styles are neither entirely negative (nor entirely positive), which the helping character in particular demonstrates; when he helps too much, one needs to talk about the co-dependent character. The "distant", "self-demonstrating" and "determining and controlling" are more neutral terms, in contrast to "aggressive and devaluing", which can only be classified as a virtue or vice. Through the addition of other attributes Schulz von Thun assumes that each of us contains all styles and experiences "a preferred style through the form of contact coupled with certain avoidance styles"[44]. For example, someone using the needily dependent style makes contact with other people by showing his neediness and allowing others to help him. Someone in the aggressive devaluing style makes contact by provoking others. The former avoids displaying strength and the latter weakness. Thus, through the external reality of sensory perception he unlocks the internal psychic relationships. He always places two characters opposite each other, who could lock themselves into vicious circles. Figure 4 shows these pairs, where I have translated the negative names into something positive (lower line of each pair) and added to the only positive name (helping) a negative counterpart:

[41] cf. Schulz von Thun 2006/1, Band 2, P. 170–190.
[42] cf. Schulz von Thun 2006/1, Band 2, P. 191–227.
[43] cf. Schulz von Thun 2006/1, Band 2, P. 228–243.
[44] Ebenda, P. 58.

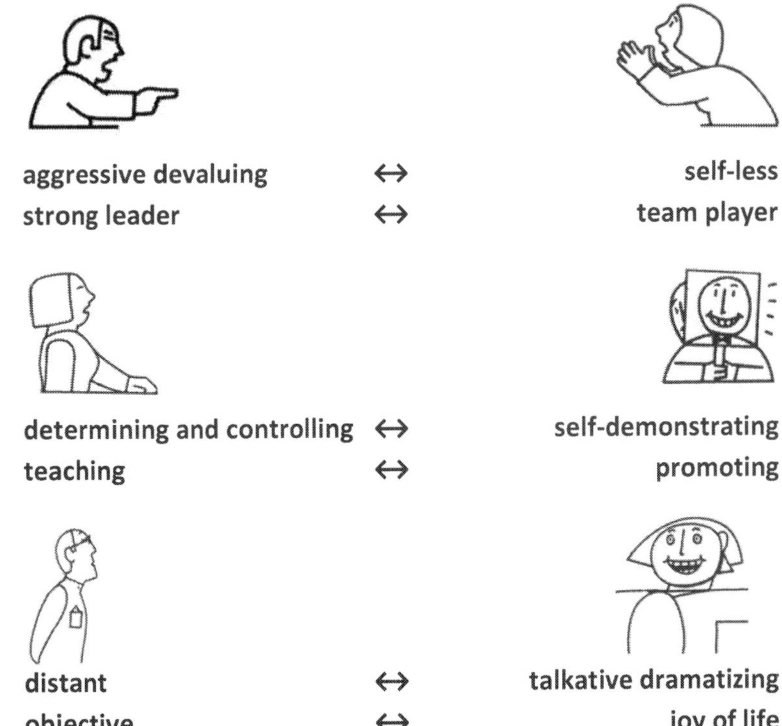

Figure 4 Schulz von Thun's communication pairs

The classification arises from the perception of the counterpart's communication, i.e. what she shows of herself. For this, the coordinate system of Riemann-Thomann's four psychological cardinal points is valuable. During a lecture by Schulz von Thun on 20 November 2006 at the University of Hamburg I was able to recognize, thanks to his lively presentation of the four psychological cardinal points, how these fit into the eight communication styles of the PDC. This results in a closed and consistent system. As part of a psychology term paper I had the opportunity to discuss this insight with Schulz von Thun. In a personal note to me on 20 June 2007 he commented, "you have gained interesting insights with which I on the whole agree."

He would have preferred to see the self-less style on the Closeness side, as he considers her to be relationship oriented. In my opinion, this character corresponds to Type Six in the Enneagram, who serves people not out of emotional closeness, but in an impersonal manner due to their position and role in order to fulfill a common task.

Each pole in this diagram contains two communication styles. Therefore the first step in perceiving one's counterpart is to locate him in which of the four poles he currently resides, e.g. if he's closer to Closeness or Distance. The next step involves refining this view by noticing, for example, if the person at the Closeness pole attempts to approach others and help them (helping communication style) or opens himself and allows the other to help him (sensitive communication style). In contrast to the Change Type, the Steadiness Type attempts to keep hold of the reins; the task-oriented Distance Type flees from the relationship-oriented Closeness Type. This diagram illustrates in many ways the interaction of the Types between themselves and serves as a valuable instrument to recognize correlations and develop solutions for communication, cooperation and conflict. Each area has its own special forces that reflect themselves on a collective operational level in the individual functions or departments in an organization.

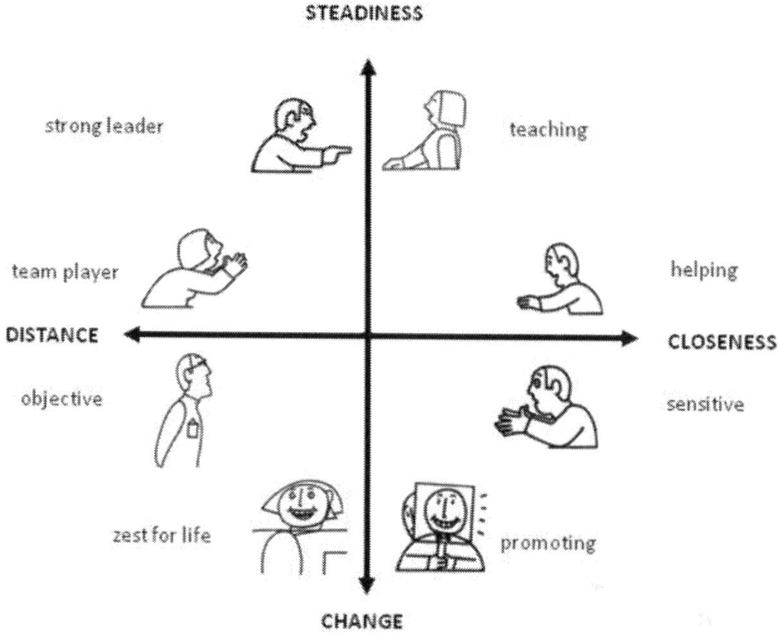

Figure 5 The 8 PDC communication styles aligned with the Riemann-Thomann Cross

So, for example, the bustling Marketing (function), which happily shows itself to the outside world, is to be found on the Closeness side of the Change pole (this corresponds to the self-demonstrating communication style). Beside it, on the Distance side the bustling, but task-oriented Sales, which understands how to excite people about new topics, is to be found (this corresponds to the talkative dramatizing communication style). This is where people work, who like to go outside the organization and present themselves, those who do not primarily need the closeness and security of the company. Both like to be rewarded and motivated through freedom, the other poles through interesting tasks (Distance), responsibility (Steadiness) and public recognition (Closeness). This brings to a close the description of Prof. Schulz von Thun's PDC, coupled with the four psychological cardinal directions of the Swiss psychologist Christoph Thomann, who in turn built on the four forms of fear from the German psychiatrist Riemann, together with a glance at the professional-collective level from group dynamics.

Building a bridge to the Enneagram

You already know the Enneagram with its nine personality types. To start with, I'll sketch the Types briefly and connect them to the eight communication styles of the PDC ("Communication" below). These descriptions are based on the career-oriented Enneagram literature from Goldberg, Mächler, Palmer, Tödter and Werner, and Salzwedel, the communications literature from Schulz von Thun, as well as my own observations, experiences and insights.

Type One[45]

experiences his anger as inwardly directed in the form of discipline and being principled; is highly engaged to reach self-defined and reform-oriented higher ideals, goals and values. Reliably delivers perfect work and expects that from others.

Behavior with others:	serious, critical, reserved, determining, conscientious.
Working style:	diligent, practical, structured, organized, efficient.
Leadership style:	objective, role model, responsible, reliable, strict.
Areas:	organization, HR, quality control, controlling, (corporate) management.
Position:	leader, teacher, trainer, lawyer.
Communication:	a clear correspondence to the determining and controlling style. Both live according to the principle, "I know what is right"

Type Two[46]

ashamed of her own needs, projects them onto others and helps graciously, going even beyond her own boundaries and those of others. Works so that she can be in contact with others and to receive attention.

Behavior with others:	affectionate, helpful, flattering, empathic, proud, loud.
Working style:	versatile, emotional, supportive, helping, capable, energetic.
Leadership style:	personal, encouraging, caring, generous, manipulating.
Areas:	personal assistant, HR, deputy, right hand, consultant.

45 cf. Goldberg 1998, P. 31–61; cf. Hauser 1995, P. 46–48; cf. Mächler 1998, P. 135–137; cf. Palmer 2000/2, P. 59–92; cf. Palmer / Brown 2000, P. 56–88; cf. Salzwedel 2008, P. 56f; cf. Tödter and Werner 2006, P. 72–83.

46 Cf. Goldberg 1998, P. 62–92; cf. Hauser 1995, P. 60–62; cf. Mächler 1998, P. 114–116; cf. Palmer 2000/2, P. 93–118; cf. Palmer and Brown 2000, P. 89–122; cf. Salzwedel 2008, P. 58f; cf. Tödter and Werner 2006, P. 84–95.

Position:	personal assistant, social fulcrum, "power behind the throne".
Communication:	a clear correspondence to the helping style. Both are afraid of their own neediness and are fully there for others.

Type Three[47]

is ashamed of his own feelings, without being aware of them. Identifies himself through tasks, performance and success to please others. Concentrates more on the goals than the way to achieve them; builds up a pleasing image.

Behavior with others:	charming, competitive, promoting, sufficing, sugar-coating.
Working style:	effective, flexible, quick, success-oriented, ambitious.
Leadership style:	motivating, inspiring, task-oriented, dynamic.
Areas:	marketing, trade, sales, director.
Position:	best in the group.
Communication:	a clear correspondence to the self-demonstrating style. Both attempt to gain recognition through performance.

Type Four[48]

shames herself for her own inner strength and shows herself as weak. Wants to distinguish herself from others and be somewhat special. This also applies in terms of tasks and approaches to them. Penetrates to the kernel of a topic.

Behavior with others:	sensitive, individual, cultivated, preoccupied, withdrawn, different.
Working style:	creative, aesthetic, unconventional, sensitive, complicated, audacious.
Leadership style:	gentle, headstrong, emotional, intensive, authentic, radical.
Area:	creative design, designer, architect, artist, coach.
Position:	special position.
Communication:	this correspondence is particularly tricky, since the creative-artistic side of the Type is emphasized in the Enneagram. In contrast, the PDC emphasizes the lack of self-confidence in the needily dependent style, which is the corresponding style. The connection is to be found in the sensitivity of the Type, which allows her to

47 Cf. Goldberg 1998, P. 93–126; cf. Hauser 1995, P. 73–75; cf. Mächler 1998, P. 117–119; cf. Palmer 2000/2, P. 119–145; cf. Palmer and Brown 2000, P. 123–159; cf. Salzwedel 2008, P. 60f; cf. Tödter and Werner 2006, P. 96–108.

48 Cf. Goldberg 1998, P. 127–156; cf. Hauser 1995, P. 87–88; cf. Mächler 1998, P. 119–121; cf. Palmer 2000/2, P. 146–170; cf. Palmer and Brown 2000, P. 160–190; cf. Salzwedel 2008, P. 62f; cf. Tödter and Werner 2006, P. 109–120.

perceive her own inner needs in a particularly intensive way, weaknesses and contradictions. This sensitivity often finds its artistic expression through creative acts. Both like to lean on strong people and are afraid of self-reliance.

Type Five[49]

is afraid of human closeness and therefore withdraws. Precise observer who thinks sagaciously and gets to the bottom of topics. He is modest and reserved with his emotions, knowledge and personal presence. He hoards readily.

Behavior with others: shy, observing, neutral, rational, deflecting, cool or even cold.

Working style:	analytical, concentrated, independent, objective, systematic.
Leadership style:	minimalistic, sober, philosophical, impersonal, formal.
Area:	research and development, expert, analyst.
Position:	self-employed, staff position or leading at a distance.
Communication:	a clear correspondence with the self-distancing style. Both require a safe distance and live according to the motto "don't come too close to me".

Type Six[50]

projects her fears on the outer world and feels secure in a system with clear hierarchy and rules, into which she can willingly insert herself and fit in unobtrusively. Clears away obstructions and problems and is problem-focused.

Behavior with others:	fearful, doubting, unsure, conscious of hierarchy, task-oriented.
Working style:	reliable, preventative, dutiful, loyal, risk-conscious.
Leadership style:	cooperative, reliable, loyal, mistrustful, pessimistic.
Area:	production, technology, trades, security.
Position:	one among equals, or team lead.
Communication:	this corresponds to the self-less communication style. Neither Type not Style sees herself as important and allows herself to be instrumentalized for the aims of others.

---

49 Cf. Goldberg 1998, P. 157–188; cf. Hauser 1995, P. 101–103; cf. Mächler 1998, P. 122–124; cf. Palmer 2000/2, P. 171–199; cf. Palmer and Brown 2000, P.191–223; cf. Salzwedel 2008, P.64f; cf. Tödter and Werner 2006, P. 121–132.

50 Cf. Goldberg 1998, P. 189–217; cf. Hauser 1995, P. 115–117; cf. Mächler 1998, P. 124–127; cf. Palmer 2000/2, P. 200–227; cf. Palmer and Brown 2000, P.224–255; cf. Salzwedel 2008, P. 66f; cf. Tödter and Werner 2006, P. 133–144.

Type Seven[51]

flees from fear through change, adventure, fun and non-committing. Above all, one can never have enough, always has too many projects on the go, loves the possibilities and the ideas more than the real result. Can realize new, unusual and complex things and motivate others to help.

Behavior with others:	fascinating, narrating, amusing, non-committal, erratic.
Working style:	quick, imaginative, planning, innovative, process-oriented.
Leadership style:	*laissez-faire*, visionary, optimistic, motivating, spontaneous.
Area:	sales, networking, planning, idea generator.
Position:	autonomous with a direct boss or reportees.
Communication:	this has a direct correspondence to the talkative dramatizing style. Both like to perform and bring some life to the party, in order to avoid the inner emptiness.

Type Eight[52]

Experiences her anger directly and immediately, highly prepared to enter into conflict, dominant and confronting, energetically controls her space and territory, needs power, takes over leadership willingly and pushes things through, is strong and robust. Has a hard shell and a soft center.

Behavior with others:	self-confident, provocative, present, demanding, direct, loud.
Working style:	practical, focused on usefulness, action-oriented, full of energy.
Leadership style:	open, honest, fair, direct, autocratic, rough, protective.
Area:	production, (corporate) management.
Position:	boss, generalist.
Communication:	this corresponds directly to the aggressive devaluating communication style. For both, being on top is a question of survival and they avoid weakness.

Type Nine[53]

has turned his sensors far enough down so that he doesn't need to experience

---

51 Cf. Goldberg 1998, P. 218–245; cf. Hauser 1995, P. 128–130; cf. Mächler 1998, P. 127–129; cf. Palmer 2000/2, P. 228–255; cf. Palmer and Brown 2000, P.256–290; cf. Salzwedel 2008, P. 68f; cf. Tödter and Werner 2006, P. 145–156.

52 Cf. Goldberg 1998, P. 246–274; cf. Mächler 1998, P. 130–132; cf. Palmer 2000/2, P. 256–283; cf. Palmer and Brown 2000, P. 291–322; cf. Salzwedel 2008, P. 70f; cf. Tödter and Werner 2006, P. 48–59.

53 Cf. Goldberg 1998, P. 275–309; cf. Hauser 1995, P. 158–160; cf. Mächler 1998, P. 132–134; cf. Palmer 2000/2, P. 284–312; cf. Palmer and Brown 2000, P. 323–359; cf. Salzwedel 2008, P. 72f; cf. Tödter and Werner 2006, P. 60–71.

anger. This leads to a stunted emotional and mental presence; he doesn't take himself seriously, doesn't respond well to external pressure, needs harmony and can generate it.

Behavior with others: passive, friendly, non-judgmental, conflict avoidant, absent, obstinate.

Working style: peaceful, sits things out, reactive, steady, peaceful.

Leadership style: fair, comradely through consensus or stubborn through boycotting changes.

Area: everywhere, in particular in the administration and works council.

Position: facilitator, administrator, leader.

Communication: there is no clear correspondence to one communication style. After all, one will be left over when a system of eight is being made compatible with a system of nine. It's not so surprising that this happens with Type Nine. They don't become entangled in their communication with others due to their need for peace and quiet, unlike the other styles which form dialectic parings as opposing poles, according to the philosophy of Schulz von Thun.

Communication Enneagram

The correspondence between the eight styles of communication in the PDC and the Enneagram Types yields the following picture:[54]

Figure 6 Communication Enneagram 1

In the symbol it is easy to recognize that the Nine stands in between two halves, left and right. He has no opposite pendant and equally represents both the start and the end of the circle. From a communications perspective, this Type is an intermediary between the other eight. Thus it makes sense that at first glance this Type seems to be missing in the Schulz von Thun model. During a training on the Riemann-Thomann model he explicitly stated that he

[54] *priv. comm.* on 20 June 2007, Schulz von Thun agrees "by and large" with this mapping of the styles to Type.

integrated "rooted down-to-earthness" into the Steadiness pole[55]. To complete the communication icons I commissioned a suitable cartoon for this Type[56].

The advantage of this approach is that the numbers receive memorable pictures and so it is easy to recognize the connection between the inner world of experience and the external communication style. A disadvantage is the judgment that the Types experience by being drawn at a particular point in their development. An interesting variant emerges when one connects the pairings that Schulz von Thun selected in his PDC, because they get caught up in vicious circles, with lines on the Enneagram symbol:

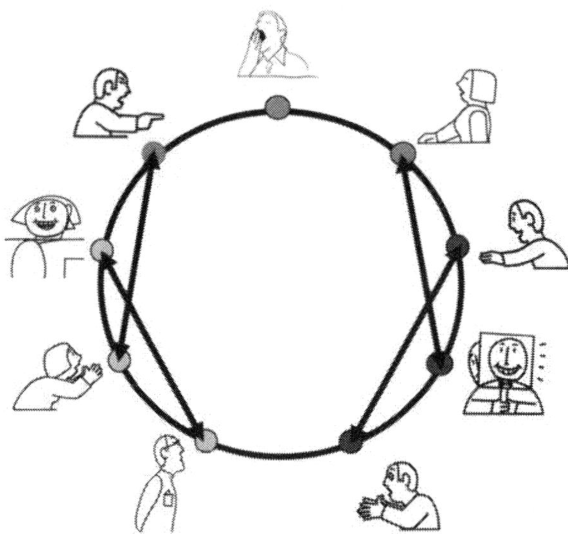

Figure 7 Communication Enneagram 2

As if by magic, one has a new symmetric figure. The lines between Type Two "Helper/Co-dependent" and Type Four "Sensitive/Needily Dependent" and between Type Five "Objective/Distant" and Type Seven "Joy of Life/Talkative Dramatizing" are known. These show connections that in Enneagram terms are due to the flow and stress points. The line between Type One "Teaching/Determining and Controlling" and Type Three "Promoting/Self-Demonstrating" is new. This reflects a teacher-pupil or governess-child relationship. The line between the "Strong Leader/Aggressive Devaluing" Type Eight and "Teamplaying/Self-less" Type Six is also new. This reflects a master-servant or boss-subordinate constellation. Both pairings have a lot to do with power, which is not clearly visible in the Enneagram symbol. These insights, gained through the application of the PDC, correspond to Riso & Hudson's Harmonics.

The Enneagram supports the analysis of the strengths, non-strengths and weaknesses (i.e. over-used strengths) of one's own personality as well as typical qualities. I like to use it in professional coaching for profiling and development. I have some reservations about its use in written test form[57]; in my opinion it shows its true strength in the narrative tradition[58]. In a seminar Type recognition

---

55 04.–06. May 2010, Kloster Kappel, Switzerland.

56 by architect Rainer Lißner, Leonberg (Germany).

57 Cf. Simon (2006), P. 213 f.

58 Cf. Palmer 2000/1, P. 24–26.

is a consensual act in which the individual recognizes himself or herself in the mirror on the basis of the possibilities contained in the model. It must be said that this requires an experienced and skillful teacher who can act as a guiding and mindful midwife for the recognition of one's own self.

The Riemann-Thomann Cross with its differentiation of the eight communication styles is for many participants in business seminars more accessible than the Enneagram, since it better reflects the dialectic thinking of our modern world. The four-component system enables us to consciously perceive people's different preferences in behavior though the four qualities of the poles (closeness—distance—steadiness—change), each with two fine distinctions (e.g. the helping and sensitive styles either side of the Closeness pole), which gives us a first way to understand the associated attitudes to life. As I already mentioned, this is looking from the outside at other people, since people usually first appear to others through one of the four polarities.

At the same time, it opens up the possibility to expand one's own repertoire of communication styles so that one can deal with people of different Types, since one speaks differently with each one. This is a particularly important skill for leaders and managers. Professionally I like to use this to help clarify and harmonize professional relationships; I use it in mediation as a building block towards the resolution of the conflict. In particular, the Helwig's Values Square, which Schulz von Thun popularized, plays a key role. For space reasons, I need to leave that for another article.

System transition

They complement each other all the way from self-knowledge through personal development and insight into human nature. The clarity and simplicity of both systems together with their memorable symbols greatly simplify the understanding of complex personality and relationship structures. It is also fascinating that both systems deal with the same archetypes from different perspectives. It never ceases to amaze me how compatible the two systems are, which I will now illustrate.

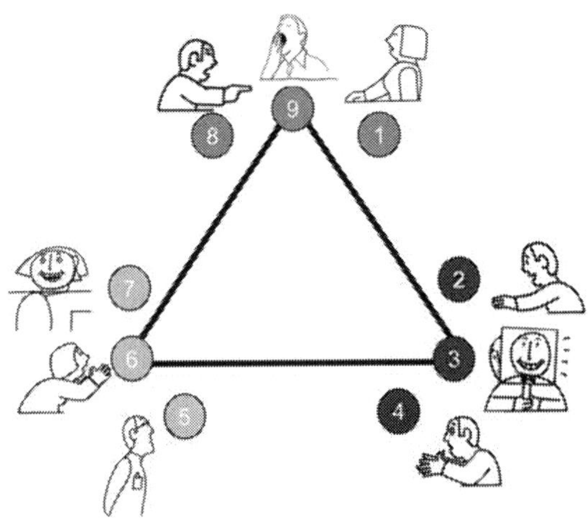

Figure 8 Enneagram without circle or hexagram

Starting from Fig. 7 and placing the different characters in one of the three Enneagram centers (Gut-Heart-Head), we obtain Figure 8.

To make the transition to the four-component model of the Communication Diagram (Fig. 5), we need to extend the existing three dimensions by a fourth dimension (Fig. 9):

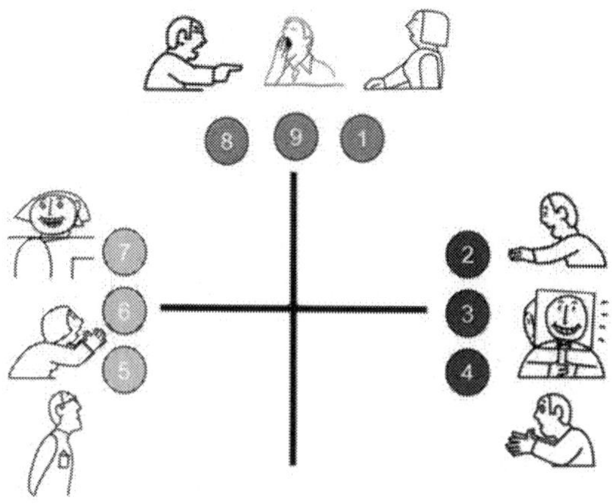

Figure 9 Transition between the systems 1

Four-component models look from the outside at how people present themselves and what they show of themselves. Starting from this thought, two Enneagram types, Three and Seven, show themselves as particularly exuberant and lively. At the same time, one Type shows very little profile and is most difficult to place. That's the Type that prefers that everything stays as it is, but can still deal with changed conditions pretty well; Type Nine, who doesn't belong to any of the poles and thus is placed in the middle. If the two Types, Three and Seven, together form an outwardly exuberant pole and Type Nine is placed in the undifferentiated center, the following changes result (Fig. 10):

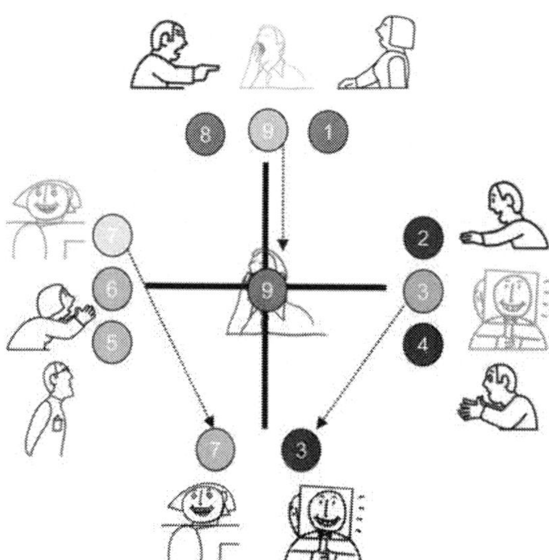

Figure 10 Transition between the systems 2

The result is that the communication diagram (Fig. 5) has been extended through placing Type Nine in the center (Fig. 11).

This completes the transition between the systems of the Enneagram and the psychology of differential communication, embedded in the Riemann-Thomann Cross. This allows us to find an explanation for why Types Three and Seven are so fundamentally different in their inner world, although they both appear to be similarly outgoing: the Three is agile and flexible, in order to impress others and is motivated through the feeling (Heart Center Type) or wish to come closer to other people. Type Seven loves the show and euphoria behind which he hides, so that he doesn't need to really show himself. It is his disguising ploy to keep others at bay by appearing to be rational Head Types. Interestingly, in this system at three of the four poles we find two Types which are not Enneagram neighbors (the exception is the Distance pole, where Types Five and Six are placed). In recent years, thanks to this perspective, I was able to observe that a slight change between these two Types at the pole is possible, similar to the effect of wings, due to their connection as flow and stress points of each other. This means that a Type Four can behave from time to time as a Type Two, and *vice versa*. Equally so for Types Three and Seven, which is astonishing if one only knows the Enneagram symbol, where the two have nothing to do with each other. Observe for yourself how easy it is for a Type Three from time to time to act like a joyful child, without striving for success or competing.

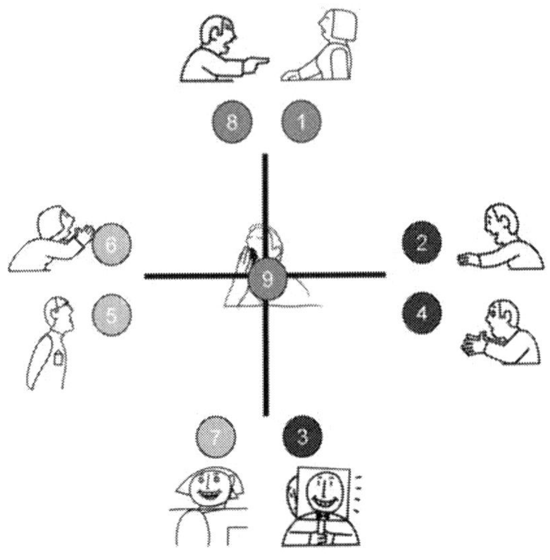

Figure 11 Communication Diagram 2

What irritates some people by this transition is that twice one Type is removed from the middle of its center (Nine as central gut type and Three as central heart type) to position it anew, and once from the edge of a center (Type Seven, which is not the central head type). In each case, the Type that suppresses the primary characteristic of its center is moved: the Nine suppresses anger, action and guilt; the Three suppresses feelings, love and shame; the Seven denies the fear and dispassion at its center). So seen it makes sense to pick out precisely these three types and to place them anew. The question that I since then ask myself about the Enneagram symbol is: Why is Type Seven not in the middle of the head center?

In practice, when I use both systems, I begin with the four poles of the communication diagram. I attempt to identify in which of the four poles of Closeness-Distance-Steadiness-Change my counterpart currently resides. When I go one step further, I attempt to differentiate in which of the two types he currently resides. Only after a closer interaction is it gradually clear whether this might be the main style at which he's anchored. Then I move on to an Enneagram perspective, also with the wings and lines. Of course, there are exceptions, people who live solely in their main type and use their main style; however, I don't assume that at the beginning. When a coachee comes to me looking for a personality profile and development, I begin with the Enneagram symbol (better said, from a variant that I show in the next section). Afterwards I come to the four-component perspective with the question, "how do I come across?"

New perspectives

During my long work with the transition between the systems, I recognized the analogy with the four elements of Empedocles and I use that now instead of Thomann's terminology: Earth for Steadiness, Fire for Closeness, Air for Change and Water for Distance. In one of my seminars a participant commented that in this model, Air is under the Earth, which contradicts our terrestrial conditions. So we flipped it 180°. By the way, after another participant question in a seminar in Switzerland, Christoph Thomann also decided it is better if the light Change is above the heavier Steadiness[59].

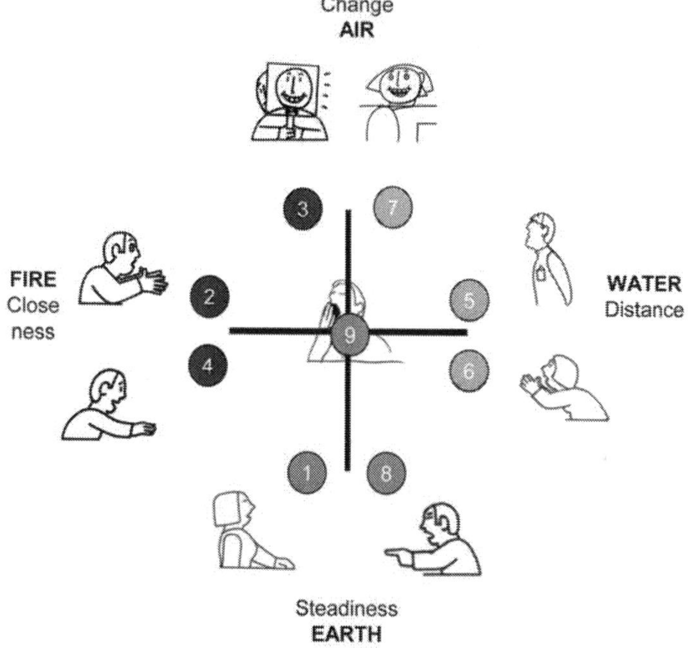

Figure 12 Cosmogram (from Sabine Gramm)

This inspired me to apply the same idea to the Enneagram and to turn this symbol around:

59 Seminar: *The Riemann-Thomann Model*, Kloster Kappel, Switzerland

Figure 13 Anthropogram (from Sabine Gramm)

I prefer this to the traditional Enneagram for the following reasons:

- The most traditional and entrenched type of all, the Nine, takes the position of the symbol's root.
- The heart center is on the left rather than the right, just as in the physical body.
- The gut center is below both head and heart centers, instead of being above – which is in reality illogical. Thus it comes closer to a real person than the traditional symbol, where the gut is on top. At present, I call this variant the Anthropogram, to distinguish it from the Enneagram.
- Instead of the threatening hole at the bottom, there is now an inspiring opening towards above: there, where the highest inspiration sits, between the creative energy of the Four, who is always looking for something higher and strives for this and the thoughtful creativity of the Five, who gains insights "from above"; this is where divine light can fall, so that it may be manifested on earth.

Summary

Professor Friedemann Schulz von Thun did not know the Enneagram[60] before he developed his psychology of differential communication which he published in 1989, contemporaneously with the first Enneagram book in German. Thus two systems of personality developed independently, in different languages and at different times, and yet lead to quite similar results in their archetypical insights. They give us different ways of looking at the same truths, which supplies reciprocating evidence for the authenticity of both systems and their archetypes. This confirms my firm belief that one always comes to the same truth when one thinks things through, irrespective of one's starting point: many paths lead to Rome! It was only by comparing and connecting both systems that I was truly able to appreciate each of the for the first time. This gave me a 360° view of how a personality type presents itself to the world, its inner emotional life and that to which it strives. These insights inspire me each day in my own life and in particular in my professional work with people who try to resolve their conflicts and improve their relationships – both private and professional. Although a central finding from my research over the past thirteen years, the compatibility between these two systems is not the only match between systems of personality that I have found. Seen in this light, human typologies are not only helpful, but also justified through the human ability to reflect and think abstractly, to recognize the laws that hide behind the veil of everyday forms. Here I present these connections to international experts for the first time, to trigger a discussion and would be delighted to receive constructive feedback that might help to rethink, enrich or further develop the presented relationships. For me the exchange of opinions with other forms of truth is the key, not who is right.

Bibliography

Translator's note: The author draws on German translations of some literature that was translated from the original English. Where appropriate, the equivalent title in English is added at the end of the reference. Please note that the page references in the endnotes are for the German translation of the works.

Die Bibel mit Bildern von Marc Chagall (1994), Herausgegeben im Auftrag der Bischöfe von Deutschland, Österreich, der Schweiz, Luxemburg, Lüttich und Boden-Brixen,,D-Augsburg Pattloch-Verlag (*The Bible illustrated by Marc Chagall – published by all German-speaking bishops*)

Aristoteles, (1970) *Metaphysik*, D-Stuttgart, hrsg. von Schwarz, Franz F., Reclam-Verlag (Aristotle's *Metaphysics*)

---

60 In an interview with Sabine Gramm on 1 November 2006 in his office in Hamburg university.

Friedmann, Dietmar (2000) *Die drei Persönlichkeitstypen und ihre Lebensstrategien - wissenschaftliche und praktische Menschenkenntnis*, D-Darmstadt, Wissenschaftliche Buchgesellschaft

Friedmann, Dietmar (2004) Denken, Fühlen, Handeln - mehr Menschenkenntnis mit der 3-Typen-Lehre, D -München, überarbeitete Neuausgabe, 4. Auflage, Deutscher Taschenbuchverlag

Goldberg, Michael, (1998) *Die Persönlichkeitszahl im Beruf*, D-München, Droemersche Verlagsanstalt Th. Knaur Nachf. (*Insider's Guide to the Nine Personality Types: How to Use the Enneagram for Success at Work*)

Hauk, Freimut (2003) *Lust an der Erkenntnis*, D-München, Deutscher Taschenbuchverlag

Hauser, Renate (1995) *Neunmal klug statt einsam ratlos - das Enneagramm als Schlüssel zum Erfolg in Partnerschaft und Beruf*, D-Düsseldorf, München, Metropolitanverlag

Jaxon-Bear, Eli (2003) Das spirituelle Enneagramm – Neun Pfade der Befreiung, D-München, Wilhelm Goldmann Verlag (*The spiritual Enneagram – Nine Paths to Freedom*)

Küstenmacher, Werner (1998) *Von Reptilien und anderen Menschen,* Celle, Enneagramm Rundbrief Jg 8, Nr. 14

Mächler, Christoph (1998) *Change Management mit dem Enneagramm*, D-München, Wilhelm Heyne Verlag

Niederwieser, Christof (2002) *Über die magischen Praktiken des Managements*, D-München und Mering, In: Schriftenreihe Organisation & Personal, Bd. 11, hrsg. von Neuberger, Oswald, Rainer Hampp Verlag

Palmer, Helen / Brown Paul B.(2000) *Das Enneagramm im Beruf*, D-München, Droemersche Verlagsanstalt Th. Knaur Nachf. (*The Enneagram Advantage: Putting the 9 Personality Types to Work in the Office)*

Palmer, Helen (2000) *Das Enneagramm – Sich selbst und andere besser verstehen* (D-München), Droemersche Verlagsanstalt Th. Knaur Nachf. (*The Enneagram: Understanding Yourself and the Others In Your Life)*

Palmer, Helen (2000) *Das Enneagramm in Liebe und Arbeit*, D-München, Droemersche Verlagsanstalt Th. Knaur Nachf. (*The Enneagram in Love and Work*)

Riemann, Fritz (2002) *Grundformen der Angst*, D-München, 34. Auflage, Ernst Reinhardt Verlag

Riso, Don Richard/ Hudson, Russ (2000) *Die Weisheit des Enneagramms*, D-München, Wilhelm Goldmann Verlag *(The Wisdom of the Enneagram)*

Rohr, Richard / Ebert, Andreas (2002) *Das Enneagramm – Die 9 Gesichter der Seele*, D-München, 42. Auflage, Claudius Verlag (*Discovering the Enneagram: An Ancient Tool for a New Spiritual Journey*)

Rosenstiel, Lutz von / Regnet, Erika (2003) *Führung von Mitarbeitern*, D-Stuttgart, hrsg. von Domsch, Michel, 5. überarbeitete Auflage, Schäffer Poeschel Verlag

Salzwedel, Martin/Tödter, Ulf (2008) *Führen ist Charaktersache*, D- Berlin, Cornelsen Verlag Scriptor GmbH & Co. KG

Schanz, G. (2000) *Personalwirtschaftslehre: Lebendige Arbeit in verhaltenswissenschaftlicher Perspektive,* Vahlen Verlag

Schimmel-Schloo, Martina / Seiwert, Lothar J. (2002) *Persönlichkeitsmodelle – die wichtigste Modelle für Coaches, Trainer und Personalentwickler*, D-Offenbach, hrsg. von Wagner, Hardy, Gabal Verlag

Schirm, Rolf W. (1997) *Die Biostruktur-Analyse 1 – Schlüssel zur Selbstkenntnis*, CH-Baar, IBSA 20. Auflage in völliger Neubearbeitung

Schulz von Thun, Friedemann (2006) *Miteinander Reden 1 – Störungen und Klärungen*, D- Reinbek bei Hamburg, Sonderausgabe, Rowolth Taschenbuch Verlag

Schulz von Thun, Friedemann (2006) *Miteinander Reden 2 – Stile, Werte und Persönlichkeitsentwicklung*, D-Reinbek bei Hamburg, Sonderausgabe, Rowolth Taschenbuch Verlag

Simon, Walter (Hrsg.) (2006) *Persönlichkeitsmodelle und Persönlichkeitstests*, D-Offenbach, Gabal Verlag

Thomann, Christoph / Schulz von Thun, Friedemann (2006) *Klärungshilfe 1*, D-Reinbek bei Hamburg, 3. Auflage, Rowolth Taschenbuch Verlag

Tödter, Ulf / Werner, Jürgen (2006) *Erfolgsfaktor Menschenkenntnis*, D-Berlin, Cornelsen Verlag

Werner, Helmut (2006) *Lexikon der Numerologie und Zahlenmystik*, D-Köln, Komet Verlag

Winkler, Werner (2001) Lehrbuch Psychographie: Menschenkenntnis mit System, D-Fellbach, Werner Winkler Verlag

EXPLORING ENNEAGRAM TRITYPE™: THEORY AND PRACTICE

Katherine Chernick Fauvre & David W. Fauvre, MA

Abstract

When theory building for a system like the Enneagram, it is important to base new distinctions on a solid empirical and practical foundation. With the breadth of fine distinctions already built into Enneagram theory, it seemed that most avenues of distinction had been fleshed out. However, upon working with a multitude of clients, a fascinating pattern emerged. Research and test results with clients revealed that people utilize one type in each center of intelligence: head (5,6,7), heart (2,3,4) and gut (8,9,1), and that these types were used in a preferred order, with one being dominant. These Tritype™ combinations also reveal specific character archetypes that enrich and enhance current Enneagram theory and provide Enneagram researchers and enthusiasts with a new typing language. Understanding the basics of Tritype™ can help those working with the Enneagram (enthusiasts, clients, therapists and coaches) communicate in a new typological language. Aristotle suggested that true internal harmony could be achieved only when internal conditions allow each aspect of the psyche to perform what it was primitively meant to perform. The authors have found that one's Enneagram Tritype™ reveals critical aspects of the psyche and how they were meant to perform, thus allowing one to develop the self-awareness needed to create internal harmony and live a more fulfilling life.

Keywords: Tritype™, Enneagram, Instinctual Types, Instinctual Subtypes

Part I: Research, Design and Analysis

What is the Enneagram Tritype™?

Extensive research, beginning in 1995, has shown that individuals have not one, but three Enneagram Types used in a preferred order. These three Enneagram Types always occur in each of the three centers of intelligence: head (567), heart (234) and gut (891). The Enneagram Tritype™ combination identifies these three Enneagram Types, adding significant precision, accuracy and scope to the Enneagram Typing process.

One of the three types in one's Tritype™ is dominant (or primary) and represents the ego's preferred defense strategy. However, when the strategy of the dominant Enneagram type fails, the ego uses the strategies of the other two types within the Tritype™ in a repeating, descending order. In an attempt to solve a problem, the ego will continue to deploy the other two types in the Tritype™ until the issue is resolved. The dominant type in the Tritype™ is always in charge, therefore, ultimately the individual will always return to the resources of their core or dominant strategy.

The combined defense strategies of the types within the Tritype™ create a unique focus of attention with a shared worldview. Research suggests that the common theme found among the three types within one's Tritype™ will be one's archetypal life purpose and a critical blind spot to self-awareness. Research emerged from diverse studies: Enneastyle: The 9 languages of Enneagram Type, (1995), Enneagram Instinctual Subtypes (1995), Enneagram Core Fears (1996), Katherine Koch Horpel Chernick, Enneagram, Instinctual Subtypes and Intimacy (1998), Katherine Chernick with Victoria Ruderman and Kit Snyder (1998), A study of Instinctual Subtypes (2005), A Study of Trifix (2007), A Study of Tritype (2008, 2009, 2010 and 2011), Katherine Chernick Fauvre and Katherine Chernick Fauvre and David W. Fauvre, MA, (2010). In addition, the shared view by the types in one's Tritype™ gives important clues as to what is needed to live a more conscious and meaningful life.

The high side of the intersection of these three Enneagram Types is that they define what gives life direction, focus and purpose for the individual with that Tritype™ combination. The low side of this intersection is that the type's defense strategies collude, narrowing one's ability to accurately self-assess, thus impeding personal growth. One's strengths are the gifts that emerge as a result of the specific focus created by these three types working in concert with one another. One's weaknesses are a result of this intersection as well, limiting self-awareness and spiritual growth, thus creating what the authors term an egoic 'blind spot.'

Illuminating this blind spot often releases neurotic symptoms. Further, aligning one's self with the archetypal energies found in the three types in one's Tritype™ can align one with his or her higher life purpose and mission. Identifying one's Tritype™ Archetype also creates an opportunity to discover one's innate abilities, develop expertise and experience a greater sense of satisfaction.

Research Origins

In 1995, Katherine Chernick began her first empirical research exploring the self-image of the nine types with the "Enneastyle Questionnaire," a testing instrument made of 20 questions on image, self-projection and style. This research revealed that each Enneagram type has a self-image that includes positive attributes accompanied by a set of core fears. More importantly, the image statements, combined with the corresponding core fears, reveals the more hidden, 'internal experiences' of type. This data further explained the underlying motivations that drive the behaviors of the nine types.

Inspired by unexpected findings during her initial study, Katherine immediately followed with a research study on the instinctual subtypes. These studies led to the development of an entirely new research endeavor including significant findings centered on the types, instinctual subtypes, the instinctual subtypes and intimacy, and the aforementioned Tritype™ theory which will be expounded upon later. What emerged from the initial research was the discovery that lexical patterns that were used by participants and clients on their Enneastyle Questionnaire and during "In-depth Inquiry Process" coaching sessions, consistently organized ego strategies around three Enneagram types. In other words, clients consistently utilized the language and lexicon of three Enneagram types when revealing their personal psychological experiences. Clients preferred a dominant Enneagram type, but also identified with the core fears of two other types; a type from each center of intelligence: head (5,6,7), heart (2,3,4) and gut (9,8,1). More importantly, many used the language of types that do not connect to their primary type by a line or a wing. This is an important distinction in the discovery of Tritype™, as most theorists believe that all Enneagram behaviors can be attributed to one's dominant style, wings or lines of connection, yet it was found that clients repeatedly utilized the personal lexicon of a type in each center. So, it became apparent that an expansion of traditional Enneagram theory would need to be explored to explain this deviation.

Circa 1996, Katherine attended a presentation given by a teacher from the Arica School and learned that Enneagram pioneer, Oscar Ichazo, had added the term "tri-fix," (the use of three fixations) to his teachings. This concept intrigued her and appeared to validate initial findings that one uses three types. This complimented her ongoing research. In 2008, after 12 years of research, Katherine coined the term Tritype™ to distinguish Katherine (and David Fauvre's) vast body of work from Ichazo's early teachings of "tri-fix."

In 1996, Katherine met David W. Fauvre, MA and began collaborating with him on Enneagram projects. In order to lend greater validity and scientific weight to this emerging theory, a methodology was conceptualized by David and developed along with Katherine, to uncover how these three styles could be derived from personal lexicon use.

Methods

In 2003, David commissioned Michael Tsai, Ph.D., a MIT computer science expert (who specializes in software to detect complex language patterns) to program software for Enneagram Explorations. Together they developed two methodologies, the "Enneastyle Bayesian Classifier" and the "Enneagram Lexicon Tagger" to confirm and further investigate the complex language patterns that emerged in Katherine's research. The language patterns revealed that each Enneagram type, instinctual type and Tritype™ consistently described themselves and their life experiences in a unique and identifiable lexicon set.

The "Enneagram Lexicon Tagger" software classifier was developed by examining the language patterns found in the responses on the Enneastyle Questionnaire. The words (and word combinations) the participants used to describe themselves were weighted based on Katherine's assessment of how frequently a particular word, or combination of words, was utilized by a particular type on the Enneastyle Questionnaire. This was based on hundreds of questionnaires, typing interviews and participant corroboration. The word weighting system is based on a +2 to -2 scale, with +2 indicating a high probability of use by a particular Enneagram type, instinctual subtype or Tritype™ and a -2 being a low probability of use. Then the word-tagging system was programmed into the classifier and questionnaires were entered into the classifier and analyzed utilizing the weight system to help ascertain possible Enneagram type, instinctual subtype and Tritype™ combinations. After the data was analyzed utilizing the classifier, researchers corroborated classifier assessments to help create validity. Initially, the classifier was programmed using 1000 questionnaires. The classifier was able to canonically detect the correct Tritype™ based on questionnaire responses with 80 percent accuracy (N=1000). It was able to detect two of the three types in one's Tritype™ with an over 90% accuracy. After the initial questionnaire analysis, over 15,000 questionnaires have been subsequently collected and substantiated with both the algorithm and inter-coder confirmation. Personal lexicon became a remarkably accurate predictor of Enneagram type, instinctual type, wing and Tritype™.

The Enneastyle Classifier has been used to statistically validate the language choices in the Enneastyle Questionnaire, and confirms the hypothesis that each Enneagram type speaks in their own lexicon, regardless of language, age, gender, education, nationality or race. Further, it also confirms that they use the lexicon of the three types in their Tritype™ as well as the language of their dominant instinctual type. Thus, the typing process proceeds through five basic steps 1.) The Enneastyle Questionnaire, 2.) The Enneacards Enneagram Test, 3.) The Instinctual Subtypes Test, 4.) The Enneastyle Language Classifier and 5.) Coaching.

With this software revealing empirical and statistically verifiable data on language use by type, Enneagram type research has moved beyond the traditional heuristic or experience-based style of research. This previous method of research often left gaps in understanding, analogous to the mapping of a forest by walking amongst the trees, versus the statistically verifiable, robust research methodology of mapping a forest from aerial photographs.

Sample Data and Analysis

The analysis process consisted of four primary steps: 1.) Analysis of the questionnaire utilizing the classifier 2.) Corroboration of the classifier assessment of Enneastyle questionnaires 3.) Corroboration of Enneastyle questionnaire and Enneacards Enneagram Test 4.) Inter-coder reliability assessment of the Enneastyle Questionnaire and Enneacards Enneagram test.

The questions: greatest strength and why and greatest weakness and why along with or saying were added after the initial 400 Enneastyle Questionnaires. These additional questions further confirmed the initial findings of probable type, instinctual type and later, Tritype™.

Example 1, shows the test taker's responses to the Enneastyle Questionnaire and scoring by the Enneastyle language classifier software. The Enneastyle Questionnaire asks the test taker to describe themselves as if to a stranger using five adjectives. This is followed by a series of questions to further elicit self-image. A blank Enneastyle Questionnaire appears before example 1.

Enneastyle Questionnaire

Name ______ Date ______
Address ______ Phone ______
Email ______

Enneagram Point ____ Wing ____ Subtype ______ MBTI ______

Presentation

Considerations:
Please list the five adjectives that would most fully describe your personality character traits.

______ ______ ______ ______ ______

Greatest Strength ______ Why ______

Greatest weakness ______ Why ______

Favorites:
Color ______ Symbol ______ Creature ______

Image

Please fill in the blanks with appropriate words that describe your personal image.
Remember to include your attitudes in your early 20's, especially if they are different.

Desire	To look
Need	I need
Fear	I'm afraid of styles that are
Avoidance	I avoid
Image Personality	My personal image style is
Image Statement	I am
Image Theme	I dress for

Example 1 Enneastyle Questionnaire responses as scored by the Enneastyle Language Classifier

Terms: 'ActualType' is the actual Enneagram Type of the test taker as determined by the Enneagram Enneacards Test results, test taker interview and corroboration. The same applies to 'Actual Tritype™'

ActualType	7
ActualTritype™	729
Adj1	sincere, creative, innovative
Adj2	caring
Adj3	outgoing
Adj4	thoughtful
Adj5	listen

Strength:	aware
Strength: Why:	able to understand impacts my actions and words have on others and relations
Weakness:	details
Weakness: Why	tend to look at large picture and not work out details completely
Color:	blue
Symbol:	zen circle
Creature:	fish
Desire:	healthy
Need:	food and sleep
Fear:	abrasive
Avoid:	conflict
Image Style:	clean cut
Image Statement:	soul
Image Theme:	comfort and to be interesting
Saying:	rumi poems

Notes on Score Interpretation:

The score below is the predicted Tritype™ Archetype of the test taker based on analysis of the language patterns found in the test taker's Enneastyle Questionnaire responses.

The score is canonical and as such does not take into consideration the weight of the score between the three types in the test takers Tritype™.

Often the score weights of the words will correctly predict not only the Tritype Archetype™ but the preferred order in which the test taker uses these types in their Tritype™. For example, the language classifier accurately predicted type 7 as the dominant type in the test takers Tritype™.

Report Terms

Tag: Enneagram Type

Score: The weighted score of the language combinations found indicative of a single Enneagram Type.

Math: The word combination indicative or counter indicative of a specific Enneagram Type.

Score from Language Classifier

Canonical Tritype™: 279 (predicted); 279 (actual)

(The weighting given to each word has been removed to protect the intellectual property of Enneagram Explorations. The score is the sum of the weights assigned to the words listed.)

Tag	Score	Math
7	17	abrasive + caring + clean + comfort + conflict + creative + healthy + innovative + interesting + outgoing
6	12	abrasive + actions + caring + clean + comfort + conflict + outgoing + sincere + thoughtful
9	11	caring + circle + comfort + conflict + details + others + thoughtful
2	11	caring + comfort + interesting + others + outgoing + sincere + thoughtful
3	6	caring + comfort + healthy + outgoing + work
1	6	caring + clean + comfort + healthy + thoughtful
8	5	comfort + creative + innovative
5	3	blue + comfort + conflict
4	3	aware + comfort + creative + thoughtful

In the above example, the classifier was able to isolate the dominant lexical usage of three types. Type 7, 9 and 2 are shown to be the highest rated types in each center of intelligence (head, heart and gut). The classifier indicates the possible Tritype™ canonically (hence 2-7-9). However, because this respondent utilized the most words from the Type 7 lexicon, it ranked Type 7 with a score of 17, followed by Type 6 (indicating this person is likely a 7 with a 6 wing, followed by Type 2 and Type 9 equally weighting at 11 points. After careful review from the researchers, the Tritype™ of 729 is confirmed first through analysis of the Enneastyle Questionnaire and then through a typing interview. In this particular example, the Enneacards test corroborates the classifier assessment.

In some examples it is vital to weigh the respondents test results against the classifiers prediction of Tritype™, particularly when there is overlap between a person's wing and a possible Tritype™ type. In the second example we can see this principle at work:

Example 2 Enneastyle Questionnaire Responses

Actual Type	8
Actual Wing	7
Actual Tritype™	873
Adj1	Confident
Adj2	Creative
Adj3	Enthusiastic
Adj4	Strong
Adj5	Fidgety
Strength:	My complete confidence in the fact that I can do anything—I am not afraid to try.

Strength Why:	This has been put to the test time after time, and when I am bold and dare I can and have made great things happen.
Weakness:	I have problems dealing with emotions--I'm either too much or too little, except with certain people I trust completely. Then it's easy.
Weakness Why:	I don't know, honestly. I can blame my father (who was sort of like this), but that seems too easy, doesn't it? :)
Color:	Purple
Symbol:	Spiral
Creature:	Dragon
Desire:	To look elegant, confident, relaxed
Need:	Something in my hands all the time; to be connected (online), to be in control fear overly busy, floral. Loud is OK but not WITH flowers!
Avoid:	Clingy people. Mediocre people, Crowds of people.
Image Style:	Simple but with bold colors and neutrals, great jewelry,
Image Statement:	Successful, relatively content but master of my domain! :)
Image Theme:	Myself!
Saying:	Boldness, boldness, and again boldness (paraphrased from E. Roosevelt, I think)

Scores

Canonical Tritype™: 378 (predicted); 378 (actual)

(The weighting given to each word has been removed to protect the intellectual property of Enneagram Explorations. The score is the sum of the weights assigned to the words listed.)

Tag	Score	Math
7	12	busy + clingy + colors + control + creative + enthusiastic + people + trust
6	9	afraid + blame + certain + confidence + loud + trust
8	8	afraid + bold + confident + creative + dragon + loud + myself + strong
3	7	busy + confident + elegant + successful
9	6	content + easy + loud + simple + too
2	6	enthusiastic + people + too
1	1	afraid + control + elegant
4	0	confident + creative + enthusiastic + purple

In example two, the classifier isolated the 378 Tritype™ as the probable Tritype™ for this respondent. The Type 7 was indicated as the top probable type (with a score of 12) based on the lexical choices in the questionnaire, with type 8 (with a score of 8) in the gut center, and type 3 (with a score of 7) in the heart center. However, the respondent's Enneacards questionnaire indicates a dominant type of 8, with a wing of 7. Thus, the questionnaire must be measured against the Enneacard test results to reach greater confluence between the Enneacard results and classifier assessment. The final typing of 873, as opposed to 783, seems to be accurate when analyzing the data utilizing inter-coder validity. Due to the preponderance of type 7 in this person's lexical usage, the 7 lexicon is more heavily weighted, however, after review of the Enneacards test results and researcher validation of the respondents type, the core style of Type 8 can be confirmed over Type 7 (which concurs with the Enneacard test results). The 8 with the 7 wing, with 7 in the Tritype™ will seem very 7ish, however, if we return to the motivation of the types and the core fears of the types then we can isolate in the above mentioned example, a core strategy of 8 as opposed to Type 7. Words like "strong," an indication of avoiding "mediocrity" and "weakness," as well as the desire to look like "themselves" and be "master of their domain," all indicate 8 as a core strategy, and 7 as both a wing and the preferred type in the mental center (confirming the classifiers illumination of a high preponderance of 7 words). Thus, in this example, utilizing the classifier in conjunction with the Enneacards test and typing interviews allowed for greater accuracy in predicting the probable type of the respondent based on their lexical usage and Enneacard selections.

Part II: Deeper Into Tritype™ Theory

Enneagram Centers of Intelligence

The nine Enneagram types are grouped into three triads or centers. There are

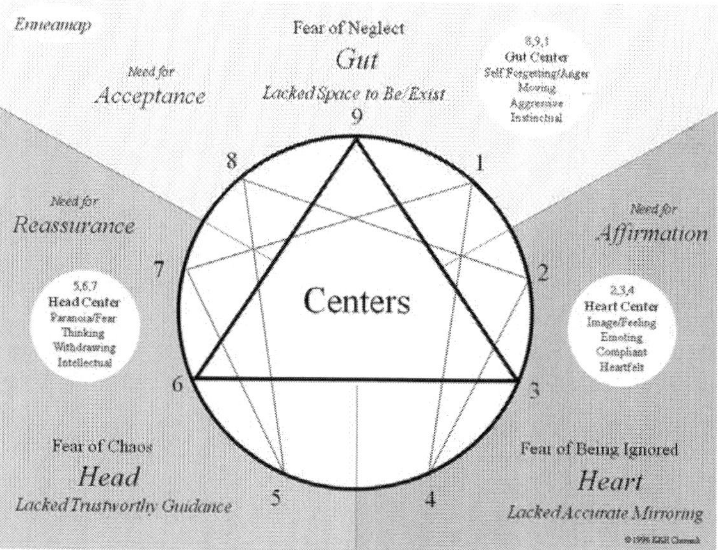

three Enneagram types in each triad. Each triad represents a different center of intelligence: head (5,6,7), heart (2,3,4) and gut (8,9,1). In human nature, we use all three centers but tend to primarily use one of these three centers. In the center that we predominantly use, one will use one of the three types. This is one's dominant Enneagram Type. Tritype™ demonstrates that one utilizes a type in each center, in a particular order. So once the primary center (and type in that center) is unable to resolve a problem, one will move to one's wings and lines of connection, and then move to the secondary and tertiary center of intelligence (and the preferred types within those centers).

Gut Center

The instinctual or gut center (8,9,1) is body-based and can be seen as having a desire to direct their course and take action in the world. They focus on their physical environment. They are gutsy, instinctive and visceral. Their primary issues are judgment, denial and resistance. They may struggle with being asleep to their true self. Whether or not they overtly express it, they are motivated and take action when they are angry. They fear being unimportant, neglected or overlooked. They seek acceptance and a sense of well-being.

Heart Center

The emotional or heart center (2,3,4) is feeling-based and can be seen as having a desire to positively affect others. They focus on their relationships. They are heartfelt, emotive and adaptable. Their primary issues are of craving attention, needing affirmation and wanting to be attached to others. They may struggle with being identified with their image or 'false' self. Whether or not they overtly express it, they are motivated by and take action when they feel emotional anxiety. They fear being ignored and unseen. They seek attention and mirroring.

Mental Center

The mental or thinking center (5,6,7) is thought-based and can be seen as having a desire to give greater importance to the interior world of ideas. They focus on their thoughts. They are knowledgeable, intellectual and visionary. Their primary issues are aversion, avoidance and projection with a focus on authority. They struggle with preconceptions that can manifest as prejudices and the fear of being alienated. Whether or not they overtly express it, they are motivated by and take action when they feel fear and anxiety. They fear chaos and their ability to cope with it. They seek reassurance; whether from an authority, a theology, a philosophy, or a kind word.

Understanding the importance of the centers helps to lay the basis for our discussion. The core fears of the individual Enneagram types reveal the underlying fear of their corresponding center. One uses all three centers, and the center one prefers is the center that houses the core Enneagram style. However, Tritype™ theory states that as one shifts focus (outside of the dominant style, wings and lines of connection) one will employ the other two centers in a particular order, whilst utilizing a particular style in those other secondary and tertiary centers.

Core Fears and Self-Image

Research not only revealed consistent self-image statements but also consistent "core fears" reported by each of the nine Enneagram styles (Chernick, 1995, 1996; Chernick-Fauvre & Fauvre, 2010). These fears have been found to be one of the most significant factors in determining one's Enneagram type. The core fears and image statements are reliable indicators of one's Tritype™ preferences as individuals report the core fears of a type in each center of intelligence.

Type	Idealized Self-Image and Core Fears
1	I am good, I am right, I am in control, I am diligent, and I am appropriate. Resentment with the fear of being wrong, bad, evil, or corruptible.
2	I am caring, I am nurturing, I am helpful, I am altruistic, and I am appealing Pride with the fear of being worthless, needy, inconsequential, or dispensable.
3	I am successful, I am efficient, I am competent, I am focused, and I am productive Vanity with the fear of failing, being incompetent, inefficient, exposed, or unable to do.
4	I am unique, I am special, I am deep, I am accomplished, and I am tasteful Envy with the fear of being inadequate, emotionally cut off, defective, or flawed.
5	I am perceptive, I am knowledgeable, I am observant, I am wise, and I am different. Avarice with the fear of being ignorant, invaded, not existing, annihilation, or obligation.
6	I am dedicated, I am dutiful, I am provocative, I am loyal, I am compliant, and/or rebellious Fear of Fear itself, submitting, being alone, blamed, targeted, or physical abandoned.
7	I am happy, I am optimistic, I am fun, I am enthusiastic, and I am playful. Gluttony with the fear of being incomplete, inferior, limited, bored, or missing out.
8	I am invincible, I am powerful, I am protective, I am straight-forward, and I am authentic Excess with the fear of being weak, powerless, harmed, controlled, or manipulated.
9	I am agreeable, I am easy going, I am peaceful, I am humble, and I am unassuming Indolence with the fear of being in conflict, loveless, shut out, discordant, or inharmonious.

The core fears of the types have been found to have nine distinct methods with which to manage the core fears of each center of intelligence. For example, the type 2 fears being worthless, needy, inconsequential and/or dispensable which, when interviewed, were found to be more specific ways in which the 2 manages the heart center's core fear of being ignored. Being helpful and nurturing is the 2s way of compensating for the core fears of being ignored, worthless, needy, inconsequential and/or dispensable

With knowledge of the image statements and the core fears, one can observe the primary triggers that influence one's ability to successfully respond to any given situation and can learn to avoid habitual, self-defeating over-reactivity.

Tritype™, Wings and Lines of Connection

Research indicated that individuals utilize the lines of connection (defined as the lines in the Enneagram symbol that connect one point to another) and wings (the types that lay on either side of the primary type), but that these lines and wings were not the only strategies used by individuals. Thus, research endeavors moved toward uncovering why individuals were reporting core fears, lexical preferences, core triggers and desires that have no direct connection with their dominant type. What was uncovered is that quite often people utilize the types in their Tritype™ that may or may not be a wing type or the types along the lines of connection.

For example, a type 9 may or may not have type 3 and/or type 6 as part of their Tritype™ (9 connects to 6 and 3 on the Enneagram symbol). A type 9 could have a Tritype™ of 925, 926, 927, 935, 936, 937, 945, 946 or 947. Each Tritype™ combination of type 9 creates a different expression of the type 9. If the 9 has the 3 and 6 in their Tritype™ as with the 936, the influence of 3 and 6 is greater and creates a very focused 9 that matches the traditional descriptions of 9s. However, if the type 9 has types in their Tritype™ that are not connected by a line such as the 945 or 947, they will appear to be very different from 9s that have the 936 Tritype™.

In addition, a person may or may not have a wing type in their Tritype™. For example, a type 7 may or may not have the type 8 in their Tritype™. If the type 7 has a wing type of 8, and has an 8 in the Tritype™, the 7 will be heavily influenced by the 8 defense strategies and can often be mistyped as an 8. Further, the type 7 with the 8 wing with the 782 Tritype™ will have access to 8 through a wing type and by having 8 in the Tritype™. The 782 Tritype™ also has access to the 8 through the line of connection to 8 coming from the 2 in the Tritype™. So, the 782 will be a 7 with a very strong flavor of 8. With this understanding one can begin to see a source of common typing mistakes and look-a-likes and illuminates the potentially rich nuances available to people in working with Tritype™ potentialities.

Ways to work with the Tritype™

There are several ways to work with the Tritype™ material. One way is to study the differences within type by looking at the nine Tritypes™ of each Enneagram type. A second way is to study the similarities of those sharing the same three Enneagram types by looking at the shared view of those with the same Enneagram Tritype™ Archetype. A third way is to study the influence of the 27 Tritypes™ in conjunction with the 27 Instinctual Subtypes.

Tritype™ by Type

Tritype™ by Type explains the variations within Enneagram type. Those sharing the same dominant Enneagram Type can be very different from one another depending on which types are in their Tritype™. Examining the nine Enneagram Types in conjunction with the types in the Tritype™ reveals the reasons for the differences. We will look at four examples of how understanding Tritype™ through this method can help to explain aspects of the psyche that may be missed by current theory.

Ex. 1) Tritypes™ for type 1: The type 1 has nine different possible Tritype™ combinations: 125, 126, 127, 135, 136, 137, 145, 146 and 147. With this approach, one can quickly see that there are nine Tritype™ combinations for each type, creating 81 Tritypes™. Furthermore, one can readily see that the 145 is more introverted and introspective (due to the two withdrawn types; 4 and 5 in the Tritype™ configuration) than the 137 which is more positive and outgoing (with two positive and assertive types (3 and 7) in its Tritype™ configuration. Both have type 1 as the primary type, however, the other two types significantly change the presentation of type 1.

Ex. 2) Difference between the 874 and the 826: The 874 has secondary strategies that are very different from those of the 826. Both 874 and 826 are protective as 8 is the primary type for both. However, the 874 is a fast-paced (7), creative (4, 7 & 8) feelingful (4) and optimistic (7) type 8, whereas the 826 is a more cynical (8 and 6), loyal (8 and 6) and helpful (2, 6 & 8) Type 8.

Ex. 3.) A Type 4 with a Tritype™ of 468: With the 468 Tritype™ the type 4 is the primary Enneagram type, and as needed, would also use the strategies of type 6 and type 8. Enneagram type 4 is always in charge. However, when the strategies of type 4 fail to produce results that will satisfy the ego, it will use all permutations of type 4 (wings and lines of connections) to solve the problem. Once all facets of type 4 have been exhausted, this individual will then shift to using the dominant type in each of the other two centers to manage the problem and create a solution. In this case, the type 4 in the 468 would use the strategies of type 6 and then type 8.

Ex. 4) Types within the 147 Tritype™: The 147 is an individual with a Tritype™ configuration that includes types 1, 7 and 4. The primary Enneagram type is the type 1. This Tritype™ combination indicates someone that would most likely be hardworking (1), positive (7) and deep (4) that seeks standards (1), options (7) and meaning (4). If the strategy of type 1 for diligence fails to give the desired results of being thorough and responsible, this person would then employ the strategy of type 7, and as needed, type 4. This cycle continues until the personality feels that the problem is resolved. These three types cascade into one another and continue everyday throughout the day.

Tritype™ by Archetype

Tritype™ by Archetype, which groups the types in the Tritype™, canonically, (without regard to order) sheds light on the similarities of those sharing the same types in a Tritype™, and provides a fuller composite of the energy created when the three types are combined. This yields 27 distinct Tritype™ Archetypes.

The Tritype™ Archetype approach allows one to look at the influence of the psychological and energetic archetype that is created when the three Enneagram types are combined. For example, 127, 217, 712, 271, 217 and 721 are each constructed of the same types, archetypal energies and defense patterns regardless of the order in which the individual's ego deploys them. This produces a common archetypal expression and experience for anyone having that combination of types in their Tritype™ regardless of what order they are used.

Tritype™ Archetype also explains why individuals sharing the same three types in their Tritype™ have more in common with each other than those sharing the same Enneagram Type. Research has shown that those with the same Tritype™ Archetype have a natural affinity for one another because they use the same three strategies to handle problems differing only in the order in which they are used. We will look at three examples that demonstrate how sharing the same three types produces a natural affinity for those with the same Tritype™.

Ex. 1) The 126 Tritype™: The 'Supporter' is the Tritype™ Archetype of the 126, 261, 612, 162, 216 and 621. All six of these Tritypes™ feel that they need to be responsible according to the values of the respective center (head, heart or gut) in which the primary Enneagram type resides. When the three types in this Tritypes™ are combined, an archetype is created that needs to feel safe by doing what is right (1), needed (2) and free from blame (6). Therefore, this individual is hyper-focused on assisting and supporting others. In addition, this Tritype™ is also focused on doing what one should (1), what is helpful (2) and what is seen as dutiful (6), resulting in a highly responsible person.

Ex. 2) Comparing how the centers are used in terms of feeling (234), thinking (567) or acting (891): The 468 and the 459 are both Tritypes™ that feel, then think and then act, however, the type 4 with the 468 Tritype™ is more reactive (6) and aggressive (8) than the type 4 with the 495 Tritype™ which is a more passive (9) and avoidant (5).

Ex. 3) Difference between the 972 and the 935: the 972 has a very "rosy" and positive outlook, and desires comfortable relationships that are easy to manage. The 2 and 7 make the 972 a people-person and increases the 9s need for harmony. In contrast, the 935 is more intellectual and somewhat avoidant. The 5 and 3 make the 935 more reserved and focused on competency. This is why, the

953 is more mental and may mistype as the 5, especially if the self- preserving instinct is dominant.

Enneagram Tritype™ Archetypes ©1995-2012 Katherine Chernick Fauvre & David W. Fauvre, MA	
Tritype™	**Archetype**
Mentor 125, 251, 512	If you are a 125, you are very diligent, caring, and knowledgeable. You want to be ethical, helpful and wise. You are very idealistic and see what needs to be done and simple and effective ways to do it. You are intensely private but care about people. You seek practical systems and procedures to measure results and effectiveness.
Supporter 126, 261, 612	If you are a 126, you are diligent, caring and inquisitive. You want to be ethical, helpful and supportive. Highly responsible and cooperative, you are most comfortable when you do things by the book and know what to expect. Focused on the needs and concerns of others, you seek ways to be of service. You enjoy being the power behind the throne.
Teacher 127, 271, 712	If you are a 127, you are diligent, caring and innovative. You want to be ethical, empathetic and inspired. Engaging, fun loving and outgoing, you want to be with people. You seek fun with a purpose, needing goals as well time to celebrate and enjoy life. You love discovering new things. You have a gift of being able to squeeze the boredom out of anything tedious.
Technical Expert 135, 351, 513	If you are a 135, you are diligent, focused and knowledgeable. You want to be ethical, efficient and wise. Highly rational, you seek systems and procedures. Detail oriented, you like mathematical concepts and finding ways to breakdown and understand complex material. You are very precise and good with exacting details that others find difficult to manage.
Taskmaster 136, 361, 613	If you are a 136, you are diligent, ambitious and inquisitive. You want to be ethical, efficient and dutiful. Highly industrious and responsible, you are focused on achievement. You feel obligated to be orderly and create a successful image as dictated by society. Most importantly, you focus on your duty and finding certainty.
Systems Builder 137, 371, 713	If you are a 137, you are diligent, ambitious and innovative. You want to be ethical, efficient and upbeat. You are self-motivated and want to achieve your goals in a positive and effective way. You want to do your best and want look good doing it. You focus on success and seek ways to measure it.
Researcher 145, 451, 514	If you are a 145, you are diligent, intuitive, and knowledgeable. You want to be ethical, original and wise. Highly intellectual, you are focused on what you perceive is correct and above reproach. Motivated to be informed, you are research oriented. You seek and quote the opinions of experts to avoid being uncertain and seen as ignorant.
Philosopher 146, 461, 614	If you are a 146, you are diligent, intuitive, and inquisitive. You want to be ethical, original and certain. Morally focused, you have strong emotions and are inclined to voice your feelings and intuitions. You care deeply and want to help others improve their lives and the expectations they have of themselves.

Visionary 147, 471, 714	If you are a 147, you are diligent, intuitive and innovative. You want to be ethical, expressive and positive. You are passionate and idealistic. You want to make a difference in the world and see the many possible approaches to different situations. Perfectionistic, you seek standards that improve lives.
Strategist 258, 582, 825	If you are a 258, you are caring, knowledgeable and protective. You want to be helpful, wise and straight- forward. Highly sensitive, you are an empathetic, intellectual 'people' person. You are both introverted and extroverted and can be direct and easily move towards others and can 'over' give and pull away to recharge.
Problem Solver 259, 592, 925	If you are a 259, you are caring, knowledgeable and accepting. You want to be helpful, wise and peaceful. You have a very shy, gentle and reserved nature and tend to focus on what is harmonious. You need companionship and avoid feelings of loneliness by focusing on the needs and concerns of others. You can struggle with inaction when you feel overwhelmed.
Rescuer 268, 682, 826	If you are the 268, you are caring, supportive and protective. You want to be helpful, engaging, and straight-forward. By nature, you want to be in charge of your world and are attracted to the noble cause. You wish to shield others from harm and challenge what is unjust. You want to know the rules are to feel safe and to know when you can break them.
Good Samaritan 269, 692, 926	If you are the 269, you are caring, inquisitive and accepting. You want to be helpful, supportive and peaceful. You like people and want to find ways to engage with them. Your sense of pride comes from getting along with others and being of assistance. You are known for your easygoing, and friendly disposition. You hate conflict and struggle with being passive.
Free Spirit 278, 782, 827	If you are the 278, you are caring, innovative and protective. You want to be helpful, loving and straight-forward. You are assertive, funny and outgoing. You like to use your charming and sunny disposition to create an upbeat, positive and action-packed environment. You are also very nurturing to those in your circle of care.
Peacemak er 279, 792, 927	If you are a 279, you are caring, innovative and accepting. You want to be helpful, upbeat and peaceful. You are very kind and tend to see the best in others, and focus on easy and comfortable ways of relating. Very optimistic and positive, you hate conflict and strife, and use your sense of humor to smooth out difficulties.
Solution Master 358, 583, 835	If you are a 358, you are ambitious, knowledgeable and protective. You want to be efficient, wise and straight-forward. Tough-minded, you are good at studying a problem and finding both original and practical solutions others miss. Highly tenacious, you work tirelessly until you find solutions and prevail against adversity.
Thinker 359, 593, 935	If you are a 359, you are ambitious, knowledgeable and accepting. You want to be efficient, wise and peaceful. Intellectual and clever, you find amenable and pleasant ways to manage difficult situations and relationships. Often shy, you are very private and are slow to trust others. You are ambitious but seek admiration is a subtle way.
Justice Fighter 368, 683, 836	If you are a 368, you are ambitious, inquisitive and protective. You want to be accomplished, loyal and straight-forward. Verbally adept and a good reader of people and situations, you have the ability to identify unjust authority, rebel against tyranny and verbally spar against it. You want to get along with others but can struggle with being too outspoken.

Mediator 369, 693, 936	If you are the 369, you are ambitious, inquisitive and accepting. You want to be successful, engaged and peaceful. You seek balance and harmony. You want to know what is expected of you and will adjust your behavior to succeed. You need affirmation, reassurance and a sense of wellbeing to feel connected to yourself and others.
Mover Shaker 378, 783, 837	If you are the 378, you are ambitious, innovative and protective. You want to be efficient, happy and straight-forward. You are a dynamic go-getter, focused on the prize. An expansive powerhouse, you see the big picture and have the will to make it happen. Obstacles are seen as competitive challenges.
Ambassad or 379, 793, 937	If you are the 379, you are ambitious, innovative and accepting. You want to be focused, upbeat and peaceful. You like people and are outgoing even if you are shy. You are easygoing and seek comfort but strive for success and a feeling of personal importance. You are identified with what you do and achieve but are soft, gentle and kind.
Scholar 458, 584, 845	If you are the 458, you are intuitive, knowledgeable and protective. You want to be original, wise and straight-forward. You study what makes people tick and form strong opinions about what you learn. Somewhat introverted, you are identified with being an intuitive, strategic thinker and see interconnections that others may miss.
Contempla tive 459, 594, 945	If you are the 459, you are intuitive, knowledgeable and accepting. You want to be original, wise and peaceful. Highly self-aware and reflective, you are very shy, reserved and self-conscious. You need regular quiet time to reflect on your thoughts and emotions. Easily flooded with emotion, it is difficult for you to voice your ideal and feelings.
Truth Teller 468, 684, 846	If you are 468, you are intuitive, inquisitive and protective. You want to be original, certain and straight-forward. You are highly sensitive and emotional. You track inconsistencies and are like the 'canary in the coal mine,' calling off hidden agendas, deception and ulterior motives. You are very intense and can at times be emotional and over reactive.
Seeker 469, 694, 946	If you are 469, you are intuitive, inquisitive and accepting. You want to be original, certain and peaceful. You are very sensitive and can experience intense feelings of self-doubt and uncertainty. As a result you need multiple sources of confirmation. You want to be individualistic but can fear being separate from others so avoid confrontation.
Messenger 478, 784, 847	If you are the 478, you are intuitive, innovative and protective. You want to be original, creative and straight-forward. A cutting-edge tracker of both your internal and external worlds, you are an unconventional, passionate and self-possessed master of solutions. Outwardly, you are confident but inwardly you are emotionally vulnerable.
Gentle Spirit 479, 794, 947	If you are a 479, you are intuitive, innovative and accepting. You want to be original, positive and peaceful. You are identified with the defense of optimism and tend to hide your painful feelings and pessimism for fear of being rejected. You see the wonder in beauty and are tender-hearted, lyrical and idealistic. You are attracted to the healing arts.

Tritype™ with Instinctual Type

The Tritype™ Stacking (the order in which one uses the three types) and Instinctual Stacking (the order in which one uses the three instincts) are interacting parts of a complex defense system designed to ensure survival. One's Instinctual Stacking identifies one's more 'primitive' nature and is the most fundamental part of the personality structure. One's Tritype™ combination is the more specific way in which one will handle incoming threats to one's security, as identified by the values of the Instinctual Stacking.

There are three instinctual drives that govern the manner in which one will focus on survival. In the context of the Enneagram, these three drives, or 'instincts,' are referred to as self-preservation (sp)--the search for safety, security and well-being, social (so)--the search for others, groups and community, and sexual (sx)--the search for a mate, excitement, closeness and one to one bonds.

Whether consciously expressed or not, one will exhibit all three of these instinctual drives to varying degrees throughout the day. Each Enneagram type is influenced by these instinctual drives, but one is dominant, and more influential than the other two. This is called one's dominant instinctual type. The nine Enneagram types combined with the three instinctual drives results in 27 Instinctual Subtypes.

When the needs of the dominant Instinctual Subtype are unmet, the personality goes on "red alert." The instincts are automatic and cannot relax if there is *any* perceived threat, whether real or imagined. The personality reacts to *all* threats even if they are minor. The personality compulsively seeks a solution to meet the demands of the dominant instinct in the Instinctual Stacking, and the dominant type in the Tritype™ Stacking. *Therefore, combining the core fears of the Instinctual Types with the core fears of the types in the Tritype™ reveals one's habitual way of relating to the world.*

For example, a sexual 874 is someone who focuses on having a mate (sx) and power (8 + sx) to survive. If there is a threat to the primary relationship (sx), the 8 within the Tritype™ will attempt to secure the mate and restore calm. The Tritype™ of 874 with the sexual instinct dominant is someone that is focused on maintaining the strength of the intimate bond (sx) by having power and influence (sx + 8). In addition to focusing on a mate (sx), this person would also focus on being strong and direct (8), positive and innovative (7) and seeking unique and meaningful solutions (4).

The unmet need of the sexual instinct triggers the defense strategies of the 874. The sexual instinct deploys the Type 8, which in turn deploys the 7 and 4 in the Tritype™. So, if the Type 8 fails to overcome an obstacle (and all lines of connection and wing defenses), the ego would then employ the strategies of Type 7 to lighten up and examine other potential options. If the problem remains unresolved, the Type 8 would then use the strategies of Type 4 to delve more deeply into the problem to find an answer.

Also, combining the Tritype™ Stacking with the Instinctual Stacking can help to explain why people with the same Enneagram type and instinct can still behave differently from one another. For example, we can compare and contrast the sexual type of the earlier example of the 874 with the sexual 826. With the sexual 874 and the sexual 826, we will notice that the sexual 874 has different secondary and tertiary motivations than a sexual 826. All sexual 8s want to have a mate, as well as power to avoid being harmed, controlled and/or manipulated. However, the 874 is the 'Messenger' 8 that must be protective, autonomous (8), innovative (7) and deep (4) to feel satisfaction, whereas the 826 is the 'Rescuer' 8, that must be protective (8), helpful , loyal and dutiful (6) to feel satisfaction.

Levels of functioning within Tritype™

Just as with the primary Enneagram type, one will experience the other types in their Tritype™ in both positive and negative ways. They act in concert with one another.

Any Tritype™ Archetype can be delightful or difficult depending on the psychological health of the individual. To understand how this works in practice, one needs to examine the psychological health and spiritual awareness of an individual. If one is functioning at an average level or higher, one will display the positive traits of the types in the Tritype™. If one is functioning at a lower level, one will display the negative traits of the types in the Tritype™. The level of health and spiritual awareness will be the same for all three types in the Tritype™.

Conclusion

The Tritype™ can thus be an incredibly rich addition to existing Enneagram theory and helps to explain important distinctions in type that could not otherwise be explained through dominant type, lines of connection, wings or instinct. The notion that individuals employ three type strategies, which create an archetypal composite, provides individuals with rich insight into their core fears, core triggers, life purpose, and blind spot, which in turn can affect personal growth. Extensive research and in-depth coaching sessions have revealed that understanding one's Tritype™ has created greater self-understanding, and been particularly useful to those who have been working with Enneagram concepts for some time and hit a proverbial "wall" in self-growth and discovery. Further research will focus on the intersection of the Instinctual Types, Subtypes and Tritype™ Archetypes, as it is clear from the research studies of the Instinctual Types and Tritype™s, that it is the primary instinct that sets the Tritype™ strategies in motion. Since this is such a vast and complex body of work, the authors will conduct additional studies to more fully understand how the instincts affect the deployment of the types in the Tritype™.

References

Chernick, K. K. H. (1995) *Enneastyle: The 9 Languages of Enneagram Type* (3rd ed.). Menlo Park, CA: Enneagram Explorations.

Chernick, K. K. H. (1995). *Enneagram Instinctual Subtypes* (4th ed.). Menlo Park, CA: Enneagram Explorations.

Chernick, K. K. H. (1996). *The Enneagram and the World of Image and Self-Projection Part I.* Enneagram Monthly, January, 1.

Chernick, K. K. H. (1996). *The Enneagram and the World of Image and Self-Projection Part II.* Enneagram Monthly, February, 12.

Chernick, K.H., (1996) *Reflections on Type; A Workshop with Claudio Naranjo,* Enneagram Monthly. July. 13

Chernick, K.K.H., Ruderman, V. and Snyder, K. (1998). *Enneagram, Instinctual Subtype and Intimacy.* Menlo Park, CA: Presentation for the Association of Enneagram Teachers in the Oral Tradition, Asilomar, Monterey CA.

Chernick, K.K.H. (1998) *A Study of the Instinctual Subtypes.* Enneagram Educator. Winter, Volume IX number 2.

Chernick, K. (1998) *Enneagram Instinctual Subtypes.* IEA Conference Presentation, Denver, CO. July/Aug. '98, pg. 18

Chernick, K.K.H., Ruderman V. and Snyder K. (1998) *Enneagram, Instinctual Subtype and Intimacy.* Menlo Park, CA: Presentation International Enneagram Association Conference 2004, Washington, DC.

Fauvre, K. C. (2005) *A Study of Instinctual Subtypes.* Enneagram Monthly, *Jan* (111), 1.

Fauvre, K. C., & Fauvre, D. W. (2010). *The 27 Tritypes™ Revealed: Discover Your Life Purpose and Blind Spot* (6th ed.). Menlo Park, CA: Enneagram Explorations.

THE AMERICAN MYTH OF PROGRESS: AN ENNEAGRAM PERSPECTIVE

Gina Thomas, MA

Abstract

The Enneagram and depth psychology inform each other in this analysis of American culture, and together they provide a richer view of the cultural psyche of the U.S. than either field could do alone. Utilizing archival material from depth psychologists and mythologists, the author suggests that the United States operates under a collective "myth of progress," and explores the distinct parallels between how these scholars have assessed the origins and development of this myth in American culture and how the Enneagram describes the type Three pattern. Manifestations of types Six and Nine, the two points connected to Three, are discussed, along with insights from Jungian typology. Bridging the Enneagram with depth psychology allows for a fuller interpretation of the American myth of progress and how the type Three pattern plays out on a cultural level.

In Enneagram literature one finds sporadic but consistent references to United States culture embodying the type Three pattern. Statements like, "America is the land of the Three" (Goldberg, 1999, p. 88) and "North American culture is largely Three" (Palmer, 1995, p. 89) reflect what has in effect become common knowledge in the Enneagram field. The United States' cultural norms of progress, achievement and competition seem to match Enneagram type Three's personality fixation, in which personal feelings are neglected while image, performance and success get priority.

When we participate in a culture, we also participate in its collective myth. The ethos, or collective spirit, of a country can often be identified by a few predominant qualities that motivate and affect its citizens as a collective body. During the 20th century, America reigned as the most prosperous country in the world, full of resources, capital, entrepreneurship, and the prospect of unlimited growth. How do we reconcile this with the fact that Americans today are the most in debt, addicted, busy, obese and medicated society in the world? (Brown, 2010) Taken together, these phenomena illuminate a prevailing psychological pattern that dominates our collective identity in the United States, a pattern that I call the myth of progress.

This American cultural myth has political and economic roots as well as implications, but the focus of this essay is on its psychological aspects. This paper[1] examines the American myth of progress through both the Enneagram, a model of psychological functioning most commonly applied to individual personality (Palmer, 1995), and depth psychology, the study of unconscious patterns, myth, dreams and symbols. Both fields pay close attention to the psychological structures that shape our beliefs and filter our perceptions. Depth psychology calls these archetypes (Tarnas, 2006), while the Enneagram refers to these simply as types, describing nine basic type structures in total (Daniels & Price, 2009). These types or archetypes are patterns of meaning, showing up in both conscious and unconscious experiences. They can be applied to individual personality as well as to larger scales of psychological functioning, including cultural patterns (Singer & Kimbles, 2004). The Enneagram literature has demonstrated that while one Enneagram type tends to characterize our psyche, several other types play supporting roles (Palmer, 1995; Riso & Hudson, 1999). The same can be said for cultural patterns. This paper therefore explores one of the major collective myths of U.S. culture—the myth of progress—which I suggest parallels the type Three pattern in the Enneagram. This is not to say that other Enneagram patterns or other archetypal themes are not at work as well; only that type Three is currently very pronounced. Furthermore, the purpose of this paper is not to pathologize any particular Enneagram type, but rather to more deeply understand what happens when a stressed Enneagram pattern plays itself out on the cultural stage.

The Case for America as a Type Three Culture

The Enneagram describes type Three as a success-oriented performer, a pattern that revolves around image, efficiency, competition, goals, and a can-do attitude. These qualities result in an adaptable achiever, one who understands what it takes to succeed in a given environment and has the ambition to do so. Underneath this drive for accomplishment lies the belief that a successful performance is the way to secure value and approval (Palmer, 1988). However, confusion can arise around identity, as "what I do" becomes "who I am," and high productivity masks deeper feelings. Perhaps even more than achieving actual success, achieving a successful *image* is the hallmark of type Three. Chameleon-like Threes assess the values and ideals shared by an admired other and then masterfully adapt themselves to display those preferred qualities. In short, Threes seek to impress. They work hard to appear successful in the eyes of others.

Enneagram authors who describe type Three can sound like they are describing American values, from packaging the self as a commodity (Riso & Hudson, 1999) to working hard to be the best and maintain a good image (Daniels & Price, 2009). In the type Three paradigm, "Your worth depends upon

---

1 I often use the word "we" when referring to Americans as a way of acknowledging that as the author of this essay, I include myself (as an American) in this psychological analysis.

how well you can sell yourself or how marketable you are" (Wagner, 1996, p. 60). Helen Palmer sums up the North American type Three outlook: "We reward youth and vitality. We support a competitive marketing system. We expect to be propagandized by the media" (Palmer, 1995, p. 89). Indeed, America is immersed in media that feed on advertising, where products and lifestyle images are sold as tickets to health, wealth and happiness. This focus on selling and promotional advertising reinforces the type Three motto of "Sell yourself." America is famous for its systems of efficiency in transportation, industry and commerce, and as Americans we are infamous for our fast pace, busy lives and multi-tasking abilities. Adults and children alike spend many of their waking hours in competitive jobs, competitive schools, and competitive sports, so much so that being highly active and involved becomes a marker for success even as they become overworked and under connected (Doherty & Carlson, 2003). Rather than having to contend with the dilemma of too much leisure time and a four-day work week, which was predicted in the 1960's as the social problem of the 21st century, Americans today are instead facing more hours on the job for less pay than their 1960's counterparts (Taylor, 2003). "Lots of folks pretend to be Threes, sometimes without knowing it," writes Michael Goldberg, "in a culture where our identity seems to hinge on our material achievement and success" (Goldberg, 1999, p. 88).

In his observations of American culture, Swiss psychoanalyst C. G. Jung noticed this national obsession with success and productivity, and described the European view of Americans as being, "a very active, business-like, and astonishingly efficient people, concentrated upon a single goal" (Jung, 1964, p. 502). But he was insightful enough to see that it was not simply about money. In his essay titled, "The Complications of American Psychology," he wrote:

> America has a principle or idea or attitude, but it is surely not money. Often, when I was searching through the conscious and the unconscious mind of my American patients and pupils, I found something which I can only describe as a sort of Heroic Ideal. Your most idealistic effort is concerned with bringing out the best in every man, and when you find a good man you naturally support him and push him on, until at last he is liable to collapse from sheer exertion, success, and triumph. It is done in every family, where ambitious mothers egg their boys on with the idea that they must be heroes of some sort, or you find it in the factory, where the whole system anxiously tries to get the best man into the best place. Or again in the schools where every child is trained to be brave, courageous, efficient, and a "good sport," a hero in short. There is no record which people will not kill themselves to break, even if it is the most appalling nonsense. The moving pictures abound with heroes of every description...America is perhaps the only country where 'greatness' is unrestricted, because it expresses the most fundamental hopes, desires, ambitions, and convictions of the nation. (Jung, 1964, p. 512-513)

Jung's astute assessment of the American attitude aligns remarkably with Enneagram type Three. Two powerful forces fueling the American dream are the rags to riches story and the collective fantasy of unlimited progress. Type Three is built to perform, and the American paradigm of earning one's worth through hard work and merit reinforces the type Three psychological pattern.

America as the land of the self-made individual

The roots of type Three as a quintessentially American motif can be traced back to the nation's focus on individualism. For most of human history, survival meant conforming to and supporting the group. Joseph Campbell wrote, "To sum up the whole lesson of the world of the past, one may say that in traditional societies all meaning is in the group, none in the individual" (Campbell, 121). Only in the last few hundred years has the term "individual" had meaning of any consequence. Now people are encouraged to be self-sufficient, to follow their personal dreams and goals, and to accomplish something for themselves. Indeed, personal ambition has practically become a requirement for adulthood in America. Campbell noted that today, "Heroism has become democratized" and each person is expected to pursue his own goals and chart her own course. He refers to this phenomenon as, "that precious respect for the individual which is the spiritual banner of our Christian-Democratic state" (Campbell, 121). The task of the individual is nothing less than to create his or her own identity, to fashion it out of one's own impetus, ability and interests. This is the American version of free will.

Type Three in many ways epitomizes this spirit of individuals on their own trajectories. For a Three, hope lies in one's accomplishments, buoyed—for better or worse—by one's own merit, talent, and resources. When we succeed, we congratulate ourselves and expect to be congratulated by others on our efforts. The scant social supports America has built into its government sends a not-so-subtle message to its citizens that we must depend on ourselves and build up our own resources. We make it or break it on our own abilities. Indeed, capability may be the strength America values most. What other nations might call interdependence or even basic rights, Americans would call "asking for a handout." For Americans, there's no such thing as a free lunch. In America, we must earn it ourselves, and we are taught to be proud to do so. Although this brief analysis of individualism in America is compelling in and of itself, Jung suggested that underneath the American's self-reliant façade was a group-oriented conformist.

Identification with the group

Jung noted how dependent Americans are on the approval of peers, how susceptible we are to popularity, and how public are our identities:

You are simply reduced to a particle in the mass, with no other hope or expectation than the illusory goals of an eager and excited collectivity. You just swim for life, that's all. You feel free—that's the queerest thing—yet the collective movement grips you faster than any old gnarled roots in European soil... If it were possible, everything would be done collectively, because there seems to be an astonishingly feeble resistance to collective influences. (Jung, 1964, p. 505-506)

Jung was astute in seeing through the individualistic ideal of American culture to what runs beneath: collectivity and conformity. His analysis prompts us to ask ourselves: Are we Americans in fact pursuing our personal dreams and goals, or are we caught up in replicating the collective values around us and channeling our ambitions toward external goals sanctified by the culture? Are we truly individualistic at all? I offer the perspective that many of our personal ambitions and competitive impulses conform to the collective myth of progress, best illustrated in the slogan, "Keeping up with the Joneses." The American dream of wealth earned through opportunism and hard work propels us ever forward, and we measure our worth against the images propagated by advertising media. Our perceived value lies in our ability to project the right image, acquire the right stuff, and achieve the right goals. Comparison of status is fueled by an extraverted orientation, in which we look primarily outward instead of inward. Jung had something to say about this:

The most amazing feature of American life is its boundless publicity. Everybody has to meet everybody, and they even seem to enjoy this enormity. To a central European such as I am, this American publicity of life, the lack of distance between people, the absence of hedges or fences round the gardens, the belief in popularity, the gossip columns of the newspapers, the open doors in the houses... the defenselessness of the individual against the onslaught of the press, all this is... positively terrifying. (Jung, 1964, p. 506)

This public persona is outwardly focused and necessarily extraverted, which is why Jung, a self-identified introvert, would have found it so terrifying.

Jungian analyst Joseph Wheelwright elaborated on Jung's personality typology when he described the extraverted American psyche: "An unconscious extravert values the outer object and fears his own inner self. In our riotously extraverted country, this attitude is evident in our love of groups, good-mixers, and outgoing people" (Wheelwright, 104). Two things are important in Wheelwright's observation. First, the description of extraversion as "unconscious" in the American psyche, and second, the corresponding fear of one's inner self. I argue that it is this quality of unconscious, collective extraversion that contributes to the tension between the individualistic ideal and our collective conformity. Perpetual extraversion leads one to place more attention and value on what is happening in the outside world, with other people, places and events. The unconscious aspect can cause one to forget, resist and repress what is going on inside, in the inner world of subjective feelings and values. If this happens for too long, the estrangement from one's inner self can lead to fear and to further repression. Wheelwright's observation aligns with the psychology of Enneagram type Three, where competition and efficient performance are hallmarks:

> In our highly competitive life, one attitude is more or less dammed up to produce an apparently more efficient performance, and a definite type is established. However, it is never possible to completely suppress introversion, as both attitudes are basic psychological factors in every individual. (Wheelwright, 104)

Type Three should not be conflated with extraversion, for many individuals who identify with type Three also identify as introverts. Jung originally described extraversion as an externalized attitude, or outward orientation, rather than the quality of sociability (Jung, 1971). For type Three as an archetypal pattern, the inward orientation of feelings—especially so-called negative feelings—might slow down efficiency, especially if they contradict with external goals. When we are in the grip of type Three, our own desires, emotions and opinions are undervalued for the sake of embodying the right image and achieving the goal. To pursue a goal directed by one's own inner feelings may not be rewarded or noticed by anyone else. In fact, it may directly oppose collective values. When we are in Type Three we use a psychological process called *identification* in order to shape ourselves to become like the valued people or prototypes we were exposed to when young: a parent, a favorite teacher, a performer, an athlete. Threes are "particularly susceptible to identification because they look to others for approval and can therefore mobilize a lot of energy to change into what other people want" (Palmer, 1988, p. 156).

Depth psychologist James Hillman encourages us not to condemn identification. He considers it a beginning stage in the development of feeling and relationships. "No stage of a relationship should be discarded," he writes. "Identification, in fact, helps understanding, grasping the basic need of the other which we can only feel through identification with him" (Hillman, 130). In the Three pattern if our worth is attached to gaining others' approval, then identification is necessary. If we don't stop and identify what our parents, teachers, peers and/or bosses value, we risk not knowing how to relate to them. We say the wrong thing. We pursue the wrong goal. If we don't look outward for successful prototypes to model ourselves after, how are we going to succeed? We might risk looking different or being cast out. Our survival depends on identification. The result? The Enneagram describes the type Three's fixated state bluntly: deception (Palmer, 1988). In a Three culture, we are vulnerable to deceiving ourselves and others in our quest to impress.

Type Three manifested in national events

To support this interpretation of America as the land of the Three caught up in the myth of progress, we can look to national events and patterns. America continues to uphold the myth of unlimited progress while ignoring dwindling resources, ecological disasters from oil spills to hurricanes, and increasing disparity between the wealthy and the poor. This cultural myth of progress faced a severe challenge with the banking crisis of 2008 and the collapse of financial markets not just in America but worldwide. Deception—the Achilles heel of type

Three—played out on several levels in this financial drama. At one level, consumers were deceived by lenders and financial authorities by promises of material goods that until then had been beyond their reach. At another level, the lenders and traders deceived themselves by ignoring predictable cycles of the market, placing their hopes in a never-ending Bull market, and inflating the value of what they were buying and selling. The financial crisis is a painful but excellent example of what happens when a cultural myth—in this case, the myth of progress—plays out its story in the collective. In some way, perhaps Americans were willing to be deceived, in that self-deception was necessary in order to keep the myth alive, to keep believing that growth is unlimited and that perhaps we, too, cannot just keep up with the Joneses, but can become them.

Such self-deception creates enormous stress. Two outlets for this stress are fear and apathy, hallmarks of Enneagram types Six and Nine, respectively. In the Enneagram, psychological functioning is viewed as a dynamic system, in which each type is connected on the diagram with two other types. For type Three, these dynamic movements are toward Six and Nine. Highlighting the Six and Nine perspectives helps to further demonstrate how the psychological pattern of type Three operates in the American psyche.

Type Six: The hyper-vigilant watchdog

Fear and paranoia are typical of type Six when stressed, and as a nation the United States moved into this position after the attacks on the World Trade Center on 9/11. We as a nation are now on constant high-alert with a daily warning from the government that we are at "Threat Level Orange." This results in intense feelings of vulnerability, which is managed defensively by becoming hyper-vigilant. A typical Six reaction to such threat is to draw a sharp distinction between the in-group and the out-group. Patriotism and solidarity are key, and the "other" is identified as an enemy to be avoided or defeated. After 9/11 the "other" was explicitly named the Axis of Evil, activating a typical stressed Six response of in-group favoritism and out-group hostility. The Patriot Act, which allowed unprecedented access into private lives, showcased a Six-like paranoia and suspicion. The dominant question was, "Who can be trusted?" There was a high need to know who was friend and who was foe. From the Six perspective, the world is uncertain, and great defenses are erected in order to create the illusion of security. Formerly called the War Department, the renamed Department of Defense symbolically reflects the Six mode of defensively reacting to what is unknown[2]. For example, the President's proposed federal budget for fiscal year 2013 outlays 57% of discretionary spending for the military (Federal Budget, 2012). The banking crisis of 2008 reinforced the message that we live in uncertain times, and the collapse of the housing market in particular threatened one of our basic forms of security. Finally, the government's launching of the

2 I credit my colleague Charles Miller for sharing this insight with me.

"War on Terror," in which the enemy is everywhere and nowhere, amplified the emotional core of type Six—fear—to epic proportions.

Anxiety and fear are key terms for the Six position, and the consequences of this shift from Three to Six show up in rates of anxiety in Americans. According to the National Institute of Mental Health, 25% of American teens and 28% of adults are diagnosed with an anxiety disorder (NIMH, 2012). In a meta-analysis of psychopathology rates of adolescents from 1937-2007, psychologist Jean Twenge notes significant generational increases in anxiety and depression, meaning that as time has passed, recent birth cohorts have more incidents of these disorders, even after controlling for changes in diagnostic criteria (Twenge, 2010). Twenge offers several potential contributors to this phenomenon: increased narcissism; individualism; a consumer culture; unrealistic expectations for success; and the tendency to focus on extrinsic goals (such as status and money) rather than intrinsic goals (such as community and affiliation). Her conclusions support what the map of the Enneagram symbol charts as the logical progression of a stressed Three, with its focus on extrinsic goals, to the land of the anxious and fearful Six.

As archetypal patterns, each Enneagram type contains positive and negative manifestations of the core psychological structure. This means that when Three enters the territory of Six, both positive and negative tendencies can be accessed. Six emerges positively as the archetypal watchdog, and this development can also be seen in recent national events. Soon after the financial crisis of 2008 new agencies and committees sprang to life, including the Congressional Oversight Panel, designed to monitor financial regulation and the U.S. Treasury's actions, and the Consumer Financial Protection Agency, which aimed to create more transparency in financial markets and thereby protect citizens from deceit. Given the role of the United States as a global superpower, its political and economic crises cannot be easily contained within its borders. On a global scale, we can see the American myth of progress that has transformed industries and markets worldwide shifting to type Six with the birth of WikiLeaks, an international non-profit organization dedicated to exposing critical information formerly kept "classified" and hidden from the general public. For a Six, uncovering hidden motives is crucial in a world that feels threatening. With WikiLeaks, the Six watchdog turns whistleblower, exposing secrets that aim to dismantle oppressive regimes.

Type Nine: The numbed consumer

Stress on type Three can also lead to apathy, the position of type Nine. The Nine defense mechanism is narcotization, which translates into numbing feelings of discomfort, pain or conflict. Depth psychologist James Hillman noted this tendency in the American psyche when he wrote that one of the consequences of repressed feeling was *approxia*, a close cousin to apathy. "In modern day language it would mean the taking of tranquilizers" (Hillman, 130). This desire for a freedom from pain lands us squarely in the pharmacy. Although arguments can be made both for and against the use of anti-depressants, the objective facts show that physicians saw a 400% increase in antidepressant use between 1994 and 2008 for both teens and adults in the U.S. (Wehrwein, 2011). We can read these increases in anti-depressant usage as well as the high anxiety rates cited earlier as symptoms of a pattern gone too far.

Self-medicating takes many forms, from food to pharmaceuticals, compulsive shopping to workaholism. Our culture of consumption encourages this, illustrated pointedly in both our obesity rates and our credit card debt. The endorsement to go out and shop as a way to demonstrate our patriotism after the 9/11 attacks reinforced what the Enneagram calls "appetite" in the type Nine psychology—the instinct to consume in order to numb any type of discomfort. These self-medicating patterns aid us in repressing internal feeling states that we are not prepared to deal with. To acknowledge them might only upset the entrenched belief in unlimited progress and impede the unrelenting drive for success. But high rates of unemployment have already threatened this belief, and a lack of productive work can lead to apathy.

We have seen that while the U.S. culture has accessed positive aspects of type Six, such as protective vigilance and an increased sense of responsibility, the virtues of Nine – stillness, idleness, the ability to not "do" anything but to simply "be" – have largely remained untapped in the American psyche. Stillness and idleness are often pre-requisites for creativity and contemplation (Storr, 1988), outcomes which can get derailed by the need for stimulation and entertainment during downtime. Instead of reaping the potential for restorative idleness at Nine, we heed the magnetic pull of our addictions – shopping, watching television, plugging into our various devices, working, eating, drinking, etc. – all of which invite self-neglect rather than self-care.

Type Three as the wounded feeler

The American dream promised that with enough hard work, ingenuity and verve, we could indeed accomplish whatever we set our minds to. That spirit—what Jung called the Heroic Ideal—has in many ways served America well, and it is also part of the gift of the type Three. However, the myth of unlimited progress and personal success, which has sustained our capitalist market and democratic forms of government for the past several hundred years, appears to be fracturing. What, then, are we to do? This is a quintessentially type Three question. The Three psychology is built on self-propelled action. The starting point for resolving the current crisis, however, may not be to "do" anything, but rather to "feel" something. In fact, the habit of type Three is one of "shifting attention from real feelings in the interest of efficiency in order to 'do' the image that a task requires" (Palmer, 1988, p. 156). Accomplishment becomes a tangible way of securing acceptance. If one neglects inner subjective feelings—if they are dismissed, rationalized or otherwise ignored—then external goals can be pursued without obstacle. Repressed feeling is a necessary ingredient for self-deception, the vice of type Three.

James Hillman cites modern American culture as an example of exhibiting what he calls "wounded" feeling. "Feeling in our culture has become a problem, and our personal feeling problems are partly a collective result of ages of repression" (Hillman, 130). Hillman's assessment of wounded feeling aligns with the psychology of Enneagram type Three, which is understood as being most out of touch with one's own feelings and most attuned to collective attitudes (Riso & Hudson, 1999). Jung defined feeling as a process of imparting a value judgment. "Feeling is a kind of *judging*, differing, however, from an intellectual judgment, in that it does not aim at establishing an intellectual connection, but is solely concerned with the setting up of a subjective criterion of acceptance or rejection" (Hillman, 130). This is an accurate representation of how the feeling function appears in type Three. There is sensitivity to being accepted or rejected, liked or disliked. The focus is on how other people are affirming and approving them, and the Three's own internal evaluation rests on these external reflections. Type Three's curious position of holding the center point of the Feeling triad on the Enneagram diagram while at the same time manifesting a psychological pattern built on the neglect of feelings, can be partially understood by the distinctions of introverted and extraverted feeling in Jung's typology.

Insight into type Three from Jungian typology

Jung described extraverted feeling as harmonizing with externally held values generally held by the group or culture at large (Jung, 1971). Motivations for the expression of extraverted feeling include maintaining a cordial atmosphere, being sensitive to the politics of a situation, and adjusting oneself to how others are feeling. Without extraverted feeling, "a harmonious social life would be impossible" (Jung, 1971, p. 355). Such accord with external, "objective" factors, (e.g. current trends, the atmosphere, other people, etc.) can sometimes curtail the expression of internal, subjective feelings if these feelings clash with the generally accepted attitudes or values "out there." When taken to an extreme, extraverted feeling loses any authenticity, and a person can give the impression of posing, playing a chameleon, of saying "the right thing" without any genuine spirit behind it. This description is in accord with Enneagram type Three.

Meanwhile, an under-development of the introverted feeling function results in a lack of connection with subjective feelings, values, and preferences. In the mode of introverted feeling, the feeling states are intensive rather than extensive and "develop in depth" (Jung, 1971, p. 390). The expression of feelings is intimate and selective, often shared within the boundaries of trusted relationships, a private journal, or creative outlets in which the internal world can be articulated, processed and interpreted. However, in an extraverted culture such as America, a focus on outward attitudes, goals and relationships help to distract one from this inner world, and this can create a split between inner feelings and public self.

Viewing type Three from the Jungian typology lens—as tending to over-do extraverted feeling and under-do introverted feeling—sheds light on a potential path of growth for our type Three culture. "Our feeling problems are not just *our personal* problems," writes James Hillman. "They are a collective problem. And therefore any change you or I make in ourselves in the differentiation of feeling can only be seen as heroic, because this change is part of the collective redemption of repressed feeling life" (Hillman, 130).

The psychological task of a type Three culture

Developing the feeling function may itself be a heroic act. Our psychological task as a type Three culture may be to re-connect specifically with introverted feeling. Paradoxically, type Three with its heroic energy can actually help us develop this feeling function. The spiritual and higher psychological qualities of type Three include hope and honesty, and it is these two qualities that are especially necessary to heal wounded feeling. In dark times, hope chases away fear. Hope gives us a reason to believe in ourselves again; it gives us the energy and commitment to look inward. As for honesty, part of developing our feeling function is accepting the range of feelings we have. Anxiety, sorrow, disappointment and anger are just as much a part of introverted feeling as are joy, satisfaction, awe and enthusiasm. Introverted feeling takes us to the task of re-examining our values and evaluating our standards for love, work, and ethics, and then aligning our lives with a credo that conveys our own unique spirit and authentically connects us with the spirit of the collective. Because the collective American feeling function is under-developed, we may at first be immature at locating it and expressing it. Here is Hillman's advice:

The development of the feeling function therefore requires only two things: involvement with people, and involvement with oneself. The first is given us by life, and the second too, through our own feeling reactions to our own inner world of dreams, emotions, conflicts, and experiences, best carried out in a kind of diary or intimate journal, which gives form to what we are feeling. (Hillman, 130)

During the past few years, social media via the Internet has created multiple forums for people to express their own feelings—through blogs, chat rooms, Facebook updates, and Twitter accounts, just to name a few. But is this the development of the feeling function that Hillman says our culture needs? Perhaps not. My assessment is that social media is exactly that: social. It fuels our ability to do *extraverted* feeling, but for the most part still leaves our "inner world of dreams, emotions, conflicts, and experiences" unattended to in an intrapersonal way. Instead we are tempted to parade them through the public sphere. We deliver them to an audience to be commented on and rated with a "Like" on Facebook by hundreds of "friends." We thereby run the risk of reproducing the type Three pattern: treating feelings as commodities to be valued and traded, accepted or rejected, by the evaluation of the social group. In the meantime, introverted feeling, that wounded function of American culture, continues to starve in the basement of our collective shadow.

Introverted feeling requires time, solitude and silence, states not easily obtained in our extraverted culture, with its ubiquitous media, traffic and pressure to perform. As Anthony Storr noted in his book *Solitude*, "What goes on in the human being when he is by himself is as important as what happens in his interactions with other people" (Storr, 1988, p. xiv). This is not the self-absorption or isolation that can come with an exclusive focus on the self, but the creativity and reflection that can emerge from time spent in solitude. Such creativity and reflection are necessary if we are to confront the private crises of apathy and fear, and the public crises of ecological and financial collapse. Releasing ourselves from the need to succeed or be accepted according to external standards starts to release us from identification and self-deception. It gives us permission to dig down and reconnect with our values and face feelings that may be uncomfortable, painful or full of regret. This type of honest self-reflection may be a starting point to balance the tendencies toward extraversion and extrinsic goals that are so representative of being in the grip of type Three and the American myth of progress. Introverted feeling can be seen as the bright light at the end of the Three's tunnel, with its psychological virtues of hope and honesty, and represents also a bright light for American culture. It will not be easy, and it will not solve all of our crises. But it is something we can do, and we have the tools in our type Three American psychological make-up: hope, honesty and the will to succeed.

Acknowledgements

This research was made possible by a New Mythos research grant from the OPUS Archives at Pacifica Graduate Institute in Santa Barbara, CA. Many thanks to OPUS Librarian Richard Buchen for his guidance and insight during my time at the archives. Thank you to Dr. Meredith Sabini, Sandi Peters, and Benjamin Long for providing feedback and suggesting revisions to this paper.

References

Brown, B. (2010). The power of vulnerability. Retrieved February 15, 2011, from http://www.ted.com/talks/brene_brown_on_vulnerability.html.

Campbell, J. OPUS Archives and Research Center. Joseph Campbell Collection, Box 121. Series: Outtakes, The Modern Condition.

Campbell, J. Transcription of a Lecture at The New School for Social Research, NYC. Myths to Live By. No date. OPUS Archives and Research Center. U42 X-Ref: L991.

Campbell, J. (1970) Audio Lecture. The psychological basis of freedom: Is modern man different? OPUS Archives and Research Center.

Daniels, D. and Price, V. (2009) *The essential Enneagram*. New York: Harper Collins.

Doherty, W. and Carlson, B. (2003) Overscheduled kids, underconnected families. In *Take back your time* (J. de Graaf, Ed.). pp. 38-45. San Francisco: Berrett-Koehler Publishers, Inc.

Federal budget 101: Where does the money go? (n.d.). Retrieved May 13, 2012, from http://nationalpriorities.org/en/budget-basics/federal-budget-101/spending/

Goldberg, M. (1999) *The 9 ways of working.* New York: Marlowe and Company.

Hillman, J. OPUS Archives and Research Center. James Hillman Collection, Box 130. Series: Feeling Function—Notes on various lectures.

Hurley, K. and Dobson, T. (1991) *What's my type?* New York: Harper Collins.

Jung, C. G. (1964) The complications of American psychology. (R.F.C. Hull, Trans.), *Civilization in Transition.* (pp. 502-514). Pantheon Books.

Jung, C.G. (1971) General description of the types. (R.F.C. Hull, Trans.), *The collected works of C.G. Jung.* (2nd ed., Vol. 6, pp. 330-407). Princeton, NJ: Princeton University Press.

National Institute of Mental Health. (2012) Retrieved January 30, 2012, from http://www.nimh.nih.gov/statistics/1ANYANX_ child.html.

Palmer, H. (1988) *The Enneagram.* New York: Harper Collins.

Palmer, H. (1995) *The Enneagram in love and work.* New York: Harper Collins.

Riso, D. and Hudson, R. (1999) *The wisdom of the Enneagram.* New York: Bantam Books.

Singer, T. and Kimbles, S. (2004) *The cultural complex: Contemporary Jungian perspectives on psyche and society.* New York: Brunner-Routledge.

Storr, A. (1988) *Solitude: A return to the self.* New York: Free Press.

Tarnas, R. (2006) *Cosmos and psyche.* New York: Penguin Books.

Taylor, B. (2003). Recapturing childhood. In *Take back your time* (J. de Graaf, Ed.). pp. 46-52. San Francisco: Berrett-Koehler Publishers, Inc.

Twenge, J., *et al.* (2010) Birth cohort increases in psychopathology among young Americans, 1938-2007: A cross-temporal meta-analysis of the MMPI. *Clinical Psychology Review, 30,* 145-154.

Wagner, J. (1996) *An Introduction to the Enneagram.* New York: MJF Books.

Wehrwein, P. (2011) Astounding increase in antidepressant use by Americans. In *Harvard Health Blog.* http://www.health.harvard.edu/blog/astounding-increase-in-antidepressant-use-by-americans-201110203624. Retrieved January 30, 2012.

Wheelwright, J. OPUS Archives and Research Center. Joseph Wheelwright Collection, Box 104. Series 1: Jung's Psychological Types.

ENNEAGRAM ENRICHMENT

Clarence Thomson

All right. You know your nine styles, 18 stress and security points, 18 wings and 27 subtypes. With this basic Enneagram, you have a formidable diagnostic tool and template for personal growth. So how might one use all the lovely lively self-help books as you try to integrate all their helpful insights into your template?

I will employ the traditional debate axiom, "Never deny, seldom affirm and always distinguish." That is, I am not going to try to demonstrate some kind of superiority of the Enneagram, nor will I even approve of the self help books I treat. Instead, I will try to integrate the Enneagram with some of the popular books. This may entail distinctions the Enneagram can bring to the discussion of personal and business growth.

Full disclosure. The Enneagram acknowledges bias. I do style Seven, so I will begin with a book whose title seduces a Seven's attention: *The Happiness Advantage,* by Shawn Achor. a Harvard professor. His seminal thesis is that the traditional formula is broken. Conventional wisdom has it that "If you succeed, you will be happy." We, as a culture, hold this truth to be self-evident and Achor says this is backwards. You begin by being happy and then you will be successful. He slithers from "happiness" to "being positive," early in his work, but this Harvard researcher (and his work fairly bristles with academic footnoted credentials) has evolved far from the Norman Vincent Peale tradition of smiling in the rain.

Achor provides seven principles of happiness. Neurological bliss flows from being positive, our aperture determines what we see, we need to see what we haven't seen before, focus is crucial, we need to be creative after a setback and our experience is (almost) determined by our outlook. He has another principle that says that we need to "invest socially." We deal with stress and difficulty best by having a strong network of family, friends etc. This is not a happy meal for the Fives among us. He has a principle I've not seen before: "The tetris effect," which means that if you think of something a lot, you'll see possibilities that you couldn't see before. (Tetris is a computer game that plays with shapes).

An Enneagram student will see all these as good ideas and workable practices, but we have a deep appreciation of how difficult it is to change one's view of the world. We also know that, as with most self-help books, the advice is usually a bit too conscious. Telling someone, or resolving to make a conscious change has a trail littered with broken conscious resolutions.

This cognitive confidence shows up in friendly advice like "to be happy, do something you are good at." If you oblige him by confining this to technical things like baking, driving a forklift or playing the piano, that might work. But let's say you are a Five and what you are good at is collecting information. To solve or salve your problem, you go get some more information. Not if you know the Enneagram –that's how you mired down in the first place.

Achor, Harvard sheltered, assumes a definition of success that is all-American and commerce-tested. One wonders what he would say about a vivid Four like W. F. Nietzsche who was brilliant, influential and "best-seller," but who dealt with his misery by giving us encouraging sayings like "What does not kill us, strengthens us."

Jennifer White had (she died young a few years ago) a column read by 750,000 a week and her book, *Work Less, Make More* is easy to read and has lots of good advice, especially if you are a style Three. I can't prove it, but it seems to me that most time management books are written by Threes for other Threes. The book's subtitle is *"Stop Working So Hard and Create the Life You Really Want."* That seems like the advice an Enneagram coach would give most Threes.

Other Three footprints show up like this passage. *Make sure you focus your talents around something people want to buy....Having talent is not the issue, we all have unique gifts and talents. The key is honing what you do well that people will pay for.* (p. 59) One can hear a style Four indignantly refusing to do just that.

Her special section on breaking the adrenaline habit is wonderful for Threes who can live on caffeine, applause and dopamine.

White's advice is good all the way through, providing you accept that one size fits all. She has advice on procrastination and as an Enneagram coach I assume people procrastinate for nine different reasons and each one procrastinates different stuff. Ones may procrastinate if directions are not clear or detailed, but Sevens don't worry about the clarity of the directions because they may not follow them anyway. Eights have been known to acknowledge directions before doing things their way anyway.

Daniel Pink's bestselling book on motivation, *Drive,* reinforces and brings to the business community the thesis of Alfie Kohn's great book, *Punished by Rewards* that intrinsic motivation is superior to extrinsic motivation. An Enneagram student will accept their thesis with no problem but then will wonder if every style is motivated by the same things. Pink's motivations are general enough so that they don't conflict with most Enneagram styles (except for style Three who is largely motivated by external rewards like money, applause, recognition and status). But the Enneagram could add nuances that would really help. One of Pink's universals is that everyone wants control. Eights want to be in control and have much less need for security than Sixes, who would like control over smaller assignments and who would prefer security to control if the control position requires much risk. Pink's clear thesis illustrates a general principle for reading self-help books: most authors will have a "one size fits all" understanding of inner dynamics that Enneagram students will need to divide nine ways. Pink's banner reads "The Surprising Truth About What Motivates Us," and to that we would add, the nine different motivations we employ when we work.

Chip and Dan Heath have an unusually helpful book, *Switch.* It's about change –always a tantalizing topic for a coach. They employ a nice metaphor for the rational and emotional-intuitive parts of us: Elephant and Rider. The Rider is our conscious intention and resources; the Elephant is the unconscious emotional-intuitive part of us. They employ this metaphor effectively through much of the book and an Enneagram student or coach can see why the book works. One can also see how to enrich their work with the Enneagram. Our emotional–intuitive side can also be described as our Enneagram style in the narrow sense of our just barely acknowledged preferences, filters and responses. If you are going to appeal to someone's "elephant," it is really helpful to know what that elephant likes. You persuade an Eight to join your cause by emphasizing the helpless vulnerability of the people you are going to help, you persuade the Three by mentioning that this will look good on her resume and the boss will be watching (or a reporter, perhaps). In either case, you know the general contours of the "elephant's" desires. Our usual moralizing about treating others the way want to be treated is wrong and the same applies to motivations: the Enneagram has discovered nine species of elephants.

Probably one of the most harmful of the self-help and success-in-business-and-in-life books is the granddaddy, *Think and Grow Rich,* by Napoleon Hill. His exhortations to work hard, desire intensely, and focus intently has seduced more students than prom parties. He assumes focus is completely under our control and all we have to do is point our attention to our goal. He assumes that hard work will be rewarded. Ask the tens of millions of people out of work today. He assumes that desire can be pointed toward the goal we set. Enneagram students know that in addition to whatever goal we set, we have this other one specific to our Enneagram style which functions like a conditional clause. Style Seven says she will work hard (as long as the work is interesting). Style Two agreed to focus on his goal (as long as he has people to work with). Style Nine agrees to the goal, which he is going to pursue avidly (any day now). His childlike confidence is purely rational effort is touching, and his continuing popularity only underscores the need for the depth of the Enneagram.

Self-help books are quite helpful, but once you know the Enneagram, you can improve on almost all of them, regardless of the depth and range of the material offered. I offer these as a sample. Arrogance is out of place, but confidence is warranted.

References

Achor, S. (2010) *The Happiness Advantage*, Crown Business, New York

Heath, C. & Heath, D. (2010) *Switch*, Broadway Books, New York

Hill, N. (1937) *Think and Grow Rich*, The Ralston Society

Pink, D. (2009) *Drive*, Riverhead Books, New York

White, J. (1999) *Work Less, Make More*, John Wiley & Sons, New York

Sex, Love and Your Personality – The Nine Faces of Intimacy

By Mona Coates, Ph.D and Judith Searle

Editorial Department, 2011

Reviewed by Susanne Povelsen

My first impression of Mona Coates was at an IEA conference some years back. I did not attend her workshop myself, but was in the room next to the one where she held her workshop. I deeply regretted not having joined her workshop, which I later found out was on the Enneagram and relationships. The workshop that I was in myself was interesting enough, but the amount of loud laughter that came through the wall from where Mona Coates was giving her workshop made us all giggle and I was curious about what she was telling her participants. Luckily I was able to buy her recorded presentation before I went home, and I now I understand why they had so much fun. With this in mind I was curious to read the book *Sex, Love and Personality Types* by Mona Coates and Judith Searle.

Mona is an experienced psychotherapist and licensed marriage and family counselor with many years of experience in helping others to understand themselves and their partners in their private relationships. In this book she presents her theory of Five Factors for a lasting relationship. These Five Factors are linked to factors of the Enneagram although the first and most important factor is an independent way of understanding why your relationships might work very well or might suffer from severe challenges.

The first factor that the authors introduce is called the Lovemaps (a concept originally developed by sex therapist and researcher John Money). In short our lovemap is our conceptual idea of what a relationship should look like. Sometimes a rather idealistic and not always realistic perspective, image or expectation of what we get involved in when we first commit to a partner in our lives. The lovemap is described as *"a mosaic of traits that make up, partly in our conscious mind but mostly in our unconscious, the picture of our ideal mate or lover and what we would do with them"*. These traits are a set of criteria that include among others social behavior, values, political persuasion, underlying beliefs and often also include physical characteristics. When we become conscious of the components of our lovemap, they become more negotiable and easier to accept for ourselves and our partner.

Mona gives an example of her own lovemap: Her preference for a man who can fix things around the house, the way her dad did; thus having little interest in a guy who has no ability as a handyman. There is also her attraction to extremely smart men who are on the quiet side; her dad was a solid, stable, and introverted man who focused on his family, doing the work and solving every problem.

Although this is often the case, your lovemap will not always be based on the image or role model of your parents. In fact it can be the complete opposite as you may have had some resistance on the way your father or mother lived their lives. The clue is to look into your own image and expectations for a partner, what you are attracted to, and why this is so important to you as a way to make your lovemap more conscious and flexible.

When lovemaps are compatible, together with one or more of the other factors that the authors point out, there is a better chance that relationships will last – or at least be without too much trouble.

Lovemaps are by far the most important factor to look at in a relationship if you want to predict the sustainability of a long term relationship, or for creating more understanding of what is going on in your present relationship, as they are a map for how we meet each other's expectations and ideals in a relationship.

The four other factors for how a relationship can be predicted to work out or not in the long term are factors related to the Enneagram. These factors are (mentioned in prioritized order): High Levels of Psychological Health (based on the theory of Don Riso and Russ Hudson), Matching Personality Subtypes (also called Instinctual Variants), Harmonic Triad Match, and Complementary Connection Line.

If you are a reader who does not yet know the Enneagram, the book offers a short description of the types, highlighting, among other things, the strategy of each type. Whereas it is always good to explore a comprehensive theory of personality in more in depth, these kinds of short introductions to the types often give you a hint of your type and from there you can choose to go deeper into the type, e.g. by reading other of the recommended books.

The second factor that is pointed out as an important one for the relationship is the Levels of Psychological Health (based on the theory developed by Don Riso and Russ Hudson). Even though your type is important, the health of your type tells a lot about how you deal with life and relations in general. The Levels of Health indicate your ability for being/not being conscious, aware, authentic, psychologically healthy, realistic and ego-driven, etc. For a couple who are at very different levels of health, the imbalances that occur will be affected by your basic Enneagram type; in short – the healthier you and your partner is, the healthier and more in balance your relationship tends to be. When both lovemaps and levels of psychological health are compatible, there is a more chance of creating a lasting relationship.

A third factor that the authors have found to be important is the personality Subtypes (or Instinctive Variants of the types) which are: Self-preservation, Sexual and Social subtypes. They have each their own strengths and weaknesses. In a relationship, partners with different Subtypes will have different challenges. As Subtype is unconscious and probably determined by biological predispositions from birth as well as early childhood experiences, it takes awareness and insight about these to cope with whatever discrepancies this may bring up in a relationship. Partners with the same subtype enjoy an easier and smoother love relationship as they feel more compatible. As we can read from the case stories in the book, your relationship is not doomed to fail if you have different Subtypes, but, again, awareness of how these Subtypes play out in our lives, gives a good standpoint for preventing too much trouble. In fact it gives you and your partner a very good hint about what it can be advantageous to pay attention to.

The fourth factor is the Harmonic Group of the Enneagram. The Harmonic groups are the way that we deal when problems or conflict as they occur: *The Positive Outlook Group* (2-7-9) responds to conflict and difficulty with a "positive attitude", reframing negatives and highlighting positives. *The Competency Group* (1-3-5) deals with difficulties by closing down their personal feelings and striving to be logical, objective, effective and competent. And the *Reactive Group* (4-6-8) reacts emotionally to conflicts and problems and have a need to know how others feel, think or sense about the situation. This factor is less significant that the others but if can be a big help to see what patterns play out when a relationship runs into problems or conflict.

The fifth and least important factor is Complementary Connections. If a couple has a shared interior line in the Enneagram, it seems to be like a flow of energy and a deeper connection where balance and correction becomes more possible. The complementary connections are more about opposites complementing each other, provoking and correcting imbalances, exchanging energies and agendas than about compatibility.

Throughout the book the authors give examples of different combinations of the above factors, highlighting both the positives and the challenging parts of the relation between partners. Although you might not fully identify with the type or issue described within your type, the case stories will probably awaken aspects of awareness in your own relationship and help you look at yourself and your partner in a more curious and objective way than when bringing in your own personal story. People often find that other peoples' stories are what help them to look at their own relationships in a different way, whereas it can be more challenging to look at our own relationship directly – especially if they do not have professional help at hand.

The book is written in a light, clear, and easily understood manner. I've enjoyed the way the authors have been able to cut down what must have been rather long stories from the real lives of the couples mentioned in the book to something that gives the reader a very realistic and to the point description of the therapeutic sessions. The book is highly recommended to everyone who is curious about relationships, whether it is for their own purposes or for counseling, coaching, or therapy.

The Enneagram of Death – Helpful Insights by 9 Types of People on Grief, Fear, and Dying

By Elizabeth Wagele

International Enneagram Association Publications (2012)

Reviewed by Kathryn Grant

Elizabeth Wagele, well-known in the Enneagram community for her witty and accurate introductory book, *The Enneagram Made Easy,* and additional volumes: *Finding the Birthday Cake,* written for children and the child-like within each of us; *The Career Within* in collaboration with Ingrid Stabb; and others, presents an ambitious, profound, and compassionate look at death and dying.

Through interviews and story submission, Elizabeth has compiled an interesting array of death-related stories. Liz, as she is best known, presents these to the reader within Enneagram reference. We hear the voices and encounter the writing style of each type as they share a story of their own close encounter with death, watching or waiting with someone who is dying, or recounting a story of someone's death, often early in their own life, that has impacted them. We get a clear taste of the struggles inherent in each type's life and death journey.

One chapter is devoted to each of the nine Enneagram types. The stories are bundled and so impact the reader with a sense of how each type deals with the death of a loved one, the process and anticipation of death, and how each type tends to relate to this experience. An ingredient that had the most impact for me was the insights that the authors and storytellers share of their personal transformation in the aftermath of journeying with death. At the conclusion of each chapter, Liz gives the reader a short, accurate glimpse of the chapter's heroes: their style of grieving and its inner impact and some of the shadow aspects of each style that are so clearly shown in the chapter.

Elizabeth writes succinctly and with accuracy about the struggles and strengths we all will meet on our journey with death, both those unique to our Enneagram type and those that are universal, as well as based on her years of Enneagram study and her own personal growth. Each type receives a humble, questioning summary and we learn about people in those types, as well as how that particular type lives in us.

This concluding piece to each chapter makes the work accessible to those new to the Enneagram as well as drawing those with deeper knowledge into the stories in a more personal way. The potential audience thus becomes anyone who knows someone who has died. Anyone who knows someone who is dying. Anyone who will die.

A topic that often holds little appeal, Liz brings us to a learning edge about one of the two inevitabilities of life. She fortunately does not speak of taxes. We journey with folks of our own type and learn about ourselves in a deeper way. We journey with folks of other types and learn to bring increasing compassion to ourselves and to our relationships. I find this book fascinating as the structure of each Enneagram style, both strengths and vulnerabilities become crystal clear as heard in the voices of those who are suffering and moving through this difficult time with vigor, tears, compassion, denial, and bravery.

Another piece for curious reading, are the stories of folks who came close to death but did not die. Faced with a chilling diagnosis or other threat (gun point!), we hear how people change and shift to a more grateful stance, more open and aware.

Second half of life issues are in the forefront of much writing and lecturing, most likely a result of many authors actually being in the second half of life. I find some of this work helpful, as I too, am solidly in second half. Yet, curiously often the words seem flat as the final moment of life is not addressed. Here, in Liz's work, we see this moment clearly and can use these stories to contemplate how we are relating to this inevitable moment.

I am left with a haunting question: Who is David Bennett? Often quoted, I perhaps should know who this is, however, I do not. It would have enhanced my relationship with the quotes to have background on this person.

Read in a contemplative fashion, we learn how to die. From some stories we learn how difficult it can be to let go – either the dying person refuses to leave or loved ones refuse to allow the peace that the dying seek and ask the patient, spouse, parent to stay. Many stories tell of that mystical moment when there is a relaxation and an agreement to let go. I heartily recommend *The Enneagram of Death* to spiritual directors, hospice workers, and therapists who will find the stories and Liz's comments helpful and enlightening. I also recommend this book to all who would like a guidebook on this most mysterious aspect of our lives, our death.

CONTRIBUTORS

David Fauvre, MA, co-founder of Enneagram Explorations and www.enneagram.net is an internationally recognized author, trainer, coach and researcher. Since 1995, in partnership with Katherine Chernick Fauvre, he has co-conducted research focused on the self-image, micro-expressions, language patterns and consumer behavior of each Enneagram Type, Tritype™ and Instinct. David is co-author of the book *The 27 Tritypes™ Revealed* and the *Enneagram Enneacards Testing Instrument.* In addition, he co-created the Enneagram Pro Certification Intensives and the award winning Enneagram television series *Types: Your Personality Revealed.* David has a Masters in Transpersonal Psychology and is a certified Enneagram teacher with Riso-Hudson and has completed the Professional Trainings with Palmer-Daniels. David attended the Barbara Brennan School of Healing and is a certified teach teacher of the 'The Work' with Byron Katie.

Katherine Chernick Fauvre, co-founder of Enneagram Explorations and Fauvre Research is an internationally recognized teacher, coach and researcher. In 1995, she began her innovative research studies exploring many facets of the Enneagram including; The Enneagram Instinctual Subtypes, Tritype, Core Fears, Spirituality, Intimacy, Lexicon Usage, Archetypes and the Self-image of the 9 Enneagram Types. Katherine is the author of *Enneastyle: The 9 languages of Enneagram Type*, *Enneagram Instinctual Subtypes,* co-author of *The 27 Tritypes Revealed,* and co-creator of the *Enneagram Enneacards Testing Instrument, the Enneagram Pro Intensives* and the television series *Types: Your Personality Revealed*. She is a former member of the Board of Directors of the IEA and is a certified teacher with Palmer-Daniels, Riso-Hudson and Hurley-Donson.

Virginia S. George received her M.A. in Integral Psychology from the John F. Kennedy University School of Holistic Studies in June 2010. She is a graduate of the Riso-Hudson Professional Enneagram Training Program and has been certified to teach the Riso-Hudson method. Correspondence concerning this article should be sent to virgeo@astound.net.

Sabine Elisabeth Gramm started in the banking sector before studying psychology and completing her communications training with Schulz von Thun. She has been working with the Enneagram since 1999 and member of two professional associations in Germany (ÖAE and EMT). Her Master's Thesis coupled the Enneagram with the Differential Psychology of Communication for use in professional contexts. She further developed this into the ProFIEL® System that she uses in leadership trainings. On 11.11.11 she founded the Institute for Human Communication in Ettlingen (Germany) with the goal to improve relationships in the workplace and elsewhere. Contact: s.gramm@pro-gramm.de

Kathryn Grant is a certified and accredited Enneagram teacher, Spiritual Director, Life Coach and family constellation facilitator. She uses the Enneagram in private practice and leads retreats, workshops and study groups. She shares her enthusiasm for the Enneagram by working with and supporting Chapters and as Chair of the Northern California Chapter of the IEA. She is a founding member of the Southern California Chapter and is an IEA Board Member.

Peter McNab is an IEA Board Member and runs his own training and consultancy organisation, excellence*for*all. He has run numerous public workshops including over fifty NLP Practitioner programmes, over twenty-five NLP Master Practitioner programmes, and several NLP Trainer Training Certifications. He is an INLPTA Master Trainer, a certified MBTI Practitioner, a qualified Spiral Dynamics Practitioner, and a Founder Member of Ken Wilber's Integral Institute. He is the author of "Towards An Integral Vision: Using NLP & Ken Wilber's AQAL Model to Enhance Communication" (2005) and the App, "NLP Models" (2012).

Dr. Claudio Naranjo, M.D. has been at the forefront of understanding, researching, utilizing and teaching the Enneagram for many decades. He is a developer of the Enneagram of Personality and founder of the Seekers After Truth Institute. Dr. Naranjo is a highly respected author of books featuring the Enneagram, Gestalt therapy, meditation, and transformational change. He has conducted countless workshops and held numerous lectures on applications of the Enneagram to personality, approaches in the SAT program, supervision of Gestalt therapy, among others. In *Mind Body Spirit* Magazine, Dr. Naranjo was listed as one of the 100 Most Spiritually Influential Living People of 2012.

Professor Alaor Passos is a sociologist and associate professor at the University of Brasilia – UNB. He also organizes and coordinates activities in Brazil as a representative of Claudio Naranjo. Professor Passos has been teaching about the Enneagram in Brazil since 1992. In addition, he has taught courses in Australia, Chile, Mexico, Colombia and Italy and participated in international conferences in Spain, France and the United States. He is a member of the international team of therapists at SAT, the founder and director of the Institute EneaSAT of Brazil and a founding member and the current President of IEA Brazil.

Susanne Povelsen is a Business and Life coach in her own company, CoachSpirit. She helps people to attain their goals and get more balance in life by efficiently combining coaching methods with the Enneagram. Her passion is to see people develop and grow, and to find the spirit in life. She is an IEA Board Member, has been a board member of the Danish Enneagram Association and has been the coordinator of two European Enneagram Conferences hosted in Denmark. In addition she has published a number of translated Enneagram books in Denmark. She has written several articles and a book called *Enneagrammet — kort og godt* (*The Enneagram — short and good*).

Anna Sutton, Ph.D., is Senior Lecturer in Organisational Behaviour at Manchester Metropolitan University Business School. Her Ph.D. thesis is titled *Implicit and explicit personality in work settings: an application of Enneagram theory.*

Gina Thomas, MA, is a coach, facilitator, Enneagram Teacher, and writer. Her graduate training is in depth psychology (Sonoma State University) and holistic health care (Western Michigan University). She is a certified Enneagram teacher (EPTP) and qualified in MBTI through the Association of Psychological Type. She currently serves on the board of EANT.

Clarence Thomson has taught the Enneagram for 20 years and with Mary Bast, co-authored *Out of the Box: Coaching with the Enneagram.* More recently he also authored *You're Fat: Your Fault?* His website is www.enneagramcentral.com.

Jerome Wagner, Ph.D. is a clinical psychologist, therapist and consultant in private practice, and a faculty member in the Department of Psychology at Loyola University, Chicago. He is the author of *Nine Lenses on the World: the Enneagram Perspective* and *The Enneagram Spectrum of Personality Styles: an Introductory Guide*; the *Wagner Enneagram Personality Style Scales (WEPSS*); *and Two Windows on the Self: the Enneagram and the Myers-Briggs.* Jerry has been researching and teaching the Enneagram for over 40 years and has offered the *Enneagram Spectrum Training and Certification Program* nationally and internationally for the past 20 years (www.enneagramspectrum.com). Jerry was on the Board of Directors of the International Enneagram Association, was recently named an Honorary Founder of the IEA, and is co-editor of the *Enneagram Journal.* He was the keynote speaker for the 2010 IEA Conference.

ABOUT THE INTERNATIONAL ENNEAGRAM ASSOCIATION

Like any vibrant, dynamic organization, the IEA continues to evolve as the needs of our members evolve.

Our vision *a world where the Enneagram is widely understood and constructively used* remains unchanged but our mission, the way the IEA will help bring that vision to fruition, has changed. The IEA's board of directors voted to revise the IEA's mission statement to:

The IEA's mission is to help our members thrive through providing opportunities for:

- *Developing greater excellence in the use of the Enneagram*
- *Education in theory and application of the Enneagram*
- *Engagement with an international community of shared interest and diversified approach*

In the past, the IEA's mission has been to serve as a hub for developments in theory and application of the Enneagram. As popularity of the Enneagram spreads we see a larger need, a need driven by the changing demographics of our membership.

Essentially, our members fall into two broad categories:

- Those who use the Enneagram in their own personal work.
- Those who also use the Enneagram in their work with others in areas such as spirituality, psychology, education, the arts, or business.

The IEA will continue to provide the same (and even more) services that we always have to the first category of members. We are committed to: insightful and informative publications covering all the latest developments in Enneagram theory and application; an international conference and an increasing number of regional conferences that bring the finest Enneagram teachers in the world together under one roof; and providing an opportunity for local and global communion with fascinating, like-minded people.

The growth in the IEA's membership has been in the second category, people who use the Enneagram in their work with others. As people take the Enneagram out into the world, it is important to all of us that we do so constructively, in a manner that is ethical and beneficial to the individual. We see our mission as supporting and encouraging those efforts - serving the community of people publicly committed to a shared set of ethical standards and commitment to integrity in our practice.

The new mission statement changes little about the spirit of the organization, but it serves as a public declaration of intent. It will help the IEA's board of directors, other volunteers, and all of us, as members, better focus our energy and the organization's resources on the initiatives that matter the most.

Benefits of Membership

Membership in the IEA brings a variety of benefits. The more-tangible benefits are listed below, but it is easy to overlook the intangible benefits of membership. Membership in the IEA sends a signal to the world that you are part of an international community of practitioners committed to excellence in their personal and professional practices. It shows that you find value in fellowship with people who share your commitment to the development of wisdom, understanding, and compassion for self and others. And, it shows that you are committed to helping to bring about the IEA's vision of a world where the Enneagram is widely understood and constructively used.

Other member benefits include

- The IEA's quarterly Nine Points Magazine
- Discounted Registration to the Annual IEA Conference and some regional conferences
- Access to Member Only section of the IEA website, which includes:
    - Members Only directory
    - Enneagram symbols for download
    - Back issues of Nine Points Magazine available for download
- Discounts on books and many training programs
- IEA podcast interviews with leading Enneagram teachers

Professional members also receive

- A free copy of the annual *Enneagram Journal*
- Free listing of their services and events on the IEA website calendar
- Eligibility for IEA Professional Accreditation
- Eligibility to present at IEA conferences and events
- Eligibility for listing on IEA Speakers Bureau
- Listing in the "Find a Professional" directory on the website
- Invitation to attend the Professional Member reception at the annual IEA conference
- Eligibility to purchase an email blast sent to the IEA database

The International Enneagram Association brings together Enneagram professionals and aficionados from around the world. Be part of a global learning community by becoming a member of the IEA today!

Visit us at www.internationalenneagram.org

Printed in Great Britain
by Amazon.co.uk, Ltd.,
Marston Gate.